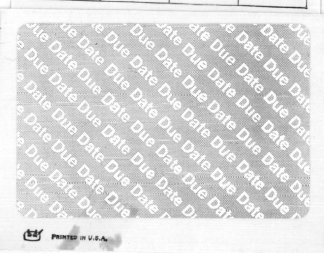

AEOLIAN HARPS

AEOLIAN HARPS

Essays in Literature in Honor of
Maurice Browning Cramer

And what if all of animated nature
Be but organic Harps diversely fram'd,
That tremble into thought, as o'er them sweeps
Plastic and vast, one intellectual breeze,
At once the Soul of each, and God of all?

Samuel Taylor Coleridge

Edited by Donna G. Fricke and Douglas C. Fricke

Bowling Green University Press
Bowling Green, Ohio
1976

This book may be ordered from
Donna G. Fricke
Center for Bibliography
Department of English
Bowling Green State University
Bowling Green, Ohio 43403

Contents

Values and the Profession

Essays in Literature

Acknowledgements

The editors wish to express their appreciation to the contributors for their enthusiasm and patience. Special thanks go to the editorial board for their learned advice, but the editors take full responsibility for the final selections and for all errata that may remain in the collection. Our gratitude to Deborah Austin, Frank Baldanza, Elmer Borklund, Charles Crow, James Harner, Karen Hopkins, Thomas Kinney, Lowell Leland, Virginia Leland, Henry Sams, and Thomas Wymer. We thank Edgar Daniels, chairman of the English department of the Bowling Green State University, for his support. And, finally, we are grateful to Connie Holman for her outstanding work on the IBM composer. Publication of this volume was made possible by the generous subscription and sponsorship of the persons here listed:

Preface

These essays and poems honoring Maurice Browning Cramer were written by his former students at the University of Chicago and The Pennsylvania State University. The editors realized only too well that such a format limiting contributors would exclude from this collection many respected friends and colleagues of Maurice Cramer who knew him or taught with him at the college and universities he distinguished as teacher, scholar, and administrator for the last four decades. Moreover, it is difficult to separate associates of Maurice Cramer into those who were his students and those who were not, for all who have known him have become his students. Yet the decision to invite only those who have shared classes with him or written under his direction seems an appropriate way of honoring a man who generously gave of his time and wisdom to those who studied with him. Not all who wished to contribute to this collection were able to do so. The exigencies of time and space intervened to keep many from appearing here, but their presence is felt in their good wishes and warm and gracious letters, remembering Maurice Cramer as teacher and friend, which were written in response to this occasion. A collection of such letters would make a timely companion to this book if the full admiration and respect accorded to Maurice Cramer were to be measured.

Coleridge's poem provides the title for this collection, as it provided the inspiration for the gift honoring Maurice Cramer on his retirement from The Pennsylvania State University in 1972. Since that date, in his continued capacity to learn and teach, Maurice Cramer has demonstrated that the first Aeolian Harp occasion, whatever reverence may have attended so senior an event, was not valedictory. The happiest aspect of this second Aeolian Harp presentation is that it celebrates the undiminished presence of a man who, in the Coleridgean metaphor, has swept over and through the lives of everyone associated with this book.

Bowling Green, Ohio   The Editors

The Professional Career of Maurice Browning Cramer

Maurice Browning Cramer was born on April 24, 1910, in Camden, New Jersey, the son of Dr. Alfred and Anna Browning (Doughten) Cramer. He was a student at the William Penn Charter School (1922-27) and received his higher degrees in Classics and English Literature from Princeton University. He married Alice Carver on August 24, 1935; they have two children, Owen Carver and Maurice Browning, and four grandchildren. Professor Cramer retired in 1972, Professor Emeritus, after teaching for thirty-eight years, to Chapel Hill, North Carolina.

Professional Education and Teaching

EDUCATION

Princeton University
> A. B. (Classics) 1931; Magna Cum Laude; Phi Beta Kappa.
>> White Graduate Scholar 1931-32.
>> Hunt Graduate Fellow 1932-34.
>
> M. A. (English) 1934.
> Ph.D. (English) 1937. Dissertation: "The Foundation of Browning's Fame, 1833-1869."

TEACHING

Mount Holyoke College
> Instructor of English, 1934-39.
> Assistant Professor of English, 1940.

University of Tampa
> Associate Professor of English, 1940-41.
> Professor of English, 1941-42.
> Chairman, Department of English, 1940-42.

Princeton University
> Lecturer in English, 1942-43.

University of Chicago
> Assistant Professor of Humanities, 1945-48.
> Associate Professor of Humanities, 1948-53.
> Professor of Humanities, 1953-59.
> Chairman of Humanities 2, 1948-50.
> Chairman of Humanities 3, 1950-51.
> Chairman, College Humanities Staff, 1951-57.
> Quantrell Award for Excellence in Undergraduate Teaching ($1000), 1957.

University of Athens, Greece
> Fulbright Professor of American Life and Civilization, 1957-58.

The Pennsylvania State University
> Professor of English, 1959-72.
> Professor Emeritus of English, 1972–.

Bibliography

VERSE

"To a Company of Scholars in English Literature," *The Atlantic Monthly,* October 1938; reprinted in "A Week of Verse," *New York Herald Tribune,* Sunday, October 23, 1938.

"Vocamur," *The Mount Holyoke Monthly,* 47 (December 1939), 8.

"Pulvis et Umbra," *The Mount Holyoke Monthly,* 47 (December 1939), 10.

"The Bait," when exhibited on National Poetry Day at the New York World's Fair 1940 and judged by Robert P. Tristram Coffin and others, won (a) a Certificate of Honor, (b) a promise of publication in *The Star Shooter,* ed. Anita Browne (Poets Press of National Poetry Center), and (c) the Florida gold medal.

"Aesthete," in "The Home Forum" of *The Christian Science Monitor,* Thursday, July 11, 1940, p. 8.

"Paternoster," *American Poetry Magazine,* 21 (September-October 1940), 5.

"Quando Ver Venit Meum," *Queen's Quarterly: A Canadian Review,* 48 (Winter 1941-42), 341.

"July Hot Spell," *Queen's Quarterly: A Canadian Review,* 51 (Autumn 1944), 296.

"Coquette," *The New Yorker,* February 24, 1945, p. 55.

"Summer Maple," *The Saturday Review of Literature,* June 23, 1945, p. 41.

"The Professor and the Prothonotary," *The American Scholar,* 19 (Summer 1950), 273-74.

"Aubade," *The Saturday Review of Literature,* June 20, 1953, p. 28.

FICTION

"Conviction of Things Not Seen," *Queen's Quarterly: A Canadian Review,* 46 (Spring 1939), 14-27, a short story.

Phoenix at East Hadley, (Boston: Houghton Mifflin, 1941), 307 pages, a novel.

ESSAYS AND REVIEWS

"Browning's Friendships and Fame Before Marriage (1833-1846)," *PMLA,* 55 (1940), 207-30.

"Henry FewSmith, Philadelphia Artist, 1821-1846," *The Pennsylvania Magazine of History and Biography,* 65 (1941), 31-55.

"What Browning's Literary Reputation Owed to the Pre-Raphaelites 1847-1856," *Journal of English Literary History,* 8 (1941), 305-21.

"Browning's Literary Reputation at Oxford 1855-1859," *PMLA,* 57 (1942), 232-40.

The Foundations of Browning's Fame, 1833-1859, a gathering of reprints of articles; general title page and binding done in Tampa, Florida 1942; distributed by Princeton University to selected libraries; Library of Congress PR4283.C7.

Review: *American Harvest,* ed. by Allen Tate and John Peale Bishop, in *The Chimera (A Rough Beast)* ed. by William Arrowsmith, Autumn 1942 (I, pp. 46-47).

"Good Neighbor Policy Begins at Home," *The Delphian Quarterly,* 26 (1943), pp. 2-5, 14.

"How Good Are Public Schools in *Your* State?" *The Delphian Quarterly,* 27 (1944), pp. 24-27, 33.

"Billy Budd and *Billy Budd," The Journal of General Education,* 10 (1957), 78-91.

"Norms for Promotion: A Symposium," *The Journal of General Education,* 10 (1957), 136-40.

"University Fulbrighting," H ANTALLAGH ("The Exchange," newsletter for the Fulbright program in Greece), July 1958, pp. 6, 8.

"Some Great Fools in Literature," *Penn State Alumni News,* May 1960.

Review: *Engraving in England in the Sixteenth and Seventeenth Centuries.*
Part III, by M. Corbett and M. Norton, in *Seventeenth-Century News,* 21
(1963), 48-49.

"Maisie Ward and Browning Biography: A New Era," *Modern Philology,* 68
(1971), 294-300.

"The Ring and the Book: 'Underthought'," pp. 168-190 in *Directions in
Literary Criticism,* ed. by S. Weintraub and P. Young, a *festschrift* in
honor of Henry W. Sams, The Pennsylvania State University Press, 1973.

"Irvine and Honan, and Maisie Ward Sheed: The New Standard Browning
Biographers," *Studies in Browning and His Circle,* 3,i (Spring 1975), 9-31.

PUBLIC LECTURES

1939 "Some Old Letters: The Life and Times of Henry FewSmith, Philadelphia Artist 1821-1846," South Hadley, Mass.

1941 "Some Early Elizabethan Dramatists," Delphians of Tampa, Palma Ceia
Golf Club.

1941 "How a Novel Is Made," The Women's Club of Tampa.

1941 "The Pleasures of Novel Writing," Tampa.

1942 "The Southern Scene in Literature," NCJW, Tampa.

1942 "Some Trends in Modern American Literature," AAUW, Tampa.

1952 "Humanities in a Liberal Arts College," Earlham College, Ind.

1955 "The Rationale of a Humanities Sequence in a College Program,"
Shimer College, Ill.

1956 "The Humanities," Government of India Commission on Higher Education, Chicago.

1957 "Symbolism in Literature and the Student," Northwestern University.

1957 "The Humanities," television broadcast.

1958 "An Interracial Community in Chicago," Palace of St. Michael and St.
George, Isle of Corfu; audience included Metropolitan Archbishop
of the Ionian Islands and the Nomarch.

1958 "Modern American Poetry," Creative Writers' Society of Macedonia,
Salonika, Greece.

1959 "Shrines and Oracles of Ancient Greece," University College, Chicago:
(1) "Sites of an Ancient Drama"; (2) "Pilgrimage to Rhamnus";
(3) "Byzantine Attica."

1959 "Reading Modern American Poetry," Blair County Teachers, Holidays-
burg, Pa.

1959 "Modern Greece," radio broadcast.

1960 "A Reading of Poems by Browning," Poet's Corner, The Pennsylvania State University.

1961 "What Is an Educated Man?" radio broadcast.

1961 "Book and Ring in Browning's *The Ring and the Book,*" colloquium for University Park and Commonwealth Campuses.

1961 "American Civilization," for the Peace Corps in training at University Park.

1961 "Dostoevsky and English Romanticism," The Pennsylvania State University.

1962 "Browning as Philosophical Poet," State College, Pa.

1963 "Browning's 'Balaustion's Adventure': An Interpretation," Armstrong Browning Library, Baylor University.

1963 "Teaching American Civilization to the Descendants of Pericles," Phi Beta Kappa, The Pennsylvania State University.

1964 "Robert Browning Nowadays," Thomas Shipley Lecture, Haverford College.

1965 "Robert Browning Nowadays," The Pennsylvania State University.

1967 "Can a man who hasn't written a novel teach a novel?" radio broadcast.

1967 "Browning's *The Ring and the Book: 'Underthought',*" The Pennsylvania State University.

PROFESSIONAL AFFILIATIONS

Phi Beta Kappa.

American Association of University Professors.

Modern Language Association; consultant on Robert Browning papers submitted for publication in *PMLA,* 1951-57.

American Civil Liberties Union.

Reader, College Entrance Examination Board, 1937-38.

Member of Florida State Conference for Teacher Training, 1941.

University of Chicago Philological Society.

Council of the University Senate, 1952-59, University of Chicago.

Association of Princeton Graduate School Alumni: Governing Board, 1964-68.

Humanities Consultant and External Examiner, New School College (New York City), 1967-68.

PH.D. DISSERTATIONS DIRECTED AT THE
PENNSYLVANIA STATE UNIVERSITY

1968 Ronnalie J. Roper Howard. The Poetic Development of Dante Gabriel
Rossetti, 1847-1872.

1970 Annette Shandler Levitt. The Poetry and Thought of William Blake in
Joyce Cary's *The Horse's Mouth.*

1970 Daniel E. Lees. Shelley's Literary Reputation: 1950-1970.

1971 Douglas Charles Fricke. A Critical Study of Swinburne's *Poems and
Ballads* (1866).

1971 John George Rudy. Theory and Arrangement in Wordsworth's Tour
Categories.

1972 John Mitchell Gotwalt. Organicism in Swinburne's *Songs Before Sunrise.*

1972 Raymond W. Kearney. Yeats, the Man of Letters.

1972 Robert James Cornet. The Structure of Unreliability in Browning's
Men and Women.

1973 Keith A. Gould. The Modern Wordsworth: A Comparative Study of
William Wordsworth and Charles Hartshorne.

1973 John E. Rogers, Jr. "Dearest Friend": A Study of Dorothy Wordsworth's Journals.

M.A. DISSERTATIONS (One Long Thesis Degree) DIRECTED AT THE
PENNSYLVANIA STATE UNIVERSITY

1961 William B. Furlong. Newman in the Light of His "1859-1879 Journals":
A Clarification.

1962 Marshall Alan Ledger. Parodies of Robert Browning's Poetry.

1963 Robert Lefcourt. "Till Time shall be no more": A Study in Wordsworth's Use of Time in the Form and Content of Various Poems.

1964 Janice Treadway Heiges. Robert Browning and Henry James: A Study
in Parallelism.

1966 Karen F. Stein. Hopkins' "The Wreck of the Deutschland": An Aesthetic Analysis.

1966 C. J. Durrwachter. John Donne and Gerard Manley Hopkins: A Comparison.

1967 Terry Howard Wallace. Wordsworth's Concept of the Pastoral.

1969 Clifford W. Young, Jr. Theme and Characterization in Tennyson's
Becket.

1969 Marilyn Giorgio. Tennyson's *Enoch Arden:* An Analysis of Criticism
Past and Present.

Values and the Profession

The Professor and the Prothonotary

Maurice Browning Cramer

"You ought to be a lighthouse keeper," said
His wife to a professor in a famous
Mid-city university last fall
When, faced with ninety-nine new students, he
Declared he sometimes wished they were not all
So keen to keep him up to snuff, so strong
In hundredfold insistence that he be
Profoundly erudite and accurate,
Invincible examination coach,
Impeccable in politics and wardrobe,
Untiring in philanthropy and wit,
Polite, theatrical and eloquent.
"Or firewarden on a northern forest tower.
There is your chance to watch the migrant birds:
The gold prothonotary fluttering south,
The white-crowned sparrow and the gray-cheeked thrush —
Their rapture of resistless flight, their wild
Serene alacrity." He shook his head.
"There's too much uproar in those jobs for me,"
He said. "What would I do, a Ph.D.,
When the wreck struck, or the flame leaped? I'd rather
Become a forest ranger stepping lightly,
Ever so lightly on the forest floor.
I'd have a sack of acorns at my belt,
And every now and then, when I would cross
A dune too open to the wind and sun
(One of the wooded dunes of Michigan)
I'd reach into the sack, and stoop, and plant
An acorn softly in the forest mould —
Brown cup, green nut among the rotted leaves."
He spoke, and saw himself gliding along
In blue jeans and a flannel shirt alone
And silent under oak and hemlock boughs.
He felt his feet sink down in moss, in layer
On layer of yielding hemlock needles, brown
Of old and green of new, while overhead
Were redstarts and blackburnians. But his wife
Laughed. "Who would pay you to do that?" she asked.

At Cap St. Jacques During The Easter Offensive

"The ancients liked to write about natural beauty."
—Ho Chi Minh, "Cam Tuong Doc *Thien Gia Thi*"

John Balaban

In earlier times poets brushed on printed silk
those poems about clouds, mountains, and love.
Nowadays, when "poems are cased in steel," poets know
that literary words only limit and lie,
that fine words only tug at the ear.
A poet had better keep his mouth shut, we say,
unless he's found words to comfort and teach.
Today, comfort and teaching themselves deceive
and it takes cruelty to make any friends
when it is a lie to speak, a lie to keep silent.
Wise to this, most men talk too much. A few
trail morning beaches studying seadrift, marveling
at curls broken bare in crushed shells,
at the sheen and cracks of laved, salted wood,
at the pearling blues of rock-stuck mussels,
each odd as friends: accidental; fragmented.

Here sunshine streams the rain-pocked sand
and glares off keening gulls
squabbling over shellfish meats.

In tidal pools the pipers wade
on twig-legs, stabbing for starfish
with scissored, poking, needle bills.

Beetles scurry dry sea weeds.
The air heaves with a heavy smell.
Even the sun is hungry.

About the brilliant beach is scattered
a seaweed-strung and rotting wrack-heap
of mussel shells with grinning gums.

Nicely like a pearl is a poem
begun with an accidental speck
from the ocean of the actual.

A grain, a grit, which once admitted
irritates the mantle of thought
and coats itself in lacquers of the mind.

1975

Near the Parthenon, Azaleas
for Maurice Cramer

Harry Fisher

Phidias craftily swung his hammer;
Showers of sparks lit the Attic plain.
Praising Athenians raised a clamor,
Feeding their deities blood and grain.

Now into dust have the statues fallen;
Time and the elements grind down stones.
Yet from the crevices bees bear pollen:
Honey will flow from these broken bones.

1973

Mekong Bus Ride

Lana Balaban

The bus was bright orange with yellow dragons painted on either side, on the rear a poster of a black man with a broad flat nose and a broad smile bearing a set of the finest white horse-teeth this side of the Saigon River. "Pour les dents blancs — Denta Trice." Red mud, baked on the sides and rear of the bus, had blotched the black man's left cusp making him look as if he had just bitten into a chunk of beef. The dragon's fire was dust, grime, and oil.

All the bus windows were open; each window framed a person's face: Delta women in checkered scarves, young children sucking sugar cane, men with streaked wrinkled smiles in coolie straw hats, and weary, silent old women. Several hawkers badgered the passengers, thrusting sugar cane, cold drinks, rice cakes, putrid, yellowing sandwiches under every nose. Melons. Pineapples. Something to cool your two-hour journey to My Tho.

In front of the bus door, the driver, sitting behind a rickety, stained wooden table told me the price to My Tho was 650 piasters but for rich, pretty Americans, 1000. I knocked down the price to 800, and the driver graciously agreed. When I climbed on I saw that the bus was already filled to capacity, three to a seat; chickens, with feet tied together, wings clipped, squawked from their places on the floor. Piglets in cheap wire baskets squealed from the narrow luggage rack running above the heads of the passengers. While I scanned for a seat, the whispers rose like a tropical storm. I decided not to sit by a window beneath one of the piglet baskets, but made my way down the bus aisle, stepping over young children, fruit, chickens, and carry-all bags stuffed with clothes and various Saigon purchases, and, as I passed, all eyes followed each awkward movement. Children peered into my face to see the eyes, the cat eyes of the young American woman. It was strange for Vietnamese to see an American woman riding on a public bus, for most of the American women they saw were middle-aged, plump secretaries who worked for the American command in Saigon and who shuffled themselves around the city in taxis or in air-conditioned, chauffer-driven Chevrolets. I managed to squeeze into a seat next to the rear door which I hoped would give me a cooling breeze once we left the dusty, sweltering city and hit the country road to My Tho.

Pulling out of the station took a lot of gesturing and swearing as five drivers scheduled to depart at the same time tried to jockey to first place. As we pulled onto the busy street from the station's dirt road, a boy began running along the side of the bus and hopped gracefully onto the steps of the open rear door. His hair was clean, shiny and black; his olive complexion caught the sun's rays, glowed healthily, and contrasted beautifully with his white, open shirt. The driver yelled something to him which made him laugh, eyes bright; his presence bright in the tropical sun.

The bus swerved and jerked its way through the outskirts of Saigon. It stopped periodically to pick up, incredibly, more passengers, and at each stop, the boy jumped from the bus steps while it was still in motion, shouting the bus's destination. He danced through those crowding to get on the bus, joked with the men, flirted with the school girls, and jostled the boys his age. His job, it seemed, was to help new passengers find a corner of a seat, or a space on the floor.

At every bus stop the young steward flirted with the young girls and women outside hawking bread, fruit, and other products to the passengers. At one bus stop, a young girl came up to my window, "Hey you. You buy." She pushed a loaf of French bread through the window and into my lap.

"No, I don't want any, thank you," I said as forcefully as I could, pushing the long loaf back into her reluctant hands.

Her eyes pinched sharply at me from their corners. Her lips pursed. "You number ten. You shit—American."

Most of the other hawkers had seen me by this time and I was besieged by six or more venders. A young woman held up a baby to me, "You buy Baby-San." She laughed, and pinched my arm which was resting on the bus sill. Older women hawkers stood away from the bus eyeing me suspiciously yet getting some good laughs at the sales techniques which their younger associates were using with me. Things were getting out of control. Excited by my youth and strangeness some venders began to pinch my arm or to pull my hair to get my attention. My good will was ebbing; I was wearying and began looking about nervously, wondering why the bus was not yet moving. Passengers seated nearby pretended not to notice my uncomfortable situation.

Meanwhile, the boy had been stowing on the roof a wire basket filled with chickens, some wicker baskets filled with long loaves of French bread, a chair, and a few battered suitcases. There had been some loud, irritated discussion between the boy and the bus driver about the loading and placement of the rooftop cargo. Passersby stopped, offered their advice, called wisecracks to the boy sweating and carrying out the various decisions and matching wits and jokes with the advisors.

Having secured the rooftop cargo, the boy moved into the bus to seat those people still standing up in the aisle. Probably the boy got a share from the driver for crushing four and five into a seat. When the seats were gone, the boy materialized small folding stools and simultaneously directed people to sit on their own suitcases wherever they could find space. I was impressed by the boy's expertise in manipulating people and things. He gently guided an arthritic old man to the seat I was sharing with two other women. From the front, the bus driver snapped some command which released a glint of anger from the boy's face. His small chest heaved; he brushed hair from his forehead. He motioned the two women and me closer together to make room for the "old gentlemen." He addressed the old man respectfully, and both the old man and the boy ignored the grumbling complaints of the two Delta women crowded beside me.

The boy noticed the crowd beneath my window. Perhaps he saw a poke or a pinch; maybe he caught a weary or nervous look on my face. His face muscles tightened as he leaned over my seat resting his hands on the window sill. "Enough" he shouted, "Go away now." I was grateful. Someone threw a piece of bread at him. He caught it and threw it back. The crowd moved away from the bus. He was smiling and talking; the hawkers were laughing. I heard him say "hippy" and lots of laughter. I didn't like being the joke, but at least the heat was off. He moved onto the steps in front of me. He yelled to the driver, and lit a cigarette as the bus lurched to a start. He took a long draw on his cigarette and watched me as I examined my pinched arm. He clucked from the side of his mouth.

"Very bad," he said in Vietnamese. He asked me if I spoke Vietnamese.

"Very little. Do you speak English?"

"Little bit," he said in clear English and shrugged, turning away from me. Another long cigarette drag. He pulled a rolled magazine from his back pocket. On the front cover was a rotogravure photograph of the one and only Vietnamese rock group, the CBC. Turning to me, pointing at the picture, "You know?"

"Yes, the CBC. They're very good."

Smiling, he said, "Boss. I hear a lot at Club. You know?"

"Yes, I like them. They're boss."

The CBC were pretty good. Little people with big voices doing good imitations of hard, American rock. The Club was a place where only rich Vietnamese and GI's could afford to go. If this kid went to the Club, I thought, he was making more money in more ways than working on these country-bound busses. He became engrossed in his magazine as we rode through Saigon suburbs.

Saigon, like any other city, has its posh section of town, only it's a much smaller posh section than other cities. Beyond this six-block radius where one finds the Presidential Palace, the National Assembly, American built government buildings, JUSPAO (Joint United States Public Affairs Office), two or three large hotels, a few expensive restaurants, and a French-built shopping mall and theatre, sprawls the most dense and desperate population in the world. Refugee families are piled on top of one another in their scavenged homes of army tarps, wood, and if fortunate, corrugated tin. Families survive in alleys, cemeteries, and in the gutters. With families in the gutters, children are left to the streets.

The boy was a street kid. Perhaps he wasn't a kid. Maybe old enough to be in the army. City boys not yet captured by the army work the streets and the foreigners; pickpocketing, pimping, heroin dealing are common professions. It takes a good, fast mind to dodge successfully both military and police authorities.

The city shacks, filth and human waste now began to thin into flat and muddly defoliated suburbs where there were few homes and many army installations. Civilian life seemed to exist at their periphery.

"Hung," the driver's snapping of the boy's name brought my attention back into the crowded bus. Hung agilely twisted his way up the aisle to the bus driver's seat. They had a whispered conversation, then back came Hung to the rear door. He lit another cigarette, brushed his hair back from his forehead, hiked his pants, straightened his shirt. Collected, he picked up his "Hot Rock" magazine and gently pushed it underneath the rubber mat which was covering the first step of the bus door. Grinding gears, the bus jerkingly slowed to a stop. Hung was hanging out the door, cigarette dangling from his tightened lips, and waving greetings to people along the roadside. I leaned out of my window and saw a military checkpoint station 100 yards ahead.

In front of the checkpoint station the bus veered to the shoulder and stopped. Hung jumped from the bus and was grabbed by the arm by a soldier. Hung pointed to the bus, the soldier nodded and released Hung's arm. A soldier came onto the bus, ordered us to do something and got off again. Everyone busily went about collecting their belongings and checking for their identity papers. I felt my purse for my passport. The babies on the bus were awakened from their hot sticky sleep and began to cry. One by one the passengers filed off the bus. A soldier standing in front of the door separated us into lines of men and boys, women and children. The bus driver was talking to an officer and two soldiers who seemed to be giving him a hard time about the papers he presented to them. I looked around for Hung and found him on the bus roof with a soldier beside him. He had opened a suitcase and was watching, one arm on his hips, the other stroking his hair, as the soldier searched through its contents.

They processed the women's line quickly. The woman in front of me had two small children, a baby, and a large shopping bag. I gestured an offer to hold the baby. She smiled shyly and gave me the baby, then juggled one child and the shopping bag in her arms. I was glad to be useful and grateful I had something to do with my hands. The baby in my arms also partially blocked my body from the gawking stares of the soldiers. One officer checked the papers of the woman in front of me, then helped himself to a piece of fruit from her shopping bag. She protested. He shrugged and bit into the fruit. He moved towards me and I handed him my passport.

Back on the sweltering bus, I watched the line of hot, weary men fanning themselves as they waited for their military papers to be checked. Alongside the station, a beer vender had set up a few tables, and was serving iced beer to Hung and the bus driver. The bus driver looked slick with his gold framed shades and baseball cap as he joked with the soldiers with whom he had recently argued. Hung and the bus driver mopped their sweating foreheads and sipped their cold beers as they waited for their passengers to pass through the checkpoint.

When the bus pulled onto the road I tried to see if we had left anyone behind because of papers that weren't in order, but the bus was as crowded as before. Hung was back on the stairs. I looked closely at his face and decided he was older than I first thought. There was a look of calculated cleverness that didn't belong to a youngster.

Once out on the country road the bus picked up speed. The air was clear, free of city exhaust fumes. The bus moved at 70-80 kph. The wind rushed in and refreshed us all. Hung was leaning out the bus door, smiling against the rushing wind. The countryside was flat. Far off, against the horizons rose small mountains. The land had been defoliated on either side of the road. For mile-long stretches there was nothing but baked mud and barren shrubs. Beyond the mud, at the edge of the cleared zone, the rice shoots swayed to a gentle breeze. In the middle of almost every paddy incense smoke rose from the ancestral tombs. I watched Hung gaze over the rice and wave to the children tending the family tomb and water buffalo.

Every six or seven miles the bus driver would pull off the road and a few passengers would work their way off the bus while Hung followed them with their packages. Usually some of the passengers' family would be waiting. Hung would hand the packages to the family members and wave goodby as they walked down a narrow path which led beyond the rice paddies to the village shaded by tall Eucalyptus trees. The bus driver got impatient at Hung's pleasantries and did a lot of grumbling and spitting. With Hung back in position, the bus ground its way through the gears, and was going 70 kph in no time.

There was a loud noise on the roof which startled me. It sounded as if the roof cargo was blowing away. Hung flung his body out the door and hopped onto a window sill. With some scraping, he scrambled onto the roof. His feet dangled, then disappeared. Some more noise came from the roof, then as quickly as he had disappeared, he reappeared on the steps. He looked at me to see if I appreciated his acrobatics.

I was laughing, but impressed.

The bus was slowing down again. This time it stopped in front of a small stucco building about 50 yards off the road. Children of all ages were thrusting themselves out of the schoolhouse door. School was out. Three teenaged girls in fluttering white *ao dais* waited by the roadside to board the bus. There were no seats, no more stools, and barely enough room for the three girls to stand. The bus moved out, but Hung wasn't in position. I was afraid we were going to leave him behind. I looked back and saw him carelessly jogging alongside the bus. The bus picked up speed and so did Hung, effortlessly he jumped aboard. The three girls giggled at him. Then they noticed me. Domino theory: the girl closest to me poked the girl in the middle in the ribs, and she whispered to the next. Hung laughed and said something which made all three giggle and demurely turn their faces away from me. The boldest of the three directed a question at Hung. He said to me in English, "They think you a French teacher."

"No, I'm an American teacher."

He relayed the message which brought surprise to the girls' eyes and comments from a few passengers seated nearby who happened to be listening.

The girls were curious about me but were pretty curious about Hung too. They peeked at him from underneath their conical hats, yet lowered their heads and voices when he glanced their way. Hung seemed to know he had their attention. Cigarette in his mouth, out of the bus he went again. This time he crawled fly-like to the rear of the bus, belly pressed against the rear window as he checked the ropes securing the cargo on the roof. Into the bus again, back onto the roof, and down again while the bus tore along the narrow country road at 70 kph.

Barbed wire, curled coils looking like tumbleweed began to appear on the shoulder of the road. Tin sheets, with the coca-cola can imprint, walled one-room shacks where women were sitting, watching babies play in the dusty earth. We were approaching a small army base. The barbed wire was the first sign. Several tanks were parked half on the road, half on the shoulder. We were slowing down. Ahead a line of traffic; ahead of the traffic a one lane bridge crossing a branch of the Mekong river. Sandbag shelters were scattered on either side of the river bank like mushrooms.

On the other side of the road was a group of cream-colored houses, with the traditional two-pillared porch, and red tiled roof. Beyond the houses were the rice paddies. A patrol of about twenty soldiers was hiking out of the jungle on the raised paths running between the two paddies. The soldiers carried their rifles across their shoulders. Waiting for the soldiers on the road was a cold drink vender.

It was apparent that we were at another checkpoint, the last one just outside of My Tho. People were climbing out of their cars, jumping down from trucks, and taking the opportunity to stretch their legs. I watched a group of four soldiers progress down the line of traffic, checking papers, car trunks, and floor space under the seats. Some drivers were directed to an official looking building to have their papers more carefully scrutinized.

The heat of the day seemed to be melting the bus. My arm could no longer rest on the window sill and my seat was slick with sweat from thighs sticky on the beaten leather seats. The children in the bus were fussing; mothers shifted their children from one leg to another as they tried to fan themselves. One woman began singing to her screaming baby boy. Finally the soldiers had made it to our bus. They boarded and we all moved to produce our identification. Two soldiers stayed outside talking with the bus driver. Hung was sitting on the bottom step, wiping the sweat from his forehead. One of the soldiers was watching Hung as he listened to the bus driver. He nudged the other soldier, and gestured with a nod of his head towards Hung. Both men ambled, swayed lazily towards Hung. As they approached Hung stood up. They said something to him, then from his back pocket he produced a battered wallet, pulled out an identity card, and gave it to one of the soldiers. The soldier looked at the card and seemed surprised. He passed on the card to his comrade and began shouting at Hung. He pushed Hung against the bus, and continued to prod the boy while he fired questions at him. The other soldier was not too interested and looked at the ID card, then back up the line of traffic towards the bridge.

I could hear the angry voice of the soldier and hear the sounds of Hung being beaten up. The soldier repeated the same question over and over, between punches, "How old are you?" Hung was whining an answer, then he was punched again. I could hear the sounds, but I couldn't see. Soon the first two soldiers finished checking the passengers and climbed off the bus. They called to the guy beating up Hung. As if nothing unusual had happened all four soldiers proceeded to the next vehicle in line. I saw the bus driver move towards the rear of the bus, and heard Hung spitting and sniffing. Ten minutes later, Hung appeared at the side of the bus, picked up his card lying in the dirt, and mounted the steps. People on the bus stared at him, but said nothing. His shirt was ripped, his cheek bone was swollen and bruised, and he was tending a bleeding lip with a soiled handkerchief. He stood on the step, looking past the army base to the jungle tree tops. Once across the bridge, Hung fly-climbed onto the roof of the bus and stayed there for the remaining twenty minutes into My Tho.

The My Tho bus station was an exact replica of Saigon's, smaller and dingier but the same design. As soon as the bus pulled off the street into the station, the cyclo drivers, fruit sellers, bread venders, street urchins gravitated towards the bus as if it were a magnet pulling society's shavings. The bus stopped, and the various venders hit every passenger climbing off the bus. I decided to stay seated until the bus more or less cleared. My cat-eyed face caught the sharp eyes of the bread woman, and she alerted the rest of the venders. Plied again with various goods and services, I prepared myself to negotiate the bus station. Hung came down off the roof where he had been unloading the cargo. He looked at me and the young man who was trying to pull my small suitcase out of my hand. Clucking his tongue, he looked at me and said in English "Good luck."

I said the same to him and watched him disappear among the late afternoon crowd at the station.

Values in the Arts and Sciences: A Course

Elizabeth Coleman

Discourse about curriculum and teaching in liberal arts education has a rich and varied history. Continuing dialogue has been generated by the confrontation between commitments to the unity of knowledge with its thrust towards interdisciplinary general education, and the intellectual and institutional powers of specialization. The allure of a core curriculum with its apparent advantage of a common experience for students and faculty and its promise of genuine intellectual community collides, again and again with the respected tradition that men of real stature teach their own course and no one else's. A core curriculum also poses the immense psychological difficulties for students and faculty of relinquishing their own individual interests, even temporarily, as the decisive principle governing curriculum. This repeated collision has assured vitality, not to mention volatility, in the articulation of means and ends appropriate to teaching and learning in the university. There are, of course, many other specific issues that provoke debate: introduction of new subject matters; relevance; the proper role of the creative and performing arts in a liberal arts curriculum; of independent study in an undergraduate education.

Nonetheless, despite the continuity of concern about education and the seriousness and discernment in much of the discussion about it, as my teaching experience has increased, so has my sense of the enormity of the gap between this discourse and what actually goes on in a classroom. I am not alone in this discovery; indeed, it is virtually a commonplace. The most pervasive explanation for this disconnectedness is that the decisive determinants of good teaching are particular innate virtues of individual teachers. As a corollary, the development of intellectual self-consciousness about what and how one teaches is seen as essentially irrelevant when it comes to the actualities of the classroom experience.

It would be foolhardy to deny the importance of the universally acclaimed qualities of dedication, native talent and devotion to one's subject matter in the art of teaching. Certainly the extent to which Maurice Cramer embodies these qualities, the occasion of this book, gives one pause about even questioning some of the claims made in the name of those virtues. To recognize that these qualities are inimitable because of their specialness is undoubtedly

reasonable. Using them, however, as the rationale for disclaiming the responsibility and desirability of thinking, scrutinizing, struggling with what we are
doing as teachers, and why, is both self-serving and limiting. Moreover, the
position that good teachers are born and not made bypasses what I think are
equally authentic, and certainly more important, reasons for the distance between theory and action in the arena of undergraduate education.

The fifteen years I have worked as teacher and administrator have been in
contexts where there has been an unusual amount of planning and thinking
about curriculum, about educational philosophy, about students, involving
faculty from colleges and universities throughout the country. One phenomenon which has emerged with painful clarity is a lack of the most minimal
consensus when it comes to action about concepts that permeate virtually
all serious discussion about liberal arts education. A particularly glaring example is in the use of a word obviously basic to any discussion of university
curriculum, that is, "discipline."

While it is probably safe to say that the widespread agreement with respect
to the existence of such things as disciplines goes a shade beyond the verbal
level, once one gets close to the dimensions of meaning that would actually
affect the selection and organization of materials and the ways of exploring
them in a classroom, it is as if people were speaking in different and alien
tongues. In the absence of such consensus what proves decisive again and
again is not what happens on the level of immediate debate and discussion,
but the prior educational experience of the participants. If one happened to
attend the University of Chicago, concepts like "grounds of a discipline"
have a wealth of associations dealing with the meta-level of various kinds of
inquiry; for others it is understood as an attempt to turn all knowledge into
philosophy; for still others it is the historical context out of which disciplines
grew. For those who experienced general education courses at Harvard, it
tends to be individuals who come to define what the fundamentals of a
discipline are. The decisive issue becomes, for example, whether a student
initially encounters literature with a Reuben Brower or a Harry Levin. A
relatively sophisticated grasp of an historical approach to the relationship of
ideas is very likely to be a product of the famed Contemporary Civilization
and Humanities courses at Columbia. There are, of course, other institutions
where these and analogous orientations exist. The point is that while all of
these experiences result in a shared commitment to the importance of curriculum and a concern for the relation of general and specialized education,
they simultaneously result in radically different notions of the implications of these concerns. These differences are obscured repeatedly because of

similarities in a language that swirls around and about these concerns.

Another example of an absence of consensus, one which exists less frequently in the literature about education, but no less so in its practice, is the notion of what a "course" is. The failures of communication that exist on such a seemingly basic issue can scarcely be exaggerated. To many the idea that a course should be subject to some kind of definition beyond the fact that it is "elementary" or "advanced," "in physics" or "in literature," that all of its books are "great," or written in the same century, is a revolutionary, if not heretical, notion. To others these are mere categories and do not begin to provide the structure necessary to select and organize the materials of a course. The difficulty here is not so much caused by the language used in seeking to communicate, but by the absence of any tradition of systematic effort to communicate at all about this dimension of teaching. It would seem that the issue of what constitutes a course is somehow beneath such attention.

In both instances the prevailing attitudes towards appropriate levels of discourse about education present major obstacles to genuine communication. The points at which understanding might be possible because they would deal directly with the shared experience of teachers tend to be bypassed as undeserving of serious inquiry. In so doing, the conditions that might yield effective communication about the more abstract issues are forfeited. Diversity, pluralism and disagreement are critical to the vitality of education; but if we are to make use of the wealth and range of experience that exists in American higher education we are going to have to start talking and thinking a good deal more than we now do about the experience of the classroom itself, where what we think is translated into what we do. There are, no doubt, any number of ways of pursuing this task; what I propose to do in this paper is to try to describe in some detail a course in which I was recently involved.

The course was offered at the New School for Social Research in a recently initiated one-year program devoted exclusively to the Freshman Year of college. Students are almost all early entrants, in most cases having completed their junior year of high school and in a few cases only their sophomore year. It was a one-semester course with twenty students. While the students were by and large gifted and highly motivated, there was a substantial range in their abilities and in their previous educational achievements.

The course was taught by two people—one (myself) immersed in a tradition concerned with the organization of knowledge, the relation of disciplines, the importance of curriculum. My specialty is literature, and my orientation is essentially non-historical (not to be confused with anti-historical) emphasizing that which provides internal intelligibility to texts. My teaching had been consistently aimed at involving students in the activities of analysis and interpretation, in which the development of their powers of inquiry generally was central. The other instructor[1] had no readily defined orientation to any of the traditional academic disciplines, and a wide-ranging interest in all of them. Her intellectual predilection was towards synthetic overarching concepts which was in sharp contrast to mine. What we shared was a commitment to the texts studied as the appropriate center of inquiry, as *the* mediating link between faculty and students, between student and student. In the words of my co-teacher, "the text was to be the 'star' of the course."

Although I had taught many courses in which several people were involved in the planning and teaching, this was the first time I had taught with another person in the same classroom. We had no elaborate plans about how we would proceed; what we had agreed upon was some division of responsibility for various sections of the course. The effect of having two instructors was undoubtedly complex and important, one which I do not begin to understand adequately. A consequence of the co-teaching that is clear was that it allowed a rare opportunity for scrutiny, placing one of us always in a position that was somewhere between student and teacher. The course was called "Values in the Arts and Sciences." Since the title was one of the last things we arrived at, it is probably best to try to recapitulate our thinking about the purposes of the course and the selection of texts as a way of making the title intelligible.

The initial idea of the course was to take a series of texts radically distinct from each other in terms of their subject matter and traditions (historical, disciplinary, intellectual), thereby stripping students and faculty of any frame of reference from which to approach these texts other than that provided by the texts themselves. The point was to "force" the issue of using one's own resources in the activity of reading without benefit of a shaping context. Behind this was the presumption that texts reveal within themselves the sources of their intelligibility, their power and their value, *however much the nature of that intelligibility, power and value might differ.* What we did not presume was that all texts had a sameness at these levels; on the contrary, the challenge of reading was precisely to develop those resources which let the texts make these determinations rather than to develop modes of reading which predetermine just those issues.[2] Our presuppositions obviously raise serious questions. Perhaps it is a valuable approach to the arts but what about the sciences? Regardless of discipline, aren't most serious texts simply inaccessible without benefit of some kind of scholarly apparatus, historical context, or mastery of subject matter? Even assuming that something could be seen in texts without benefit of some "background," some shaping context, could such "insights" be taken seriously? If we were to assure that our assumptions about the nature of texts and the resources of readers would be genuinely *tested* rather than automatically confirmed, the range and character of texts selected was a critical concern.

The first text chosen was *Genesis,* which would confront most of the above questions and thus seemed an appropriate place to start. We next selected texts that would shift the ground from under us as much as possible by moving to history—from a world where presumably fact (what is) is subordinate to value (what should be), to one where value is presumably subordinate to fact. The readings chosen were Book I of Herodotus' *Persian Wars* and Book I of Thucydides' *Peloponnesian Wars.* By the conclusion of this section of readings students would hopefully have some idea of what it meant to confront texts which made quite disparate demands. They would have begun to experience the capacity of these texts to communicate, and their own to comprehend, without benefit of the usual resources of continuity and context.

The next sequence was designed to test further the powers of text and reader by turning first to art and then to science. Shakespeare's *King Lear* and Freud's *Five Lectures on Psychoanalysis* (the Clark University Lectures) were chosen for this section of the course. In each case there were some supplementary texts—for *King Lear* the historic and literary sources and Tate's emendation; for Freud, "The Case Study of Anna O," (in Breuer and Freud's *Studies in Hysteria*) and Erikson's "The First Psychoanalyst." The reader may wonder at this point whether the use of supplementary texts wasn't fudging the issue of autonomy by adding a shaping context. There are several responses to this. First of all the particular cluster of readings selected tends to sharpen rather than diminish a reader's sense of the extent to which the focal texts attain a life of their own, *if* one examines them without presuming otherwise. Secondly, the idea of autonomy as used in this course was not that texts exist in a vacuum; it was used to explore ways in which texts themselves shape and define significant contexts (among other things that they do), rather than seeing one or another context as a necessary precondition to getting at the text. Differences in the kinds of supplementary readings reflect this. "The First Psychoanalyst" is quite different in kind, at least on the surface, from Tate's emendations. (Substantial similarities also exist;

the point here is that there are significant differences.)

Having spanned the seemingly dichotomous worlds of value and fact, and then hurtled from art to science, we decided to conclude with readings that would be reflexive with respect to prior readings. Thomas Kuhn's *The Structure of Scientific Revolutions* was a relatively clear-cut choice. Its character as an unusually provocative argument for a distinction between the actual nature of scientific inquiry and the way in which it tends to be seen by both the scientific community and the community at large had obvious resonance with respect to issues raised in the science readings. Tolstoy's *Anna Karenina* was chosen to conclude the course for several reasons, not the least of which was simply its monumental dimension. It was thought that the range of its content, the power of its art, its own claims to truth and goodness as well as art, would likely provide a context for reflecting on all of the prior readings. Along with Kuhn and Tolstoy we selected *The Communist Manifesto*. The rationale for this selection is at least as much a reflection of our concern with providing a *range* of reading experiences as its value as a reflexive text. Differences between this text and all the others in the role the audience plays in determining its value, and in the associations students would bring to it (in some respects almost the antithesis of those brought to *Genesis*) made it particularly suggestive. In addition the ways in which *The Communist Manifesto* raises the problems of the relation between thought and action would, we thought, inject a new note into our discussion and reflect back on previous discussions because of the extent to which this issue permeates all inquiry.

As the selection of texts proceeded the course began to assume added dimension in our thinking about it. The goal of teaching a kind of reading remained central, but in attempting to provide some organization to that process additional ideas about the character and potential of the course began to emerge. The art/science sequence of readings increasingly became a central point in our thinking. From this perspective the materials of the opening section (*Genesis*–Histories) could be seen as introductory to the art and science readings because of the role value and fact assume. Fact and value are critical aspects of the disciplines of art and science, but they are not themselves focal in the same sense as they are, respectively, in History and *Genesis*. The final section could then be seen as enabling us to expand from insights limited to particular texts in art and science to more general insights about them as instances of kinds of inquiry. This is not to say that because we happened to have chosen a play (albeit a very good one) and two lectures by Freud (which fine as they might be, aren't even considered "scientific" by many) that we thought we were now in a position to pursue a definitive study into the nature of art and science. What we did think was that we had provided an arena in which certain very basic assumptions about art and science could become subject to disciplined inquiry. Examples of the kinds of assumptions I am referring to concern the role of fact in art, of value in science; the role of selection and interpretation in both; the extent to which the kind of discovery associated with science is a *process* involving intuition and uncertainty rather than a set of deductive procedures starting from a collection of givens. We felt that confronting such issues was of particular value for college freshmen who were soon to face decisions which are often informed by strong preconceptions about these matters, where the nature of these preconceptions is often decidedly, indeed, shockingly, uniformed.

Once one touches on this order of preconceptions, one is very much in a world of values—values in the constitutive rather than in the substantive sense. I am referring to that level of choice, whether made with conscious freedom and reflection or unexamined conviction, which *shapes and informs* the uses of the intellect and imagination, rather than values as exhibited in judgments about substantive issues such as the merits of war, love, etc. The development of our thinking from a certain kind of textual analysis to values was more a fleshing out of the implications of the initial idea than a shift in direction. The virtues of the kind of confrontation between student and text that had shaped our planning of the course from the outset was that it could yield this level of insight into texts, and in the process, touch these levels in the readers as well. The ultimate goal of the course could now be restated as penetrating to a level where students would become aware of their determinate intellectual values as they engaged in a process of making contact with that order of values in the readings. I should hasten to add that this was the outer reaches, and most visionary, of our thoughts about the course.

Having provided this history of what existed in our minds as we planned the course, let me clarify what we saw as the relation between our guiding, synthetic concepts and the execution of the course itself. These concepts, or any others like them, that would define the purposes of the course or its structure was *not* the subject of the course. If we were to sustain what was absolutely fundamental to the course—the absence of a shaping context that would mediate between student and text—we were not about to insert our own. In short, in the context of the course itself, the only valid unifying insights were those which would emerge out of the experience of the course, whatever those insights might be. Any others, however "enlightened," were out of bounds. The purpose, then, of all of *our* ordering ideas was to enable us to select and organize texts in an effort to place the freedom and burden of discovering order on the students.

There was a brief additional section of science fiction readings added to the course as a result of discussions with students about the kinds of texts they would like to explore. On the face of it, science fiction seemed an interesting follow-up to the readings in art and science. This section of the course was to be student led with readings selected by students. An important aspect of our thinking that is exhibited in this decision was an interest in exploiting a range of pedagogical possibilities, not only that of co-teaching, which would involve shifting roles of faculty, but in this instance, one where the roles of student would shift. The point was to dramatize neither the ultimate authority of student nor faculty, but to locate that authority squarely in the texts.

To recapitulate, the readings of the course as we embarked were the following:

> *Genesis*
> Herodotus, *The Persian Wars* (Book I)
> Thucydides, *The Peloponnesian Wars* (Book I)
> Shakespeare, *King Lear* (including sources & Tate's emended version)
> Freud, *Five Lectures on Psychoanalysis* (lectures 1 & 2)
> Breuer-Freud, "The Case of Anna O."
> Erikson, "The First Psychoanalyst" (Repr. in *Insight & Responsibility*)
> Science Fiction Readings
> Thomas Kuhn, *The Structure of Scientific Revolutions*
> Marx and Engels, *The Communist Manifesto*
> Tolstoy, *Anna Karenina*

The opening class was a carefully planned session in which the instructor intended to discuss first how we were to go about reading *Genesis* and then provide an example by doing an analysis of Chapter One. Students were asked to try to leave behind their preconceptions about *Genesis* and the meaning of God. It was pointed out that this text was purported to reveal the nature of God and that we should at least look at it before we decided what the nature of that revelation was to be. As to how we would read it, it was simply stated that we would read it "as *Genesis*" and that we could not possibly know what that meant until we had confronted the text. These seemingly innocuous statements precipitated the first crisis of the course. Significantly, the most explosive issue was confronting the text "as *Genesis*." Students kept seeking some further articulation of "how" we were to read it. Were we reading it "as literature," "as history," as "the Bible"? The push for some mediating context other than the text itself was surprisingly intense. History has certainly done its part in suggesting that looking directly at *Genesis* is indeed "heretical." It is not only the role that religious institutions have played, but the ways in which scholars have continually reinforced the impression of needing to bring a perspective and/or scholarly apparatus of one kind or another to an examination of the Bible. This, in combination with the tradition of taking lines out of the text and developing interpretations as if these lines existed in a void, constituted a formidable opposition.

The other crisis was that of leaving preconceptions behind. That this would be difficult was to be expected, and from our point of view valuable in laying the groundwork for a subsequent realization of the role that preconceptions play in controlling insight and, more to the point, in precluding insight. Moreover it did so in a context where students were particularly adamant and confident about the legitimacy of their preconceptions. After repeated failure to persuade anyone who wasn't convinced before beginning, the instructor simply plowed ahead.

Chapter One of *Genesis* is the reader's initial encounter with God and it is done through an exhibition of His power—specifically that of creating a world. When one looks at how this world is created, it is by providing structure, order and intelligibility to that which is "without form," and content and continuity to that which is "void." What God *makes*, in short, is order itself, life itself, continuity itself, and the making of such "things" is simultaneous with the desire that it be so. It is a magnificent and awesome display of power, one which man at the utmost of his creativity could only hope to imitate. The very conditions for the uses of human intellect and imagination are what God makes. That light which opens the creation precedes the light of the sun, I suspect, because it is light as associated with the activity of seeing itself in its fullest sense.[3]

Such a conception of God is not exactly what students had in mind—their associations were by and large those which are attached to an authoritarian, arbitrary, all-powerful father. Wherever their presuppositions may have come from it was clear that the very different picture sketched above had emerged from the text when looked at as if it had internal intelligibility. That presumption involved a very careful scrutiny of the text, not only of what was said but when, how, etc.

The remaining sessions on *Genesis* were a continuation of this kind of scrutiny, only with much more active participation by the students. In the process came discoveries, reversals of expectations, old answers coming unhinged, questions turning on their heads. Familiar passages like the Abraham-Isaac story took on another dimension when Abraham's unquestioning obedience to God's command was seen following on the heels of Abraham's challenge to God over the justice of His decision to destroy Sodom and Gomorrah. Abraham's audacity in arguing and God's willingness to accede were every bit as remarkable as Abraham's silent acquiescence in the face of God's command to sacrifice Isaac. The effort to comprehend a conception of God, and man's relationship to Him, which involved confronting this sequence of incidents was to suggest here, as elsewhere, that we were in the face of an ethic that was a good deal more complex and compelling than had been imagined. At the very least students became increasingly aware that insofar as they had rejected the God of Abraham, Isaac and Jacob, they had done so on the basis of grounds that were a lot weaker than the text demanded of them. Suddenly it was the students' parochialism rather than that of the "religious folk" out there that had become uppermost. Religious conversion was not what happened; what did happen was an unsettling of complacent self-assurance. The atmosphere was often a charged one, as the strain of maintaining disbelief was felt amidst the excitement of seeing things freshly. In the process, questioning attitudes towards reading, one of the most presumably neutral of human activities, had become associated with one of the least neutral—religious conviction.

We next turned to Herodotus—no explanations, no transitions. By this time (we had spent three weeks on *Genesis)* the idea of plunging into a text was routine; jumping abruptly from one world to another was not. There were only two sessions on Herodotus, and the movement of the class seemed extremely rapid. The opening class shifted from arguments that "this isn't history because of what it includes" to an increasing fascination with the significance and range of that "what." Selection, choice, as an issue in the writing of history became inescapable, not because of the limits Herodotus placed on significant fact but those which the students discovered in their own reactions to Herodotus. It wasn't that Herodotus left out politics, economics, military tactics; it was all the other things he managed to include that had provoked initial skepticism. By the conclusion of the second class, interest had focused on how Herodotus had put it all together in a way that is comprehensible.

Thucydides' *History* was the first text read that conforms to dominant preconceptions. The complication now was that students had become "Herodotians," sufficiently so that they were by no means ready to accept automatically the methodological arguments of Thucydides or its concomitant limitations on what constitutes legitimate areas of historical inquiry. Students then had to wrestle with this text every bit as much as they had with Herodotus. As a result, the quality and quantity of insight was impressive, sometimes astounding. We were one-third of the way through the course and already it seemed as if many of our most exorbitant expectations were being met. This impression proved to be short-lived. The last class on Thucydides dealt with Pericles' funeral oration. Our intention was to confront the range and flexibility that Thucydides allows himself despite his commitment to methodological rigor—hardly what we thought of as a particularly explosive starting point. We never approached that issue. Instead the class erupted into fierce debates provoked by some of the students' reactions to the values Pericles exhibits towards war, death, patriotism. It was an unequivocal instance of a clash between the values of student and text in which the discipline of inquiry collapsed. There were fitful efforts by students to discuss such relatively dispassionate subjects as whether or not the speech represented Thucydides' point of view, whether or not that made any difference, why the reaction of Pericles' audience was omitted, assuming it was, etc. But they disintegrated in the face of the frustration and anger that increasingly pervaded and finally overwhelmed this session. It was also the first indication of the intensity of students' personal involvement in the course itself, an aspect of the course that was to become increasingly evident and important. Even recognizing that issues such as war, patriotism, and political leadership tend to provoke heated discussion, the sense of something incommensurate about the provocation and the response was palpable. The continual dislocations of context and value had evidently touched students at emotionally charged levels. Whereas here it was exhibited in a relatively commonplace situation, subsequently it was to surface when dealing with a very different order of values, those where the teachers' role has traditionally been to try to galvanize student involvement.

We next turned our attention to *King Lear* where history was to play a very different role. In examining the sources relative to the play, the importance of the artist as maker of significant fact rather than its discoverer began to emerge. Shakespeare's manipulations of the sources underscored the extent to which we were being carried into a world of fiction, but in the process we saw the facts within that world acquire the unequivocal character that is continually sought, but never attained, in history or anywhere else. Whatever happens in *King Lear* happens inalterably and indisputably, and these events simultaneously assume unquestionable significance just by their very existence. Once the facts of the text were seen as embodying significance simply by virtue of being there, the "mere" *seeing* of those facts assumed immense importance.

As the class proceeded to look, it rapidly became clear that in this context seeing was a complex activity, one which demanded concentration, energy and inquiry. Contact with the text itself became in this section of the course not only the starting point, but the terminal point, of discussion. "Interpreting" *Lear* had initially meant for many students abstracting some incandescent "truth" from the welter of impressions and suggestions they thought of as *King Lear*; now they found themselves instead seeking significance by immersion in its facts. Ultimately, the very dominance of the text became an issue as students began to explore the question of what role, if any, remained for our values as audience in shaping the experience of *King Lear*. For some students this intense concentration on the text exemplified and crystallized their sense of what the course was all about; for others, it remained the most enigmatic section precisely because, in their words, "We never got beyond the text." By and large the mood of the discussion had become for the moment a good deal less heated and decidedly more reflective.

Freud was next, and the atmosphere of the class was to shift almost as much as the subject matter. Using the Clark University Lectures, in which Freud reconstructs the early history of psychoanalysis, involved seeing Freud re-create a time when he was in a state of ignorance relative to the students. Leaving distorting preconceptions behind in this instance meant seeing the limits of Freud's early knowledge and putting in abeyance one's own knowledge. This is not as easy to do as it may seem. When asked at the start of a class what Freud had covered in the opening pages of the first lecture, students mentioned concepts that were not to appear in the course of the entire text. This was more than a matter of careless reading; students were genuinely baffled by our concern for looking at the details of this text with the same care we had given the others. After all, wasn't the issue here what Freud was "getting at" and didn't their comments indicate that they "knew" that. Behind this lay a notion of theory as something that comes full-blown with a complete set of terminology and conclusions. Knowing the theory then meant having at one's command an assortment of appropriate terms. Associations between theory and processes of inquiry were nonexistent. This dissociation significantly limited both the way students initially treated the lectures (the real action for them being mastery of somewhere "outside" the details of Freud's reasoning) and their grasp of how the reasoning process itself informs the shape and value of conclusions.

Breaking through these limits meant getting in touch with the text as it unfolded that process. The impact of doing so was dramatic. What turned out to be critical in Freud's capacity to make the kinds of discoveries we watched him reconstruct was his capacity to *relinquish* again and again seeming access to knowledge: first the doctor's expertise as the source of relevant information altogether, then all the available techniques for getting at what he decides is the only legitimate source of information—the patient. It is only when he has brought himself to what he describes as "the seemingly senseless and hopeless undertaking, the task of learning from the patient something that I did not know and that he did not know himself," that he takes the speculative leap which carries him from almost total uncertainty to the realm of major discovery.[4] His way of doing so is commensurate with the undertaking. He takes the patient's insistence on ignorance, the very source of "the hopelessness and senselessness," and examines *it*. In doing so, the idea of "resistance," together with "repression" conceived as its necessary precondition, emerges to become the basis of Freud's view "of the course of cyclical events in hysteria."[5]

The class in which this turning point in Freud's lecture was explored turned out to have its own drama. When someone suggested that the only resources Freud had left at this moment were his sheer genius for discovery, a student, almost leaping from his chair said, "Now I know why it isn't science." A flood of comments ensued to the effect that any use of intuition, imagination, speculative thought, one student even precluded theory, was not science. What was science?—some process of deductive reasoning from givens, and that is putting it a good deal more clearly than anything that was said. This was the first time in the course that the nature of the disciplines was made an issue, and it was, to put it mildly, a genuinely spontaneous and revealing moment. The mixture of naivete and certainty, the absence of reflection, was breathtaking. No doubt about it, we were in the land of values.

Erikson's paper, in analyzing the nature of Freud's creativity and creativity in general, played very much into our discussions of Freud. It was an interesting class because Erikson's conception of the source of Freud's genius was not only different from ours, it was directly at odds with it. Erikson makes a point of saying that the early work of Freud (precisely that which we had read) lacked the clues needed to discern the nature of his genius, and turns to the Fliess letters to find them. Differences were to be expected, given Erikson's far greater familiarity with Freud's life and work and his own indebtedness to Freud, but his turning away from precisely those dimensions of that work which we had found so compelling raised interesting questions.

From our perspective it seemed evident that there was as much of Erikson as there was of Freud in Erikson's analysis of Freud's creativity; at the same time Erikson's analysis contained insights that were of great interest to the class. Discussion of the reader's values in affecting insight now assumed additional dimension. In this context Erikson's informing preconceptions could be seen as a condition for insight, and simultaneously the cause of discernable limits to that insight.

When Erikson extends his analysis of Freud to examine other instances of comparable scientific creativity he collapses the grounds that underlie any possible distinctions between artistic and scientific creativity. This was intriguing to students and for some led to a sharp about-face. Now all scientists were wonderful because they were in fact artists. An expansion of possibilities was certainly developing, but at a substantial price. The fact that distinctions they had lived with for so long were no longer viable had been taken to mean that there were no important distinctions. For the moment efforts to reconstruct a new set of distinctions paled before the discovery of similarities.

Next came science fiction which was seen as a welcome relief by students— a relaxation from the intensity and difficulty of previous weeks. The analysis of texts in class were thoughtful and sophisticated, but there was absolutely no effort to make any connections with the previous readings in art and science, which was mildly disappointing at the time. On reflection this "staying clear" from the rest of the course was probably inseparable from the value of this section for students. They clearly wanted to get away from the world of over-reaching that we had been so thoroughly immersed in, and to have an opportunity to exhibit their talents rather than having their limits explored again and again in constantly shifting and demanding contexts.

Kuhn's *The Structure of Scientific Revolutions* also proved to be an occasion which exhibited the resources of the class, but in this instance as a culmination of all that had preceded. Kuhn's concern with the relation of fact to theory, discovery to problem solving, the real versus the apparent nature of scientific inquiry, the complex role of paradigm in generating discovery through limiting possibilities, made the entire course appear as a preparation for this text. In my previous attempts to teach this text, students' preconceptions presented serious obstacles to their recognition of the radical character of Kuhn's argument. There was a general tendency to evade the issue by, for example, confusing Kuhn's use of paradigm with theory. The idea that theory and fact have a dynamic relationship is a provocative, but scarcely a revolutionary, speculation which leaves Kuhn's real target—more basic assumptions about scientific progress—intact. Students in the "Values" course were startled and fascinated by the substance of Kuhn's arguments, but insofar as it is an assault on preconceptions relating to the nature of scientific inquiry and the role of interpretation, it was a continuation and culmination of where they were. In fact students tended to extend the implications of Kuhn's argument rather than to pull back from them. The students' capacity to go with the text rather than fighting it made it possible for us to explore freely some of the most difficult interpretive questions and, paradoxically, enabled us to subject Kuhn's own argument to the kind of scrutiny he brings to science. Was history (seen as process) perhaps Kuhn's paradigm which, while functioning as a condition of his insights also, of necessity, precluded others?

The accomplishment of the class is inseparable from a judgment of Kuhn's accomplishment. Regardless of how controversial Kuhn's conclusions about the nature of scientific inquiry may be, his capacity to get at significant dimensions of all inquiry that frequently remain unexplored does, I think, make *The Structure of Scientific Revolutions* an important text to encounter within a liberal arts education. Certainly it was a text that had a lot to do with some of the central goals of the course and the facility with which students handled it was, for us, a significant measure of the success of the course.

At this point, time forced us to change the reading list. There were only a handful of classes remaining, the *Communist Manifesto*, and *Anna Karenina* had yet to be discussed and we felt that a session prior to the concluding session should be devoted to reflecting on the course itself. It was decided, regretfully, to drop *Anna Karenina* from the required readings. While for us the *Communist Manifesto* was somewhat anti-climactic both because *The Structure of Scientific Revolutions* was a hard text to follow and because of our growing exhaustion, it was not so for the students.

Discussion focussed initially on the seeming contradiction between the profundity of the context—all of human history, past, present, and future—and an apparent indifference to the use of evidence, together with the repeated use of emotionally charged language. The view of human history and its implications seemed something that one had to accept wholesale without anything resembling adequate proof. A few students who were politically committed to the text argued as best they could to persuade others that it could stand alone, but had great difficulty. Gradually, the discussion shifted as questions were raised about why the authors had omitted detailed use of evidence, why the presence of inflammatory language, why the striking omissions such as what else one had to lose besides one's "chains." Insights, discoveries at this point were fitful, but for most students in the class there was a growing recognition that we were seeing a subordination of values. Those virtues associated with truth—thoroughness and dispassion—were submitting to another set of values which were not only different but conflicting. These were the values associated with action. Interestingly the idea that such a subordination of values could take place was somewhat shocking to a substantial number of students. The idea that one could relinquish an unqualified concern with truth in order to achieve something else, however glorious, was by no means something they accepted as self evident. It was one of the instructors, not one of the students, who suggested that if we were looking at a piece of political rhetoric, wasn't it noteworthy that it contained so *much* dimension, such a richness of thought and reflection.

Throughout the course there had been intermittent pressure from students for us to clarify the over-all purposes of the course. We responded minimally because the activity of seeking the answer to that question—the activity of *organizing* one's own experience into a coherent and significant whole—was to be the students' obligation in this course. Ours had been to provide a sequence of experiences rich in potential for various kinds and levels of meaningful synthesis. In order to focus the first effort by the students to discuss the course as a whole we asked them to think about questions that would be appropriate for the final paper.

Efforts to center the discussion on that issue disintegrated almost immediately. Discussion wandered over a wide range of areas in a relatively incoherent set of stops and starts. Two themes did, nonetheless, emerge: the relationship between the arts and sciences, and the activity of reading. Interest in pinning down the differences between art and science had revived, but efforts to develop distinctions were unsatisfactory, primarily because the levels of distinction were so broad as to be inadequate. Discussions about reading—the relation of the values of reader and text, the meaning of interpretation—were, in contrast, much more disciplined and penetrating. From our point of view the class was inconclusive. There were certain moments in it that seemed to touch on what could be called a genuinely cumulative and synthetic experience, but there were many others that didn't. In the absence of any clear suggestions from students as to the final paper topic, we worked out several very general questions which were intended to provide as open a field as possible in which students could explore the course as a whole.

The closing session (one week later) was very relaxed and casual at the outset. We had no great design in mind and made that clear at the beginning of class. Comments by the students gradually moved to the course and their experience in writing the final papers, and informal conversations began to develop into serious discussion. The atmosphere in the room changed markedly as one after another, separately and in sustained interchange, students presented us with a series of carefully developed arguments about what the course was all about and why. It was evident that their struggle to provide intelligibility and significance had been a productive one. Despite individual differences in emphasis and quality, certain concerns emerged repeatedly both in class and in their papers.

First was the issue of the connection between the readings or, more accurately, the lack of connection:

> The question I have repeatedly asked myself throughout this course is: Exactly what are we searching for in "Values in the Arts and Sciences"? Each time we explored, debated, and struggled with a text, I found myself incapable of articulating our purpose. I was unable, at first, to make any connections between the various texts and felt as if I were being bounced from history to literature to psychoanalysis to science fiction, and back to history again, without time for reflection. This feeling eventually died out, however, and my approach to the works began to change. I began to actively seek out answers to my questions, rather than expecting the answers to miraculously fall into my lap. This is not to say that I was passive in my initial explorations, but that I presumed that I could obtain answers by forcing the text into my world, as opposed to moving *myself* into the world of the text.[6]

That search for order had also been, for some, a painful as well as a difficult struggle:

> The moving from discipline to discipline has been very difficult, and the style we have done it in has almost been bizarre sometimes. The reasons for this course have been almost incomprehensible. And also, the co-teaching has produced a strain and tension for me that has been particularly unusual. It's been both destructive and productive. For a course in Values in the Arts and Sciences, it has had a peculiar quality of flinging values to the winds.

After elaborating on the "two edged blade" aspect of the above she concludes:

> It has been the same frustration of values, this almost com-
> plete lack of framework to fall back on that has in turn
> forced me to do certain things that I didn't do in Fiction [a
> first semester course used by this student for purposes of
> comparison].

What most students did do in response to this "frustration of values" was to discover value in areas traditionally dissociated altogether from its domain. The extent of this expansion of value is suggested in the following where the disciplines of knowledge as such are seen as embodying value:

> The first major strength of this course was its ability to make
> me see values in all human endeavour. . . . Seeing values in my
> experience leads me to see them in that of others. I have come
> to see the disciplines of Politics, Science, and History as value-
> laden. The very idea of a discipline implies value — what is to
> be studied and not studied.

Interestingly the discovery of values in the land of inquiry did not diminish the intensity of involvement as it shifted from the more readily provocative territory of moral/political "convictions." On the contrary:

> The difficulty I had in dealing with *Genesis* and Herodotus
> and Thucydides stemmed from an inability to move into the
> worlds created in these works. The values in each challenged
> my own and therefore posed a threat. I am not speaking of
> convictions such as pacifism, peace, brotherhood or love. I
> am addressing myself to conceptions of truth, goodness,
> reality, objectivity. I feel the latter group strikes at the core
> of values. When you have to place these concepts on the line,
> you face new questions. For a reason I cannot yet explain, I
> gradually began to move toward this new and somewhat
> dangerous level of exploration.

At the same time the ways in which traditional values can be seen was to undergo its own revolution:

In *Genesis*, where the world was at first without form, creation was an act of separation, of looking, and knowing. In much the same way, an artist may create value by selecting and revealing a world and a way of looking at a world. Shakespeare created Cordelia as a good character. Isolated facts of Cordelia's existence were not Cordelia—many of these were present in the sources. The invention and selection of the facts, their order, the focus given to them, and the control of responses (partially through controlling what the audience knows) did create Cordelia and a world of good, evil, and suffering. Yet it is not the concept of good which determines for me the worth of *Lear, Genesis,* or *Anna Karenina,* but rather the way value is created. Whether or not a work of art expresses my values it must contain the complexity necessary to develop, sustain or invent perspectives which "the reader can actively know."

Such profound transformations in the ways students saw the activities of thinking and imagining were inseparable in their minds from changes in their conception of reading:

Freud's lectures proved to be the most significant text of the course for me. They provoked the emergence of a totally new understanding of values. It was then that I began to battle out the question of the values in a work in relation to the values of the reader. The importance of details—defining and understanding new terms such as repression and resistance, for example—hit me on the head like a ton of bricks. The notion of comprehending events, processes, or ideas based solely on what the work gives me, became crucial. In trying to understand the origin and development of psychoanalysis, I became particularly conscious of how arguments were constructed to support conclusions. These three revelations caused a change in my approach to reading. It was a change that expanded my understanding of the values in a text, as well as my own set of values.

With this expanding awareness of the possibilities for discovery as they exist in the world around them and in their own resources, came a changing sense of their potential relationship to the world:

> The class has functioned as a dynamic dialogue between teachers, students and texts. Examining what is contained within a text and together discussing what it means to us as individuals and as members of a common society has opened up entirely new areas of value (not simply subjective values; here I mean positive worth) and given me a tool for reading which I will be able to use again and again. Most of all it has stimulated me to further inquiry, further interaction with intellectual material.

In somewhat more impassioned tones:

> I consider this change to be two-fold. Firstly, it provoked me to abandon the compulsion to protect myself—I no longer rejected a text simply because it challenged or threatened my own values. I was forced to enter the author's world (be he a scientist, playwright or historian) on his terms. Secondly, though very much in line with the first, my range of experience in reading was broadened tremendously. This was perhaps the most decisive effect of the course. It opened up new worlds, new modes of inquiry, new methods of approach and decision-making. It was obviously a tiring struggle.

A series of texts where unrelatedness was their most striking characteristic, and a perspective on them which seemed to be the stripping away of available perspectives, was the material available to these students. It is scarcely surprising that one of them spoke of "flinging values to the winds." Nevertheless, as we have seen, the discovery of values finally permeates and synthesizes their experience. It is best summed up by a student:

> This has been a round about way of saying that truth and good are not separable from texts and theories. They relate to what is seen, what is looked for, and how. Ability to create seems a fascinating idea of good, especially when form, order, and knowledge are what is created.

And the activity of reading pushed to its limits was to prove for students, no less than faculty, a power capable of bringing one into contact with such revelations. It is fitting that the moment in these papers when the thought of teacher and student becomes indistinguishable is on that subject:

> Our approach to reading in this class has been to look for the critical values (choices) in any work, which let us come to an understanding of the inner structure of the work, how it orders itself. This is an approach that is appropriate to all pieces of writing, since it allows each work to provide the clues of its importance. Of course, these clues are subject to interpretations by every reader, but as an approach it is more firmly anchored to the work itself.

There are any number of issues raised by this course which could be pursued. It was interdisciplinary in its range of readings, but tended to exhibit the distinctive powers of the various disciplines, rather than to collapse distinctions between them. Despite the ahistorical organization of the readings history can be seen as playing a critical role throughout, but it is history in various guises rather than as *the* decisive context and determinant of interpretation. It is a course which combines unorthodox means (the range of texts used and the way they were treated) with some of the most traditional goals in liberal arts education. At a philosophic level, the role of fact can be seen in a more complementary and interdependent relationship to value than is frequently assumed. What most concerns me here, however, is the extent to which this experience exhibits the value of the classroom as a creative context.

The classroom is a place where the effort to communicate is tested again and again, and the place where the difficulties and limits of that effort tend to be writ large. In this particular course I discovered possibilities for communication unique in my teaching experience. The talent of this particular collection of 16 and 17 year-old students is important, but what *happened* to them while in the course is infinitely more important. What I have tried to suggest here is that there can be an intelligible relationship between the thought that goes into a course and what happens in it, without denying the role of circumstance and surprise. I have tried to indicate the range and character of the thought that teaching can (and frequently does) involve. Above all I have tried to suggest the unique potential of the classroom as an arena for inquiry, discovery and communication for teachers and scholars as well as for students.

END NOTES

[1]Her name is Edith Wurtzel and my debt to her for what follows is, I hope, self-evident.

[2]This conception of texts should not be confused with the perspective of "new criticism" which makes many assumptions about the role of language in determining the sources not only of the order, but of the power and the value of texts.

[3]I am much indebted for the above observations about *Genesis* to Professor Leonard Gardner of the State University of New York, Stony Brook with whom I had taught *Genesis* previously.

[4]James Strachey, trans. and gen. ed. *The Standard Edition of the Complete Psychological Works of Sigmund Freud* (London: Hogarth Press, 1953), II, 22.

[5]Freud, II, 23-24.

[6]The names of the students who were in the "Values" course listed alphabetically are: Scott Bieber, Jonathan Boyarin, William Brown, Herbert Buchheimer, Scott Bukatman, Mark Conrad, Cheryl Fish, Larry Florin, Jonathan Haskett, Leslie Holleran, Robin Koval, Susanne Krivit, Jayme Jaffe, Eve Leopold, Tina Minkowitz, Julia Palmore, Jeff Ruhloff, Jacob Wasserman, Abigail Wender, and Grant Willis.

Essays in Literature

Handscóh and Grendel:
The Motif of the Hand in Béowulf

Marilyn M. Carens

The form of *Béowulf*, as many readers have observed, is dignified, intricate, and complex, despite the rawness and bloodiness of much of the action. The artistry and balance of the poet's design disabuse us at once of the notion that the poem celebrates a primitive and blood-thirsty pagan sociology; nothing could be less brutal and more refined than the structure and language of *Béowulf*. The diction of the epic is as rich, as ornamental, as elaborate and symmetrical as the complex geometrical ornament of Celtic monument and manuscript from the same historical period. The carefully woven patterns of motif and image in the poem are similar in design and conception to the complex spirals and interlacings of the richly-adorned Book of Durrow (Irish, seventh century) and the painstaking geometricity of the Lindisfarne Gospels (Northumbrian, eighth century); to the delicate curves and glowing enamels of the Celtic hanging bowls found at Sutton Hoo (Sussex, seventh century); to the rigid, stylized animals of Celtic shoulder-buckles, brooches, and torcs.[1]

As repetition, symmetry and interlace are the chief distinctions of the visual and plastic arts of the Celts, so they are the most striking aesthetic distinctions of the Anglo-Saxon poem of *Béowulf*. The oral formulae described by Albert B. Lord in *The Singer of Tales* (New York: Athenæum, 1971; originally published by Harvard Univ. Press as Harvard Studies in Comparative Literature, No. 24) help to create elaborate patterns of sound audible even to beginning students of the poem. More advanced students may notice not only the incidence of complex sound-patterns in the poem but also the sophisticated departures from formulae, the imaginative and vigorous variations on a theme. As John Leyerle has recently observed in his article on "The Interlace Structure of *Béowulf*," the themes of the poem are

> . . . some of the threads that form the interlace structure of
> *Béowulf*. Often several are present together, as in the Finns-
> burh episode or in the final dragon fight. The themes make a
> complex, tightly-knotted lacertine interlace that cannot be

untied without losing the design and form of the whole. The
tension and force of the poem arise from the way the themes
cross and juxtapose. Few comments are needed from the poet
because significance comes from the intersections and conjunc-
tions of the design . . . Although the poem has to be lingered
over and gives up its secrets slowly, the principle of its interlace structure helps to reveal the interwoven coherence of the
episodes as well as the total design of the poem in all its complex resonances and reverberations of meaning.[2]

It will be my purpose in this essay to follow through the poem one of the
minor "threads" of the interlace structure of *Béowulf,* the incidence of
hand-imagery, as an example of the complexity and symmetry of the poet's
design. I believe that the frequent reference to *hands* is neither accidental
nor a matter of random choice on the part of the poet, but part of a care-
fully-controlled pattern in which the hero's conscious choice of his course
of action is contrasted to the deeds and exploits of other heroes, to the poet's
conception of the cyclical nature of human destiny, and to the workings of
fate. The hand of the hero becomes a symbol of his will, and an analysis of
hand-imagery helps to reveal the ethical stance of the poet.

One has only to follow the movement of *hands* through the poem to gain
a strong sense of the poet's artistry. We see first the "banan folmum" of
Grendel at 1. 158; next the "mæzen-wudu mundum" of the Scielding coast
guard at 1. 236; next Hróthgár honors Béowulf as a man who by reputation
is a hero:

> . . . þæt hé þrítizes
> manna mæzen-cræft   on his mund-gripe,
> heaðu-róf, hæbbe. [3]

—and one thinks immediately of the thirty thanes murdered by Grendel on
the night of his first attack.

After Béowulf has offered his services to Hróthgár, who rejoices in having
found at last a champion to defend his honor, we see the ale cup go round:

> . . . þezn nytte behéold,
> se-þe on handa bær   hroden ealu-wǽze. . .
>
> (494-95)

At this point, we have found three different words for *hand (folm, mund,
hand)* which the poet will call for as his metrical and alliterative needs vary.
We will notice as the poem continues that other words are added to this

basic word-group, and that a "floating motif" centered on the image of the
hand will frequently occur in connection with Béowulf, interwoven in the
texture of the poem like a single thread of distinctive color.[4]

After Unferth insults Béowulf, for example, the hero ably defends himself
in an impassioned recitation of glorious exploits in the past. His speech
contains a whole series of hand-images, almost as though the poet had envisioned him holding out his hands in front of Unferth and boasting, "These
hands have accomplished more in their day than yours ever will."

> Hæfdon sweord nacod,   þá wit on sund réowon,
> heard on handa;   wit unc wiþ hran-fiscas
> werian þóhton . . .
>
> (539-41)

> Þǽr mé wiþ láðum   líć-sierće mín
> heard, hand-locen,   helpe ȝefremede . . .
>
> (550-51)

> heaðu-ræs fornam
> mihtiȝ mere-déor   þurh míne hand.
>
> (558-59)

Béowulf's boast is apparently successful in silencing the obstreperous
Unferth, for he does not reply. Hróthgár takes heart from Béowulf's pledge
to do battle with Grendel, and joyfully Wealhthéow passes the cup round
again. When the company is ready to retire, Hróthgár entrusts the hall to his
new retainer:

> 'Næfre ić ænigum menn   ǽr alíefde,
> siþþan ić hand and rand   hebban meahte,
> þrýþ-ærn Dena   bútan þé nú-þá.
>
> (655-57)

Béowulf disarms and vows to fight Grendel on his own terms, so to speak,
disdaining the assistance of sword and the protection of armor. When he puts
his faith in God to control the outcome of the battle, we see once again the
insistent mention of hands in connection with the hero:

> And siþþan wittiȝ God
> on swá-hwæðere hand,   háliȝ Dryhten,
> mǽrðc dǿmc   swá Him ȝemet þynće!'
>
> (685-87)

By this time we have been thoroughly prepared, not only in terms of sound-image but also in terms of theme, for the hand-to-hand combat between Béowulf and Grendel.

We see Grendel rushing up to the hall, bursting with hate; just before he breaks in, he touches the door with his hands:

> Duru sóna onarn
> fýr-bendum fæst   siþþan hé hire folmum æthrán;
>
> (721-22)

Once inside Heorot, Grendel "devours a sleeping Gautish warrior" whom Magoun identifies as Handscóh (*Béowulf and Judith*, p. 21). It is perhaps only natural for the poet to describe the hands and feet of the hapless warrior as the last of the tasty human morsels to be devoured by Grendel:

> Sóna hǽfde
> unlifiendes   eall ȝefeormod,
> fǽt and folma.
>
> (743-45)

But the references to hands and fingers in the next twenty lines pile up so quickly that one cannot help attaching more than literal significance to them. The emphasis is on hand-to-hand combat with the fiend, and as soon as the fiend realizes that he has grabbed hold of a hero for a change, he starts trying to figure out how to escape:

> Forþ néar ætstóp,
> nam þá mid handa   hyȝe-þýhtiȝne
> rinc on ræste,   [him swá] rǽhte onȝeaȝn
> fíond mid folme;   hé onféng hrǽðe
> inwitt-þancum   and wiþ earm ȝesæt.
> Sóna þæt onfunde   firena hierde,
> þæt hé ne mǿtte   middan-ȝeardes,
> eorðan scéata   on ellran menn
> mund-gripe máran.   Hé on móde wearþ
> forht on ferhþe;   ná þý ǽr fram meahte.
>
> (745-54)

As the poet emphasizes Grendel's desire to escape three times during the actual battle, the "moral" of the story, and the justification for the emphasis on hands, seems to be threefold: that heroes are up in arms against evil while other men sleep; that they are not afraid to come to grips with the devil in the hope of triumphing over him; and that God has a hand in the victory of heroes. All of these themes are implied in the four references to hands which occur between lines 745 and 753. By associating Béowulf's hand-strength with his God-given courage, the poet has vigorously anticipated the wrench-ing-off of Grendel's arm.

Strangely, after Béowulf takes hold of Grendel, all references to hands disappear for more than sixty lines, until the monster's arm is actually off. Partly this is because the hand-to-hand combat between God's champion and the devil's advocate has become a kind of internal tornado and things are moving so rapidly—mead-benches crashing to the floor, ale spilling, men and monsters screaming—that individual parts of bodies are no longer distinguish-able. Partly it is that the poet wants to emphasize the fact that ordinary swords and staves "grœtan nolde" (803) the evil incarnate in the form of Grendel. But I think that the principal reason for the absence of hand-references in the sixty lines preceding the flight of Grendel is to increase the contrast between the terrific force of the battle and the moment when Grendel knows he is done for:

> Þá þæt onfunde   se-þe fela æror
> módes myrðe   manna cynne,
> firena ʒefremede   — hé [wæs] fáh wiþ God —
> þæt him se líc-hama   læstan nolde,
> ac hine se módiga   mæʒ Hyʒe-láces
> hæfde be handa;   wæs ʒehwæðer óðrum
> lifiende láþ.
>
> (809-15)

It is just after this that the bone-casings burst and Grendel flees to his den, leaving behind what the poet calls, in a tone of exultation, a "tácen swiotul" of his utter defeat:

> Þæt wæs tácen swiotul
> siþþan hilde-déor   hand aleʒde,
> earm and eaxle   — þær wæs eall ʒeador
> Grendles grápe —   under ʒéapne hróf.
>
> (833-36)

It is interesting to observe that a relationship is being set up between the *hand* of Grendel and his very life; once the hand and arm have been torn off, death is inescapable. The same verb, *alecgan*, meaning to lay down,[5] is used in the same form, *aleʒde,* to describe Béowulf laying down Grendel's arm (see 1. 834 above) and to describe Grendel laying down his life at 1. 851:

siþþan dréama léas
on fenn-friðe   feorh aleȝde,
hǽþne sáwle;   þǽr him hell onféng.

(850-52)

This echo of sound suggests that in the poet's mind the *hand* is being used as perhaps the *heart* might be used in a modern war poem or as the *liver* was used in the classical Greek epic: as the seat of the soul. Putting down the fiend's hand is "tácen swiotul" of putting down his essential nature, the nature of evil. Human beings come to grips with evil and struggle against it; the heroes among us shall overcome, and in token of their victory they give us a sign that we may look at and recognize as an emblem of that victory. Even the Doubting Thomas (or Unferth, as the case may be) will have to admit the courage of the hero, but even the most ardent admirer of the hero will have to admit that any victory over evil, however real and however admirable, is merely a temporary stay against the winds of chaos, a one-man stand that gives way momentarily to even greater evil. Barely twenty-four hours elapse before Grendel's dam emerges, bent on revenge.

After Béowulf puts down Grendel's arm, there is a second hiatus in the development of the hand-motif; nearly 100 lines elapse with no reference to hands. One would perhaps not expect any reference to hands in the visit to Grendel's pond, but there are many opportunities for hand-imagery in the song of Sigemund and in the song of Heremód, opportunities that the poet does not seize. Swords are wielded in these songs, dragons done in, treasures loaded on board ships, horses guided and controlled. I believe that the poet, consciously or subconsciously, wishes to reserve mention of hands for those episodes in which Béowulf is the central figure.

For whatever reason, the reference to Grendel's hand at 1.927 provides a neat transition back to the main narrative line after the allusions to Sigemund, Fitela, and Heremód. To introduce what Magoun has called "Hróthgár's Little Doxology" (*Béowulf and Judith,* p. 26), the poet observes:

Hróþ-gár maðelode   — hé to healle ȝéong,
stód on stapole,   ȝeseah stéapne hróf
golde fágne   and Grendles hand:

(925-27)

In his joy at having Heorot freed (so he thinks) from what has seemed a permanent scourge, Hróthgár adopts Béowulf as his son (11.946-49) and hopes that God will reward the hero in future as he seems already to have done.

Gracefully Béowulf compliments the old king by wishing that he had been there to see the slaughter (11. 960-62). At this point a cluster of references to hands occurs, as Béowulf recounts the story of the battle for the benefit of Hróthgár and his men. The first of six references in the space of twenty-six lines occurs at 1. 965:

> Ic hine hrædlíce   heardum clammum
> on wæl-bedde   wríðan þóhte
> þæt hé for mund-gripe   mínum scolde
> licgan líf-bisiʒ   bútan his líc swice.
>
> (963-66)

Again the hand is associated with life itself, here with the verb *licgan*, and this association is echoed in the next few lines in another passage that also begins "Ic hine . . .":

> Ic hine ne meahte,   þá Meotod nolde,
> ganges ʒetwǽman   — ná ic him þæs ʒeorne ætfealh —
> feorh-ʒeníðlan;   wæs tó foremihtiʒ
> fíond on fǽðe.   Hwæðere hé his folme forlét
> to líf-wræðe   lást weardian,
> earm and eaxle. . . .
>
> (967-72)

A fine parallelism may be noticed in this part of the poem. We begin with the hand as one kind of truth-token at 1. 925 (see above) and move immediately to Hróthgár's words as another kind of truth-token. Béowulf, like Hróthgár, ends his speech with a reference to his Creator (1. 979), and all eyes turn to the awesome hand of the fiend nailed to the roof-peak of Heorot, the hand on which all eyes were fixed before the words began:

> Þá wæs swíʒra secg,   sunu Ecg-láfes,
> on ʒielp-sprǽce   gúþ-ʒeweorca,
> siþþan æðelingas   eorles cræfte
> ofer héanne hróf   hand scéawodon,
> fíondes fingras.   Foran ǽʒhwelc wæs,
> steda næʒla ʒehwelc   stíele ʒelícost,
> hǽþnes hand-sporu,   hilde-rinces
> eʒl unhíeru.   Ǽʒhwelc ʒecwæþ
> þæt him heardra nán   hrínan wolde
> íren ǽr-gód,   þæt þæs ag-lǽcan
> blódiʒe beadu-folme   onberan wolde.
>
> (980-90)

The stunning irony of the final reference to hands at 1. 992 (see below), repeating the *folme* of 1. 970 and 1. 990, is a fine example of the poet's subtle exploitation of sound-echoes and of his sensitive handling of the motif of hands, since the first two references to *folme* refer to the bloody relic left behind by Grendel and the third to the human hands decorating the hall in honor of Béowulf's victory:

> Þá wæs háten hræðe   Heorot innanweard
> folmum ȝefrætwod;   fela þára wæs,
> wera and wífa,   þe þæt wín-rećed,
> ȝiest-sele ȝieredon.

(991-94)

Heorot, in these passages of description, becomes almost a symbol for man himself, the sparring-ground for a death-struggle between God's champion and the devil. Grendel, representing the devil, is out to destroy man, particularly those aspects of man which most please his Creator, i. e. his capacity to perform noble deeds and his tendency to commemorate those deeds in noble works of art. In a monumental struggle, Béowulf succeeds in casting out the devil's advocate, but so close to human shape is Grendel that the casting-out is nearly equivalent to wrecking Heorot. Béowulf nearly loses his humanity by defeating Grendel (as John Gardner has suggested in his brilliant recasting of the story from Grendel's point of view[6]); it takes a superhero to dislodge Grendel from Heorot because the hand of destruction is implicit in the act of creation. Grendel was fatally drawn to attack Heorot; Michelangelo's *Pietà* presupposes, sooner or later, the vandal with his chains and his hammer.

Furthermore, even when destruction is held momentarily at bay by the permanence of art (the hall itself, the songs sung within it, or even the poem which describes both), Grendel's hand hovers over the dwellings of men. Only the bands of iron (1. 774) prevent the utter destruction of Heorot in the struggle to defeat Grendel. Perhaps these iron bands, made out of the same element as Grendel's nails (1. 985), signify man's capacity to resist evil as opposed to his tendency to ignore it (the sleeping thanes) or to hope it will disappear by itself (Hróthgár). The "stunning irony" of this passage of jubilation (11. 925 ff.) is that the shadow of Grendel's claw hangs over all the bedecking and adorning of the hall, and it is that claw which is going to draw Grendel's dam to the king's demesne, where another man will die.

After the account of men and women decorating Heorot, all references to hands disappear for 300 lines, until the second monster ravages the hall.

A cluster of images occurs as soon as we return to the narrative of the main action, after the long digressions that have taken place at the victory banquet, including the Song of Finn and Wealhtheow's address to Hróthgár and Béowulf. Grendel's dam is detected almost as soon as she enters the hall, and all over the benches startled thanes reach for their swords:

> Þá wæs on healle   heard-ecg togen
> sweord ofer setlum,   síd-rand maniʒ
> hæfen handa fæst;   helm ne ʒemunde,
> byrnan síde   þá hine se bróga onʒeat.

(1288-91)

Part of the mother's revenge lies in retrieving the "cúde folme" of her slain son:

> Hréam wearþ on Heorote;   hío under heolfre ʒenam
> cúðe folme;   caru wæs ʒeníewod,
> ʒeworden on wícum.

(1302-04)

Hróthgár learns of Æschere's death and summons Béowulf, who strides across the floor-boards with his companions:

> ʒéong æfter flóre   fierd-wierðe mann
> mid his hand-scole   — heall-wudu dynede —
> þæt hé þone wísan   wordum næʒde,
> fréan Ing-wina . . .

(1316-19)

Hróthgár tells Béowulf of Æschere's death in terms of a "hand-killer" or murderer, one who accomplished the fell deed with her hands as opposed to one who kills by the sword (1. 1330). Almost immediately he alludes to Béowulf having slain Grendel with "heardum clammum" (1. 1335). Finally, Hróthgár grieves that Grendel's dam has brought low a hand that would willingly have fought for Béowulf:

> Nú sío hand liʒeþ,
> sío-þe íow wél-hwelcra   willna dohte.

(1343-44)

In Hróthgár's description of the pond and in the narrator's account of Danes and Geats tracking the mere-wife to the grisly souvenir of her attack on Heorot, there is no reference to hands, but as Béowulf arms himself for his next trial, we find him putting on a byrnie "handum zebrogden" (1. 1443), and the sword Hrunting is described as never having failed those who took it up:

> næfre hit æt hilde ne swác
> manna ǽnigum   þára-þe hit mid mundum bewand. . .

> (1460-61)

Thus we have been prepared, acoustically and thematically, for the second of Béowulf's hand-to-hand encounters with monsters. Before he descends into the deeps, however, Béowulf requests of Hróthgár a father's protection for his thanes if he should not be successful against the she-wolf:

> Wes þú mund-bora   mínum magu-þeʒnum,
> hand-ʒesellum,   ʒief meć hild nime . . . .

> (1480-81)

There are plenty of references to feet, arms, heads, shoulders, and fingers in the account of the battle with Grendel's dam, but even so, the hand emerges as the principal image of battle-strength until God sets the hero on his feet again:

> Onʒeat þá se góda   grund-wierʒenne,
> mere-wíf mihtiʒ;   mæʒen-ræs forʒeaf
> hilde-bille,   hand swenǵ ne ofteah
> þæt hire on hafolan   hring-mǽl agól
> grǽdiʒ gúþ-léoþ . . . .
>
>   . . . þolode ǽr fela
> hand-ʒemóta,   helm oft ʒescær,
> fǽʒes fierd-hræʒl . . . .
>
> Wearp þá wunden-mǽl   wrǽttum ʒebunden
> ierre óretta   þæt hit on eorðan læʒ,
> stíþ and stíel-ecg;   strenǵe ʒetruwode,
> mund-gripe mæʒenes. . . .
>
> Hío him eft hrǽðe   andléan forʒeald [8]
> grimmum grápum   and him toʒeaʒnes féng.

> (1518-42 passim)

After that the head takes over as the principal focus of the hero's interest, or perhaps we should say of the poet's. It is not until Béowulf hands over to

Hróthgár the hilt of the magic sword with which he has decapitated Grendel that we have another reference to hands:

> Þá wæs gylden hilt   gamolum rince,
> hárum hild-fruman   on hand ʒiefen,
> enta ǽr-ʒeweorc . . . .
>
> (1677-79)

Once Hróthgár has the hilt in hand, the battles with Grendel and his dam are really over. The hands of warriors, coast-guards, kings, and harbor-guards are not called into play as the hero and his men exchange farewell speeches with Hróthgár and complete the sea-journey home. Almost 260 lines elapse before the next occurrence of *folm, hand,* or *mund,* and after that another 132 lines pass in which only one reference to hands is made. Thus in the 400 lines following Hróthgár's acceptance of the hilt and the next cluster of hand-images, there are only three references to hands. As we are beginning to see, the poet utilizes hand-imagery primarily in battle-scenes, and primarily in connection with Béowulf's battles rather than with the reported triumphs of other heroes.

The occurrence of hand-imagery in connection with "Offa's shrewish queen" (Magoun, p. 54) is thus an exception to the general pattern. Here the references to hands suggest treachery, the breaking of normal human relations, the violence of power unjustly laying hands upon innocent thanes:

> Nǽniʒ þæt dorste   déor ʒenœ́ðan
> swǽsra ʒesíða   nefne sin-fréa,
> þæt hire on dæʒes   éagum starode,
> ac him wæl-benda   witoda tealde
> hand-ʒewriðena.   Hræðe siþþan wæs
> æfter mund-gripe   méce ʒeþinʒed
> þæt hit scáden-mǽl   scíran móste,
> cwealm-bealu cýðan.
>
> (1933-40)

When Béowulf and Hygelác meet, there is a nice contrast between the treachery of hands observed in the allusion to Thrýth and the fidelity of hands suggested in the passages of description of Hygd, a lover of people as Thrýth was a hater:

> Medu-scencum hwearf
> ʒeond þæt [heall-]reced   Hæreðes dohtor,
> lufode þá léode,   líþ-wǽʒe bær
> Hǽþnum to handa.   (1980-83)

The next cluster of hand-imagery occurs between lines 2072-99, in Béowulf's recapitulation, for Hygelác, of his fight with Grendel. Béowulf calls the battle a "hand-rǽs hǽlode" at 1. 2072 and refers almost at once to Grendel attacking Handscóh at 1. 2076. Three further references to hands occur in quick succession in the space of seven lines:

> Him Grendel wearþ,
> mǽrum magu-þeȝne,   to mund-banan;
> léofes mannes   líc eall forswealg.
> Ná þý ǽr út þá ȝíen   ídel-hende
> bana blódiȝ-tóþ,   bealwa ȝemyndiȝ,
> of þǽm gold-sele   gangan wolde
> ac hé mæȝenes róf   mín costode,
> grápode ȝearu-folm.
>
>   (2078-85)

The gathering of hand-images in Béowulf's account of the battle is continued at 1. 2094 with a second instance of the doubtful compound "andléan" or "hand-léan," and two further references occur at 11. 2098-99, adding the rare word *swídre* to the word-group:

> Hé on-weȝ losode,
> lýtle hwíle   líf-wynna bréac;
> hwæðere him sío swíðre   swæðe weardode
> hand on Heorote   and hé héan þanan,
> módes ȝeómor   mere-grund ȝeféoll.
>
>   (2096-100)

As Béowulf moves into his account of the battle with Grendel's dam, there are two further occurrences of hand-imagery,[9] but it is clear that the main group of images is clustered around his account of the first struggle, and that this re-telling of the events among the South-Danes for Hygelác's benefit is a thematic and linguistic echo of the re-telling for Hróthgár's benefit.

In the actual account of the battle with Grendel (by the narrator, with Béowulf referred to in the third person), there are seven references to *hand*, *mund*, and *folm*, not to mention all the related words like *fingra*, *grapum*, *féng*, and *clammum*. In the first recounting (Béowulf to Hróthgár, speaking in the first person), there are five occurrences of *hand*, *folm*, and *mund*, and a sixth in the ironic echo of "folmum zefrætwod" at 1. 992, after the third-person narrator has picked up the story again. In the second recounting (Béowulf to Hygelác, again in first person), there are seven or eight hand-images, depending on whether or not one includes "hand-léan"; the new word *swidre* is added to the word-group; and Handscóh's name occurs for the first time. In between these battles and recountings of battle, one finds few references to hands even where opportunity presumably exists to mention them. The pattern of hand-imagery in the first "half" of the poem is thus one of cluster and hiatus, with the clusters of references to hands occurring when Béowulf is fighting or telling someone else how he fought.

The second "half" of the poem is equally interesting with respect to the motif of hands, but the pattern is different. There are twenty occurrences of *hand, folm,* and *mund* in the story of Béowulf's fatal struggle with the dragon, but instead of occurring in a pattern of cluster and hiatus, the references to hands are scattered fairly evenly through the final thousand lines of the poem, and the hand-imagery is perhaps more pervasive and certainly more symbolic (or more obviously so) than it has been heretofore.

One finds in this final part of the poem that Hygelác's kingdom passes on his death into the hand of Béowulf (1. 2208). Almost immediately the thief's hand rifles the dragon's treasure (1. 2216). The narrative turns back on itself, very like the lacertine animals in Celtic interlace, and there is a second reference to Hygelác's death, which came about in a "hand-zemóta" (1. 2355). (Significantly, I think, there has just been a reference to Grendel when this allusion to hand-combat occurs.) Béowulf, bulging with rage, goes to inspect the dragon's barrow; there is an interesting hand-image suggesting that the thief's hand has passed the enmity of the dragon to Béowulf in the jewelled cup.

> Hæfde þá ʒefrugnen   hwanan sío fǽhþ arás,
> bealu-níþ beorna;   him to bearme cóm
> máðum-fæt mǽre   þurh þæs meldan hand.

(2403-05)

Once again the narrative line recoils, this time all the way back to Béowulf's childhood and the successive reigns of Hrœthel, Hæthcynn, and Hygelác. As soon as Béowulf gets to the story of his own valorous deeds as thane of Hygelác, references to hands begin to occur more frequently. There is first a reference to Eofor not holding his hand back to avenge Hæthcynn's death by killing the aged Angen-théow (1. 2488); next Béowulf calls himself a "hand-banan" in the slaying of Dæghrœfn (1. 2502); finally the aged hero pledges himself to destroy this latest plague on his people with "hand and heard sweord" (1. 2509).

The fight itself is full of references to hands, not only to Béowulf's but to

Wíglaf's and to those of the faithless hand-zesteallan (1. 2596). Béowulf raises his hand and strikes when the dragon approaches, but his sword fails him in his hour of need and he is "fýre befangen" (1. 2595). Wíglaf, unable to bear the sight of Béowulf being scorched, rushes to his aid: "hand rand zeféng" (1. 2609). This is the first of several indications that Wíglaf's hand will pick up where Béowulf's leaves off.

The most powerful instance of hand-imagery occurs after Wíglaf enters the fight. Béowulf brings down Næzling on the dragon's head with the force of thunder, but "wæs sío hand to strang" (1. 2684) and the sword breaks apart ("forbærst") under the terrible pressure. Throughout the poem, the emphasis is on Béowulf's native strength, which under certain circumstances is too great to prevent catastrophe. His heroism in seeking single combat is proof of his valor, and in the battles with Grendel and Grendel's dam the outcome is victory and triumph, not only for Béowulf but for the whole kingdom. But in the dragon episode, the consequences are disastrous: the hero is killed, and his people are left with no one to protect them from their enemies. John Leyerle believes that this juxtaposition of the hero's greatness against his responsibility to his people is the major theme of the poem: " . . . the fatal contradiction at the core of heroic society. The hero follows a code that exalts indomitable will and valour in the individual, but society requires a king who acts for the common good, not for his own glory" (pp. 8-9). The fact that Béowulf's hand is too strong for his own sword may be interpreted as further evidence of Leyerle's contention that the hero's "single-minded preoccupation with the dragon" may be more dangerous than the dragon itself.[10]

After the poet has established the powerful image of Béowulf's hand-strength and Næzling has burst, the dragon snakes forth and gores Béowulf in the neck. Wíglaf, whose shield has been burnt to a cinder and who has taken refuge behind Béowulf's shield, darts out from behind it and stabs the dragon lower down. Not heeding the dragon's head, Wíglaf burns his hand: "ac sío hand zebearn" (1. 2697). In Proppian morphology, this event corresponds to J, "branding or marking the hero," which usually occurs just after victory over the villain.[11] We know from this detail that Wíglaf is taking on some of the heroic attributes of his lord; this is his initiation, his trial by fire, and he comes through marked but triumphant.

But in the struggle Béowulf has been mortally wounded. Wíglaf, the valiant thane, last of the Wæz-mundings, ministers to his fallen lord with his own hands, vainly trying to restore life by laving him with water: "Hine thá mid handa . . . wætere zelafode" (11. 2720-22). Béowulf sends Wíglaf to the barrow to bring out treasure so he may see it before he dies; the gold ensign is described as "hand-wundra mæst"(l. 2768).

After Béowulf has in fact died, his slaying of the dragon is described at l. 2835 as the "hand-zeweorce" of a *hild-fruman* or battle-chief. Beowulf's handiwork is exalted, though he died to attain his victory, when the poet says that few men have ever survived meddling with a dragon's hoard with their hands ("handum styrede," 1. 2840).

Once again the narrative line coils away from the present, this time into the future as well as into the past, as the messenger imagines the lot of the Gautish people now that their lord is slain. The Swedes have not forgotten the revenge taken on them by Eofor and Hygelác; Eofor long ago returned the "andslieht" or hand-slaughter (1. 2929 and l. 2972) that Angenthéow had visited upon Hæthcynn. The messenger goes on to describe the joyless state of the nation now that their war-chief has "laid down his laughter":

> For-þon sceal gár wesan
> maniʒ morgen-ćeald   mundum bewunden,
> hæfen on handa,   nealles hearpan swœʒ
> wíʒend weććan . . .
>
> (3021-24)

There are only two further references to hands in the poem; one is the description by Wíglaf of how he gathered up treasures for Béowulf to gaze on before his death:

> Ić on ofoste ʒeféng
> miéćle mid mundum   mæʒen-byrðenne
> hord-ʒestréona,   hider út ætbær
> cyninge mínum . . .
>
> (3090-93)

The last reference to hands in the epic is the resonant image of the warrior bearing a fire-brand "on handa" (1. 1324) as the eight chosen thanes return to the barrow. The dragon had roared out of the barrow, breathing fire; Béowulf raised his hand to earn glory and to protect his people, but his hand was too strong and he forfeited his own life and his people's safety in his desire to prove himself once again in single combat against a monster. Wíglaf went to Béowulf's aid and burned his hand but not his honor; now the eight chosen thanes carry the fire back into the barrow, as though it is a symbol of Béowulf's life-spark, by the light of which great underground treasures are revealed for all the people to behold. Those riches Béowulf wanted to see before he died are in one way at least like the riches of the human spirit, rarely brought to light until some great catastrophe makes heroes of a few of us and cowards of all the rest. It is significant of Wiglaf's heroism that it is he who gathers up the hand-wonders in his arms and brings them out for Beowulf to look upon. The thane who walks at the head of the eight chosen men, bearing the brand, is an analogue of the treacherous slave who stole the cup at the outset of the dragon episode; symbolically, the poet suggests that nobility and heroic valor may on rare occasions be "handed" from one person to another, just as the good king could be affected by the sacrilege of one of his subjects, and just as Beowulf's people are to be affected in disastrous ways by the proud king's need to follow the heroic code to its bitter conclusion.

When the flames of Beowulf's funeral pyre roar up to heaven, mingled with weeping, Beowulf's fire has at last, if only briefly, exceeded that of the dragon. When that fire dies down, the treasure is once again buried, to lie perhaps for another thousand years until such a hero is born again. The poet's skillful maneuvering of the hand-motif throughout *Beowulf* has made us keenly aware both of the hero's greatness, incarnate in physical strength but not confined to it, and of the dangers attendant upon that greatness.

END NOTES

[1]Excellent illustrations of these and other examples of seventh and eighth century visual and plastic art in the Celtic style may be found in Ludwig Bieler, *Ireland Harbinger of the Middle Ages* (London: Oxford Univ. Press, 1966). Proinsias MacCana, *Celtic Mythology* (London: Hamlyn, 1970) is also useful. John Leyerle, "The Interlace Structure of *Beowulf*," *UTQ*, 37 (1967), 1-17, provides a detailed analysis of the ways in which the structure of the poem resembles the design of Celtic interlace.

[2]Leyerle, p. 13.

[3]Francis P. Magoun, Jr., ed., *Beowulf and Judith*, The Harvard Old English Series (Cambridge: Harvard Univ. Press, 1966), p. 11, ll. 379-81. All further quotations from the text of the poem will be from this edition, with line numbers in brackets following the quotation.

[4]As far as I have been able to discover, the phrase "floating motif" originates with Professor Michael Bell, of the Department of English at the University of Colorado. He used the term to designate an artifact, usually a noun, that may occur in association with a theme in oral literature; e.g. "The motif of water is often associated with the theme of creation."

[5]J. B. Bessinger, Jr., *A Short Dictionary of Anglo-Saxon Poetry* (Toronto: Univ. of Toronto Press, 1967), p. 40.

[6]John Gardner, *Grendel* (New York: Knopf, 1971).

[7]This interesting occurrence of the word *hand* is one of many compounds in which two nouns, or a noun-adjective combination, extend the meaning of a parent word. Here, Beowulf arrives with his "hand-troop"; we mean the same when we say "hand-picked men." There are many other *hand*-compounds in the course of the poem. Perhaps the most common is "hand-zesellan" or "close companions." Most armor is "hand-locen" and swords are often said to be the "hand-ze-weorc" of gods or giants. For an account of nominal and adjectival compounding, see Bessinger, p. ix.

[8]The Benjamin Thorpe transcription of this phrase is "hand-léan forgeald" or "paid (him) a hand-reward," suggesting a possible further instance of the motif. See Thorpe, *Beowulf* (Great Neck, New York: Barron's, 1962), p. 103.

[9]Beowulf describes the conflict with Grendel's dam as "hand zemæne" at l. 2137 and the narrator, in a maximic statement, calls retainers or thanes "hand-zesteallan" at l. 2169.

[10]Leyerle, p. 9. Leyerle's point is that the constant allusions to the Swedish wars in the second part of the poem are intended to present Beowulf's heroic deeds from a different perspective. "In this way the poet undercuts Beowulf's single-minded preoccupation with the dragon by interlacing a stream of more and more pointed episodes about the human threats to his people, a far more serious danger than the dragon poses. Beowulf wins glory by his heroic exploit in killing the dragon, but brings dire affliction on his people, as Wiglaf quite explicitly states." Although the "human threats" are explicitly the Swedes, I have taken Beowulf to be a source of danger to his people as well.

[11]Vladimir Propp, *Morphology of the Folktale*, trans. Laurence Scott, rev. and ed. Louis A. Wagner (Austin: Univ. of Texas Press, 1968), p. 153.

Metaphors of the Poet and His Craft in William Dunbar

Gerald B. Kinneavy

In the last decade of Chaucerian studies we have witnessed a growing attention of critics to the "poet-as-artist" and the "poet's imagination" as motifs in various poems. Quietly ignored in this matter—as in most others—have been the Middle Scots poets, so long reputed as merely having tried to recapture the Chaucerian line, stanza, or tone in a northern dialect. But it is no longer fashionable to call Douglas, Dunbar and Henryson "Scottish Chaucerians." And in the wake of that lost tag, it would seem that we just avoid talking about them altogether. This is indeed a loss, not only because we miss some first-rate poetry, but also because we miss a good deal of material which helps to define that self-consciousness which Ernst Curtius touches upon in his treatment of "The Poet's Pride," citing the 11th century poet, Wido of Ivrea:

> Sum sum sum vates, Musarum servo penates,
> Subpeditante Clio queque futura scio.
> Me minus extollo, quamvis mihi cedit Apollo,
> Invidet et cedit, scire Minerva dedit.
> Laude mea vivit mihi se dare queque cupivit,
> Immortalis erit, ni mea Musa perit.
> Musa mori nescit nec in annis mille senescit,
> Durans durabit nec quod amavit abit.
> . . . .
> Ut semper dures, mihi te subponere cures,
> Quodsi parueris carmine perpes eris.[1]

Such pride in the profession of poetry is not unusual. My intention in this paper is to look closely at two or three of Dunbar's poems which center on poetic motifs in order to illustrate the high degree of artistic self-consciousness to be found there and to relate that self-consciousness to the traditions running through the poems.

For a number of reasons, the view of the medieval poet generally is that he is unsophisticated regarding the theory of his art; some scholars would even maintain that he is wholly unconcerned with his individual relationship to that art. And if we examine only those manuals of poetics current in Dunbar's days—those of Matthew de Vendome, Jean de Garland, and Geoffrey de Vinsauf—certainly we do find an implied simplistic, even mechanical, attitude toward the art by virtue of their almost exclusive concern with technique.[2] But there are other commentaries on poetry which indicate an interest in matters more closely related to the creative act, to the larger issues of composition—Boccaccio's discussion of poetry and the poetic act in Books XIV and XV of the *Genealogy of the Gods*, for instance; or Dante's *De Vulgari Eloquentia*, or Chrétien de Troyes' compositional commentary in his romances. This last group of commentary is being supported and expanded by the recent Chaucerian studies, particularly centering on the *House of Fame*, viewing the poem as a description, really, of the poetic flight of the imagination.[3]

I suggest further materials exist among the Middle Scots poets,[4] here— particularly—in Dunbar. Professor Denton Fox has, indeed, asserted that all Dunbar's poetry is to some extent about poetry.[5] Certainly the "Lament for the Makaris" is one poem most directly concerned with poetry as related to the poet himself. The exterior concern or the fear of death is, it seems to me, but the incentive or inspirational motif which sets the poet off on his musings about his own feelings and worries regarding his art. That the poem is a highly personalized one has been noted frequently. In fact, Professor Kurt Wittig has called attention to the fact that Dunbar is a highly personal poet generally "in the sense that he is chiefly preoccupied with such matters as are immediately of interest to him personally. . . . "[6] Such self-interest would seem obvious even from the sub-title of the poem—"Quhen He Wes Sek"—as well as from the very initial lines of the poem: "I that in heill wes and gladnes,/ Am trublit now with gret seiknes" (1-2).[7] The initial contrast is between two physical states, sickness and health. But the operative verb brings the contrast into the emotional sphere: he is *troubled*, and the refrain sustains that emotional emphasis. It is the *fear* of death which disturbs him, which is the source of the "troubling," rather than simply the physical aspects of ill health. The technique seems clearly to be the use of the health/ sickness contrast as a kind of metaphor of the more central contrast—the troubled or peaceful emotional state. The specific experience of his own variation from good health to ill health moves him to the recognizable medieval *topos* of the transitory world. "Our plesance heir is all vane glory,/ This fals warld is bot transitory" (5-6). And that thought urges itself on to a comment specifically on the estates of man which also fall under the influence and control of this transience. "Estate," however, is not simply that of the social degree. The language Dunbar employs clearly relates the thought to the emotional state of men: "Now sound, now seik, now blith, now sary,/ Now dansand mery, now like to dee' (10-11). Then follow seven stanzas devoted to an explicit listing of various "estates" as "professions" over which Death and this transitory world ultimately gain control. Again, the medieval *topos* of "estat" as sociological fact, as a tradition, is recognizable. But what is striking is the lexical duality of the term, "estat." The early stanzas of the poem contrasted physical condition or "state" with the poet's troubled mental state. And the point of it all is the realization by the speaker—the *felt* realization, not simply the conventional motif—of the inevitability of change. The effects of that essential change are what concern, what trouble the speaker. "Estate" is as much the condition of the spirit as of social class or profession.[8]

Let me speculate for a moment outside the poem. With Dunbar's concern here with emotional change, with the obvious fact that he is a poet and is dependent upon emotions in the creative act, is it not at least plausible that the speaker is also thinking of "estate" as related to "poet"? That is, has the troubled spirit no effect on the creative urge which he—or anyone, I suppose —senses as poet? If there is that possibility, it would seem to me a highly self-conscious and a highly artistic concern. And in another place, we know, Dunbar does complain that a headache prevents him from his poetic act.

What is lightly implied early in the poem is more heavily supported by the fact that of the 100 lines of the piece, 47 are devoted exclusively to the catalogue of those poets whom death has already taken. And death now is associated with the transience of the world, including a transitory emotional spectrum as well. It is, then, not without purpose that at the beginning of this catalogue of the *makars* the speaker's tone changes from the vague generalized kind of statement—"He takis the knychtis in to feild . . . " (21)— to the specifically personal observation: "*I se* that makaris amang the laif / Playis heir ther pageant, syne gois to graif" (45-46). Here the poet speaks from his own experience rather than simply from the impersonal, indirect and generalized third-person perspective. What is focused upon in terms of the death of makaris is that Death takes their "faculte"—to be sure, an indication that the troublesome point about death for the speaker is that the *poetic* power is lost, not simply physical existence. I suggest that this fact of the poem—the speaker's concern for the deaths of the makaris *because* of their lost poetic faculties—reinforces that the true concern of the speaker throughout the poem is the loss of this faculty either through literal death or through that variation in the emotional make-up, the kind of emotional ups-and-downs which would cause from time to time an inability to create.

The stanzas devoted to the listing of the dead makaris extend from Chaucer through Quentin Schaw and finally to "Gud Maister Walter Kennedy," who, it is said, now lies on the point of death. Throughout the list, the refrain somehow takes on with each stanza a more highly personal sense. That is, we recognize it simply as a refrain from the Office of the Dead at the beginning of the poem. But by the time of the Kennedy stanza (89-92), the stress clearly is on the *conturbat me*, the personal, real, felt disturbance in the spirit of the poet-speaker. And of course, the fact that Kennedy—Dunbar's close friend and fellow poet—is lying at death's door moves the speaker to himself again, to *his* liability to death. "Sen he hes all my brether tane, / He will nocht lat me lif alane" (93-94). The conclusion is inevitable: he himself must be Death's next prey. And surely at that point, "Timor mortis conturbat me" is no longer *simply* the standard refrain but has personal connotations as well.

The speaker's problem in the poem is that of a troubled spirit; the effort is somehow to calm that spirit. But in the final stanza we find that curious paradox of orthodox Christianity. There is no remedy for death, so we must dispose ourselves for death that we may live. The disposition somehow becomes the remedy. This is proper and orthodox and—given those terms—logical. But the final and further irony is that the *emotional* problem is in no way solved for the speaker: the refrain is repeated, the fear of death *still* troubles him. The end result, then, is not at all solution to the troubled spirit. And why wouldn't the problem of the transitory world—both physical and emotional, both human and "poetic"—still perplex him? The poet is in fact still writing, still wondering (in advance of Milton) will he be next taken by death or by that emotional deadness which is worse than death to the poet.

There is a further interesting irony in the poem. The refrain, *"Timor mortis conturbat me,"* is an expression of the emotion which "inspires" this particular poem. Yet ironically, by space devoted, the emphasis falls on poetry and poets as "transitory." The necessary conclusion, it would seem, is that the writing of verse—in the long run—is futile, a logic made complex by the clearly positive value which he knows is to be found in poetry. The poet himself, however, remains at center stage. The speaker is "self-conscious" in the sense that it is his personal relationship to the various motifs of the poem that concern him.

This same kind of interior musing on his poetic faculty occurs in several

other Dunbar poems, among them, "Meditatioun in Wyntir." The season is
viewed not in any objective sense but in a wholly subjective one, and specifically as it affects the poetic powers of the speaker:

> In to thir dirk and drublie dayis,
> Quhone sabill all the hevin arrayis
>   With mystie vapouris, cluddis and skyis,
>   Nature all curage me denyis
> Off sangis, ballatis, and of playis. (1-5)[9]

This is a "meditation." The poet is thinking about those kinds of things
which stimulate or stifle his poetic activity. Winter cuts off his powers and
makes him restless: "I walk, I turne, sleip may I nocht, / I vexit am with havie
thocht" (11-12). The personal qualities or powers which he refers to are
all related to the poetic process. Nature denies him "curage" (4); he speaks
of a dull spirit (8) and a langorous heart (9), qualities deemed essential in
the poetic craft: intellect, imagination and emotions. Nearly Romantic in
attitude, the season is reflected in the speaker himself. Winter is the dampener
of the poetic spirit:

> Quhone that the nycht dois lenthin houris,
> With wind, with haill, and havy schouris,
>   My dule spreit dois lurk for schoir,
>   My hairt for languor dois forloir
> For laik of symmer with his flouris. (6-10)

Summer is the revivifier of the poetic spirit: "Cum, lustie symmer! with thi
flowris, / That I may leif in sum disport" (49-50). In connection with the
emphasis in stanzas one and two on the poetic faculties as affected by winter,
the "disport" of those final lines must be seen as poetry, the state of pleasure
and ease without the interior anxiety which winter has brought on the poet.
The poem is a self-portrait, really, of the poet's actions while in this torpid
state, defined by the metaphor of winter, but expanded once again into the
context of the creative process as either cut off or in bloom, as the winter or
the summer of the poet's *creative* faculties.[10]

Finally, let us look very briefly at some qualities of "The Golden Targe."
The poem allegorically describes what C. S. Lewis calls a slight action: "the
poet's mind, though long defended by reason, becomes at last the prisoner
of beauty."[11] The conflict in the poem exists between Reason—who attempts

to protect the persona—and the subjects and qualities and personages associated closely with poetry itself:

> Thare saw I Nature and Venus, quene and quene,
> The fresch Aurora, and lady Flora schene,
>   Juno, Appollo, and Proserpyna,
> Dyane the goddesse chaste of woodis grene,
> My lady Cleo, that help of makaris bene,
>   Thetes, Pallas, and prudent Minerva,
>   Fair feynit Fortune, and lemand Lucina,
> Thir mychti quenis in crounis mycht be sene,
>   Wyth bemys blith, bricht as Lucifera. (73-81)[12]

One of the most common of medieval motifs of springtime is the rejuvenating operation seen in nature, the rebirth of spring, of life. In Dunbar's poem, we find Nature giving May a new gown, rich and bright; we find the focus essentially on the regenerative powers of Nature which causes blooms to

> Opynt and spred thair balmy levis donk,
> Full low enclynyng to thair Quene so clere,
>   Quham of thair nobill norising thay thonk. (96-99)

By virtue of such key images as "opening blooms" and "nobil nourishing," the central operation here is to be identified with that "universal genius" which as Augustine put it, is "the god set over [all things]" and who "has the power of begetting all things" (*City of God,* VII, 13). But the full relevance of this fertile "genius" in Dunbar's poem becomes clear as we recall also that other kind of genius—analogous to the first—which the Middle Ages accepted as "existing separately in each individual soul" (*City of God,* VII, 13), a concept which accounts in large part for the numerous analogies in medieval literature between the artist and God as creators.[13] It is not inappropriate, then, that immediately after Reason has been conquered, after the speaker has witnessed the creative forces of Nature resulting in beauty, the poet comes under control of Lady Beauty. In a sense, we witness the becoming of a poet. Lady Beauty and her entourage of allegorical figures fight against Reason for *possession* of the speaker, who happens to be a *poet*. He has, in fact, been won over to the frenzied, irrational world of poetry, a world inhabited by analogous creative forces, individual poets. And this is why the final three stanzas of the poem come explicitly to poetry as the appropriate conclusion of the allegory. The encomiums of Chaucer, Gower and Lydgate—poets supreme for this speaker—are presented in precisely these terms of rebirth or regeneration. As Nature brightly revests and illuminates herself, we hear of these *poets* who "illuminate," who are the "lights" of English poetry; we hear of golden pens causing both illumination and delight, the medieval aesthetic of *doctryn* and *mirthe*. The creative powers—or genius —of Nature are directly parallel to that of the poets: both result in brightness and illumination, in beauty. And this particular poet-speaker has been, we must remember, won over by Lady Beauty. That it is recognition on the part of the speaker—and a sharp one—seems obvious. He does, after all, wake up to the sound of gunshot.

We have looked at a very few instances in Dunbar which suggest a self-consciousness not only of technique but as well of his own faculty, the operation of which results in poetry. This same kind of concern has also been posited in Chaucer. It goes without saying that any competent poet in any era will have awareness of his art, of its importance and of his own relationship towards it. He will accept as self-evident its significance. But what these instances in Dunbar reflect adds a dimension to our understanding of metaphor and tradition in medieval verse. We can easily recognize the *topoi* of the estates, of "God as Makar," of *"Timor mortis,"* of Nature's regenerative power, and so on. But these are not merely leitmotifs running through the poems. The use to which Dunbar puts these traditions is as metaphors, specifically in these poems, as metaphors of his craft and of his personal concern with it. Such technique adds a further aesthetic dimension to the use of tradition in Dunbar's poetry.

END NOTES

[1]*European Literature and the Latin Middle Ages,* trans. Willard R. Trask (Princeton: Princeton Univ. Press, 1953), p. 485.

[2]One recent treatment of a poet's simplistic view of his art is that of Jerome Mitchell, *Thomas Hoccleve: A Study in Early Fifteenth-Century English Poetic* (Urbana: Univ. of Illinois Press, 1968). But see also Alain Renoir, "Tradition and Moral Realism: Chaucer's Conception of the Poet," *SN,* 35 (1963), 199-219, in which Chaucer is seen as employing tradition in nearly the same sense that T. S. Eliot suggests in "Tradition and Individual Talent."

[3]See, for example, such studies as the following: Robert J. Allen, "A Recurring Motif in Chaucer's *House of Fame,*" *JEGP,* 55 (1956), 393-405; Alfred David, "Literary Satire in the *House of Fame,*" *PMLA,* 75 (1960), 333-39; David S. Bevington, "The Obtuse Narrator in Chaucer's *House of Fame,*" *Speculum,* 36 (1961), 288-98; William S. Wilson, "Exegetical Grammar in the *House of Fame,*" *ELN* 1 (1964); "The Eagle's Speech in Chaucer's *House of Fame,*" *QJS,* 50 (1964), 153-58; "Scholastic Logic in Chaucer's *House of Fame,*" *ChauR,* 1 (1967), 181-84; Sheila Delaney, " 'Phantom' and the *House of Fame,*" *ChauR,* 2 (1967), 67-74; and J.A.W. Bennett, *Chaucer's "Book of Fame":* An Exposition of *"The House of Fame"* (Oxford: Clarendon Press, 1968), *passim.*

[4]A part of this concern is developed in my study of Gavin Douglas, "The Poet in *The Palice of Honour," ChauR,* 3 (1969), 280-303.

[5]"Dunbar's *The Golden Targe,*" *ELH,* 26 (1959), 331.

[6]*The Scottish Tradition in Literature* (Edinburgh: Oliver and Boyd, 1958), p. 63.

[7]The text of Dunbar's poetry throughout is *The Poems of William Dunbar,* ed. W. Mackay Mackenzie (London: Faber and Faber, 1932), p. 20.

[8]That such a lexical duality is possible is documented rather fully by Ruth Mohl, *The Three Estates in Medieval and Renaissance Literature* (New York: F. Ungar, 1933), pp. 15-19. The lexical movement of "estat" ranges from general state or condition of being through references to the feudal classes and professions.

[9]*Poems,* p. 26.

[10]Boccaccio, too, calls attention to the problem of a poet when his creative spirit is affected adversely by Nature: "Furthermore, places of retirement, the lovely handiwork of Nature herself, are favorable to poetry, as well as peace of mind and desire of worldly glory; the ardent period of life also has very often been of great advantage. If these conditions fail, the power of creative genius frequently grows dull and sluggish." *Boccaccio on Poetry,* trans. Charles G. Osgood (New York: Liberal Arts Press, 1956), p. 40.

[11]*Allegory of Love* (Oxford: Clarendon Press, 1936), p. 252.

[12]*Poems,* p. 114.

[13]For this tradition documented fully, see: Curtius, pp. 544-46; Jean Seznec, *The Survival of the Pagan Gods,* trans. Barbara F. Sessions (New York: Pantheon Books, 1961), *passim;* and Edgar de Bruyne, *The Esthetics of the Middle Ages,* trans. Eileen B. Hennessy (New York: F. Ungar, 1969), pp. 45 ff.

Hieronimo's Garden and "the fall of Babylon":
Culture and Anarchy in The Spanish Tragedy

Donald R. Wineke

In Act IV, scene ii of Kyd's *The Spanish Tragedy*, shortly before Hieronimo takes his catastrophic revenge, there is a violent episode that, rather surprisingly, has attracted little critical attention. There Isabella, like her husband distracted by the unavenged murder of their son Horatio, destroys the garden in which the murder took place and then commits suicide. Critical neglect of the scene is perhaps understandable, for Isabella is a very minor character—her precipitous descent into madness and suicide does not even constitute a well-developed subplot—and her attack on the garden has no explicit relationship to the main action of the play. It seems, at first glance, that Kyd is using the episode as a sensational interlude between the formulation and execution of Hieronimo's plot against his enemies, perhaps as a means of preparing the audience for the shocking and bizarre catastrophe Hieronimo has devised.

However, closer examination of this garden scene reveals that Isabella's action is thematically relevant to the issues of revenge, justice, and moral disorder raised in the play.[1] In fact, the scene may be viewed as a symbolic prologue to the catastrophe. In literal terms, of course, Isabella's assault on the garden as a substitute for revenge against her son's murderers is merely pathetic, the action of a grief-crazed woman frustrated by her inability to obtain justice. But in symbolic terms it stands as a vivid renunciation of a world gone bad. And, in combination with Hieronimo's subsequent decimation of the Spanish court, it suggests the retribution that awaits any society that abandons the rule of law, exiles justice from the earth, and declines into moral anarchy.

There are two main clues to the significance of Isabella's revenge: her choice of the garden as her target and the relation of her actions to Hieronimo's prophecy at the end of the preceding scene. There, having set his trap for Lorenzo and Balthazar, he predicts an apocalypse:

> Now shall I see the fall of Babylon,
> Wrought by the heavens in this confusion.
> (IV.i.195-96)[2]

As S. F. Johnson points out, Isabella's attack on the garden just after this brings to mind the image of Babylon and its fabled Hanging Gardens.[3] The conclusion that Isabella (though, ironically, she is unaware of her husband's plot) is unconsciously participating in the destruction of Babylon is difficult to resist.

It becomes more credible when one considers the use Kyd makes of the garden in *The Spanish Tragedy*. Now, it is true that he does not create a formal, allegorical image of the garden as Shakespeare, for instance, does in *Richard II*.[4] Kyd's garden, with its leafy arbor or "unfortunate and fatal pine," is a conventional stage setting.[5] It is presumably a formal, enclosed garden of the type common to the period, a place of retreat—or refuge—from the active world.[6] Its symbolic significance in this play is established by the contrast between the conventional symbolism attached to it and the action that takes place there. It is conceived by Hieronimo as a "sacred bower" and by the young lovers, Horatio and Bel-imperia, as a garden of love. But it becomes a place of death, the scene of a tragic reversal that provokes Hieronimo's disillusionment and drives him eventually to his revenge.

By the late sixteenth century the garden had, of course, become a familiar setting in western literature, one that permitted a wide range of allegorical associations. Whether it basically symbolized man's attempt to recover the lost Paradise or to revive the Golden Age, it served as the focal point of man's aspirations toward various kinds of perfection—perfect love, perfect order in the state, perfect harmony in the soul.[7] A symbol of man's harmonious relationship with an essentially benevolent nature, it was created as a place of safety, pleasure, and repose, providing the nearest equivalent to bliss that postlapsarian man might enjoy. But, because the garden stood for perfection, it could be (and often was) used as an ironic setting for action in a world where man and nature are perceived as less than perfect. The garden might be used to emphasize the contrast between the ideal and the actual. In *Richard II*, for instance, the Gardener compares his well-pruned garden to the disordered condition of England, emphasizing the contrast between his good husbandry and Richard's bad. Or the garden may be portrayed as a false paradise, by virtue of its dedication to inferior forms of pleasure; such is the case with Spenser's Bower of Bliss, which is consecrated to purely sexual pleasures destructive to the mind and soul. Finally, the image of the garden may be invoked as a means of commentary on some aspect of the human condition. For instance, Hamlet sees his chaotic world as an "unweeded garden" possessed by things "rank and gross in nature" (*Hamlet*, I.ii.135-37).

In *The Spanish Tragedy* Kyd exploits the garden and the imagery of gardens and landscapes in each of these ways. And, in the context he establishes, Isabella's eventual destruction of Hieronimo's garden is a symbolically appropriate, even inevitable, act. The garden is first mentioned in the play by Bel-imperia, who refers to it as a "pleasant bower" (II.ii.42) and designates it as the "field" of her amorous encounter with Horatio. Unaware that she is being overheard by the eavesdropping Lorenzo and Balthazar, she mistakenly thinks that the lovers will be safe there, hidden from the "dangerous" court:

> There none shall hear us but the harmless birds:
> Happily the gentle nightingale
> Shall carol us asleep ere we be ware,
> And singing with the prickle at her breast,
> Tell our delight and mirthful dalliance.
>
> (11. 47-51)

In her characteristically sensuous way Bel-imperia thinks of the bower as a place consecrated to erotic bliss, and in their tryst she and Horatio metaphorically transform it into a Renaissance garden of love, decorated by Flora—

> The more thou sit'st within these leavy bowers,
> The more will Flora deck it with her flowers.
>
> (II.iv.24-25)

—and ruled by Bel-imperia-as-Venus:

> *Bel.* . . . . Cupid counterfeits the nightingale,
>   To frame sweet music to Horatio's tale.
> *Hor.* If Cupid sing, then Venus is not far:
>   Ay, thou art Venus, or some fairer star.
> *Bel.* If I be Venus thou must needs be Mars,
>   And where Mars reigneth there must needs be wars.
>
> (11. 30-35)

As Moody Prior observes, the martial imagery that describes the amorous "combat" which follows is charged with irony, since the lovers are unaware of the actual danger they are in.[8] But there is a subtler irony implicit in the allusions to Mars and Venus, for they underscore the basically illicit nature of this relationship.[9]

While the wooing scene has undeniable charm, and while the love-making of Horatio and Bel-imperia is an attractive alternative to the intriguing of Lorenzo and the posturing of Balthazar, this relationship is still in fact a clandestine, hole-and-corner affair conducted in stealth and secrecy. And there is no suggestion anywhere that the eroticism of these lovers is tempered by any kind of idealism. Indeed, there is a calculating cynicism underlying Bel-imperia's passion. She falls in love with Horatio as he is telling her about the death of her first lover, Andrea; and while she is momentarily struck by the impropriety of this, she easily rationalizes her scruples away:

> Yet what avails to wail Andrea's death,
> From whence Horatio proves my second love?
> Had he not lov'd Andrea as he did,
> He could not sit in Bel-imperia's thoughts.
> But how can love find harbour in my breast,
> Till I revenge the death of my beloved?
> Yes, second love shall further my revenge.
> I'll love Horatio, my Andrea's friend,
> The more to spite the prince that wrought his end.
>   (I.iv.60-68)

The decision to use Horatio's love as a means of gaining a petty kind of revenge against Andrea's killer, Balthazar, shows that, on Bel-imperia's side, the relationship is not even a purely erotic one.

Thus consecrated to a corrupt form of an inferior kind of love, the "pleasant bower" proves to be a false paradise, as the lovers' dream of bliss turns to nightmare. The murderers attack Horatio in a spirit of savage humor that at once emphasizes their desecration of the garden of love and reinforces the irony implicit in the wooing. As they stab Horatio, Lorenzo jokes that "these are the fruits of love" (1. 55). Bel-imperia's playful thrusts ("I dart this kiss at thee" [1. 40]) have given way to real weapons wielded in earnest, as the potential destructiveness of her passion for Horatio is realized. Horatio, poetically exalted as Mars during the wooing, is grotesquely transformed into a hanging corpse, moving Lorenzo to jest, "Although his life were still ambitious proud, / Yet is he at the highest now he is dead" (ll. 60-61). The ritual of love has turned into a grim comedy, with Mars and Venus trapped in a murderous Vulcan's net.

Insofar as the lovers are concerned, the episode in the garden is a violent, but less than tragic, one. Their relationship was badly flawed and, further, their reversal was not accompanied by recognition: Bel-imperia, the survivor, never seems to realize her contribution to Horatio's death. The real impact of the murder, and of the violation of the garden, falls on Hieronimo in the subsequent scene. Before he recognizes the body hanging in the arbor as his son's, Hieronimo suspects that someone has put it there in order to implicate him, and he is affronted by such a misuse of the garden: "This place was made for pleasure not for death" (II.v.12). Shortly, he recognizes Horatio and is outraged as well as grieved:

> O heavens, why made you night to cover sin?
> By day this deed of darkness had not been.
> O earth, why didst thou not in time devour
> The vile profaner of this sacred bower?
> (11. 24-27)

Hieronimo's complaint to the heavens and earth suggests that his conception of the "sacred bower" has been a mystical, religious one. He has thought of the garden as an inviolable temple of God, protected by the agents of divine justice. It would, I think, be too much to say that it was his terrestrial paradise, but his disillusionment does indicate that for him the garden signified a connection between man and God, between this world and the divine world, that has been broken by the murder. In his tormented imagination he identifies Horatio as the most precious plant in the garden, as a "Sweet lovely rose, ill-pluck'd before . . . [his] time" (1. 46). Horatio's death forces him to recognize that the garden is not sacred after all, and near the end of the scene he commands Isabella to help him carry Horatio's body "from out this cursed place" (1. 65).

In light of Hieronimo's mystical idea of the garden, it is to be assumed that the "pleasure" for which it was made was of a more ascetic, contemplative kind than the lovers sought. And there is some irony in the fact that he is unaware of their tryst; the garden, as he conceived it, has been violated more than once. But for him the murder is enough to turn the garden into a false paradise that, Giamatti observes, "embodies the split between what seems and what is."[10] It has thus become the scene of a tragic recognition for Hieronimo and, significantly, he never reappears there. Moreover, as he continues his futile quest for justice in the play, Hieronimo becomes increasingly agonized by his awareness of the disjunction between an inaccessible heaven and an infernal earth.

Isabella is similarly affected by this recognition, though at first her outrage is less extreme than her husband's. As soon as Hieronimo discovers Horatio's body he begins to contemplate revenge; Isabella is willing to bide her time and let the processes of justice work:

> The heavens are just, murder cannot be hid,
> Time is the author both of truth and right,
> And time will bring this treachery to light.
>
> (ll. 57-59)

But the processes of justice do not work. Hieronimo is prevented from even presenting his case to the King (III.xii), and he consequently abandons his own office as a magistrate and turns private revenger. Isabella, meanwhile, goes thoroughly mad, ultimately spending her hysterical rage on Hieronimo's false paradise, the garden.

In dramatizing Isabella's attack on the garden, Kyd exploits the setting in a new way. Though the notion of the garden as a false paradise still lingers, the bower now stands as a false symbol, or mirror, of order. Significantly, when Isabella enters it in Act IV, scene ii, she blames the King for what she is about to do:

> Since neither piety nor pity moves
> The king to justice or compassion,
> I will revenge myself upon this place.
>
> (ll. 2-4)

Her indictment of the King in this context suggests a Shakespearian use of the garden as a political metaphor, although the analogy between the garden and the state is implicit rather than explicit.[11] Isabella begins to cut down the foliage, and as she works she re-consecrates the place as a waste-land:

> Fruitless for ever may this garden be,
> Barren the earth, and blissless whosoever
> Imagines not to keep it unmanur'd!
>
> (ll. 14-16)

Using images reminiscent of biblical prophecies of the destruction of Babylon, she predicts eternal desolation for the garden.[12] Henceforth, the "earth with serpents shall be pestered," and passersby, "for fear to be infect," will avoid it because of its cursed state (11. 19-20).

Isabella's condemnation of the garden has apparently been inspired by her disillusionment with the King, whose responsibility it was to cultivate the garden of state through the administration of justice. From his pivotal position in the social hierarchy he was supposed to rule in accordance with divine law for the well-being of his people. In other words, his actions were to be informed by both "piety" (reverence for God) and "pity" (compassion for his subjects). In Isabella's mind, the King has failed to fulfill his responsibilities, and it is this failure that has driven her to attack the garden.

Earlier, I asserted that Isabella's action functions as a symbolic prologue to Hieronimo's revenge. While the two episodes are superficially dissimilar, they do correspond in a way that reinforces the implicit political symbolism of the garden. In condemning the "Accursed complot" of her misery, Isabella predicts that

> An eastern wind commix'd with noisome airs
> Shall blast the plants and the young saplings.
>
> (IV.ii.17-18)

In the catastrophic scene Hieronimo, playing a Turkish assassin, uses the "noisome airs" of his polyglot playlet as a cover under which he blasts Lorenzo and Balthazar, the "young saplings" of the realm. Not content to merely strip the foliage from the garden, Isabella burns the roots "from whence the rest is sprung." Similarly, Hieronimo does not limit his revenge to his son's murderers; he also kills Castile, the root from whence Lorenzo has sprung. The deaths of Balthazar and Bel-imperia, who were to marry and produce an heir for Spain, make the ruin complete, as the King complains:

> What age hath ever heard such monstrous deeds?
> My brother, and the whole succeeding hope
> That Spain expected after my decease!
>
> (IV.iv.202-04)

Hieronimo's deracination of the royal house has been as complete as Isabella's symbolically analogous destruction of the garden.

The well-tended garden, which traditionally symbolizes order, is here destroyed because the order it is supposed to reflect has ceased to exist in

Spain. It is a false mirror, like the Spanish court itself. Early in the play Kyd takes some care to represent Spain as a traditional monarchy whose policies are informed by late-medieval notions of natural law, divine providence, and chivalry. But it soon becomes clear that these notions, which provide the ethical foundation for the political order, have deteriorated badly. In Act I, scene ii, where the Spanish celebrate their recent victory over Portugal, we are first impressed by the absolute decorum that prevails. The King dutifully acknowledges the victory as the gift of providence:

> Then blest be heaven, and guider of the heavens,
> From whose fair influence such justice flows.
>
> (ll. 10-11)

This interpretation of the outcome of the war is repeated later by the loser, when the Portuguese Viceroy accepts his defeat as a divine judgment against his ambition:

> My late ambition hath distain'd my faith,
> My breach of faith occasion'd bloody wars,
> The bloody wars have spent my treasure,
> And with my treasure my people's blood,
> And with their blood, my joy and best belov'd,
> My best beloved, my sweet and only son.
>
> (I.iii.33-38)

The unbroken chain of cause and effect in the Viceroy's speech underlines the traditional conception of natural law implicit in the King's benediction. The outcome of the battle is seen, not as the result of mere military superiority, but as an act of providence, which rewards the virtuous and punishes the guilty. Neither ruler questions the idea that justice flows unimpeded from heaven to earth.

Following his benediction, the King asks for an account of the battle from the General, who complies by painting it as a perfect chivalric spectacle:

> When Spain and Portingale do jointly knit
> Their frontiers, leaning on each other's bound,
> There met our armies in their proud array,
> Both furnish'd well, both full of hope and fear,
> Both menacing alike with daring shows,

> Both vaunting sundry colours of device,
> Both cheerly sounding trumpets, drums and fifes,
> Both raising dreadful clamours to the sky.
>
> (I.ii.22-29)

This description, with its nicely balanced phrases, conveys the impression that the battle was an orderly affair. Even in the General's picture of the carnage—

> On every side drop captains to the ground,
> And soldiers, some ill-maim'd, some slain outright;
> Here falls a body scinder'd from his head,
> There legs and arms lie bleeding on the grass.
>
> (ll. 57-60)

—the casualties fall neatly in place, as if they knew they were performers in a pageant. Under the weight of the General's decorous, conventional speech, the real horror of war is subordinated to an aesthetic notion of chivalry.

However, the concealed realities of battlefield conduct do manage to surface. For instance, when Horatio tells Bel-imperia of Andrea's death (I.iv.6-29), we become aware of a glaring inaccuracy in the General's description. He reports that Balthazar courageously killed Andrea in a duel (ll. 67-72); according to Horatio, Balthazar succeeded only because some Portuguese halberdiers unhorsed Andrea first. But even before this discrepancy comes to light the General's characterization of the battle as a chivalric tournament is suspect. When the warriors return, the festive and ceremonial atmosphere is disturbed by contention: Lorenzo makes an entirely factitious claim to the honor and rewards for the capture of Balthazar, who had actually been conquered by Horatio. In the debate that follows, Balthazar tacitly supports Lorenzo's claim with his equivocal testimony. When asked to whom he surrendered, Balthazar replies,

> To him in courtesy, to this perforce:
> He spake me fair, this other gave me strokes:
> He promis'd life, this other threaten'd death:
> He wan my love, this other conquer'd me:
> And truth to say I yield myself to both.
>
> (ll. 161-65)

The Prince's profession of neutrality is belied by his obvious sympathy for Lorenzo and scorn of Horatio, "this other." Besides revealing that Balthazar is cowardly and susceptible to flattery, the speech also indicates that even in war chivalry cannot prevail over policy. The tradition that the General celebrates is in a moribund state.

This episode illuminates an even more serious flaw in the Spanish system of justice. Before Lorenzo made his claim the King had determined that "this battle's prize" would go to Horatio. Now he hedges. He impatiently brushes aside Hieronimo's judgment, "Enforc'd by nature and by law of arms" (1. 168), that Horatio alone deserves the honor and announces a compromise that gives both claimants a share. It is, on the face of it, a politic decision, one that most critics have found praiseworthy.[13] But it is not a *just* decision; it violates the tenets of "nature" and "law of arms" cited by Hieronimo. It amounts, really, to a rejection of the "fair influence" from which justice flows and from which the Spanish have so recently benefited. And in the end it will prove destructive to the state, for it puts a corrupt, weak-minded prince into the custody of a quasi-Machiavellian aristocrat.

During the rest of the play the King is busy arranging a détente with Portugal through the unwise device of a marriage between Balthazar and Bel-imperia.[14] Meanwhile, Lorenzo begins to dominate the play, gulling Balthazar and enlisting the likes of Pedringano and Serberine in his plot against Horatio. Following the murder, Lorenzo continues to manipulate his accomplices and the processes of justice. He engineers the deaths of Serberine and Pedringano, permitting the latter's legal execution only because he wants him out of the way. Exploiting the King's ignorance of Horatio's murder, he most explicitly interferes with justice in turning Hieronimo back when the latter attempts to approach the King.[15] He thus effectively separates the King from his subjects, and the flow of justice is arrested. Following his failure to reach the King, Hieronimo is convinced of his own impotence as a magistrate and abandons his office. He tears up the bonds of the petitioners who approach him and tells Bazulto (another father seeking justice for the murder of his son) that he cannot help him, "For justice is exiled from the earth" (III.xiii.140). In the absence of justice the predators have taken over, and Spain has entered its Iron Age.

To use Hieronimo's allusion, Spain has become a modern incarnation of the biblical Babylon, symbol of corruption and injustice. As such it is ripe for destruction. So, too, is the garden, which symbolizes social and moral order. And by reducing it to rubble Isabella converts it from a false mirror to a true one, reflecting the chaos that actually exists in Spain. At the same time, Isabella's language in Act IV, scene ii also demonstrates Kyd's use of the imagery of gardens and landscapes as a means of commentary on the condition of the world of the play. Prior to Horatio's murder, references to nature are infrequent and entirely conventional. Nature is implicitly conceived as a benign force, as the emphasis on the pleasant character of Hieronimo's garden suggests. Following the murder, however, Hieronimo thinks of the earth as a place invaded by demons:

> The ugly fiends do sally forth of hell,
> And frame my steps to unfrequented paths.
>
> (III.ii.16-17)

The earth has become a wilderness, a dark wood of error,

> . . . where the soul, that should be shrin'd in heaven,
> Solely delights in interdicted things,
> Still wand'ring in the thorny passages
> That intercepts itself of happiness.
>
> (III.vi.91-94)

Nature, revolting against the injustice Hieronimo suffers, has become a hostile force, denuding the landscape:

> The blust'ring winds, conspiring with my words,
> At my lament have mov'd the leaveless trees,
> Disrob'd the meadows of their flower'd green,
> Made mountains marsh with spring-tides of my tears,
> And broken through the brazen gates of hell.
>
> (III.vii.5-9)

As his distraction becomes more extreme, hellish landscapes abound in Hieronimo's imagination. He tells a pair of messengers that they may find the devilish Lorenzo

> Within a hugy dale of lasting night,
> That, kindled with the world's iniquities,
> Doth cast up filthy and detested fumes.
>
> (III.xi.21-22)

And, when he contemplates suicide, he pictures himself trudging "Down by the dale that flows with purple gore" (III.xii.7).

The evolving image of the earthly landscape as an infernal one is set off by contrasting images of heaven. As her madness peaks, Isabella imagines that she sees Horatio sitting in heaven,

> Back'd with a troop of fiery cherubin,
> Dancing about his newly-heal'd wounds,
> Singing sweet hymns and chanting heavenly notes,
> Rare harmony to greet his innocence,
> That died, ay, died, a mirror in our days.
>
> (III.viii.18-22)

The image of Horatio as a mirror of innocence is interesting, in light of her subsequent attack on the false mirror, the garden. Even more striking here is Isabella's conception of heavenly harmony. The "sweet hymns" are in sharp contrast to the violent rhetoric of the play, which becomes absolutely discordant in Hieronimo's multilingual playlet.[16] The musical harmony in heaven reflects a social harmony among its inhabitants as well as the internal harmony of the saved—Horatio's wounds are healed. On earth, by contrast, the social harmony we saw at the beginning of Act I, scene ii has disintegrated, while Hieronimo and Isabella have come apart emotionally.

Hieronimo, too, thinks of heaven, but with a painful consciousness of its inaccessibility. He complains that his "broken sighs and restless passions"

> Beat at the windows of the brightest heavens,
> Soliciting for justice and revenge:
> But they are plac'd in those empyreal heights
> Where, countermur'd with walls of diamond,
> I find the place impregnable.
>
> (III.vii.13-17)

The bewildered victim of an austere and inscrutable system of justice, he is impressed most by its vertical distance from earth and the hardness of its diamond walls.[17] In consequence, he is forced to turn his gaze back to a cursed earth, where "a path on your left-hand side" leads directly into hell.

Through his use of landscape imagery and his exploitation of the garden as a setting for crucial actions, Kyd has managed to enrich his story of revenge with the larger drama of a society sliding toward its destruction. The successive violations of the garden are of a piece with the abuses of justice dramatized in the play, and the increasingly grotesque image of nature that is presented corresponds to the morally grotesque condition of society. In the end, of course, there is justice. The guilty are condemned to replace their criminal archetypes in Kyd's Virgilian underworld, while the innocent gain Elysium. Andrea promises to "lead Hieronimo where Orpheus plays / Adding sweet pleasure to eternal days" (IV.v.23-24), as the old Marshal is finally rewarded with his true paradise. But this closing scene is less than convincing. For instance, one must question the logic of putting the sensuous Bel-imperia with the vestal virgins (11. 21-22). More convincing are the lingering images of the wasted garden and the bloody court in the aftermath of Hieronimo's revenge, which was indeed the fall of Babylon.

END NOTES

[1] Until the last fifteen years or so, criticism of *The Spanish Tragedy* was dominated by the Boas-Bowers view of it as an imperfectly wrought revenge play, marred by such apparently extraneous elements as the overplot of Andrea's revenge and the Portuguese subplot. Recent critics, who see *The Spanish Tragedy* as primarily a play about justice, attribute a *thematic* unity and coherence to it; they argue that the overplot, which demonstrates the ultimate efficacy of divine justice, and the subplot, which illuminates the frailty of human justice, provide a context for Hieronimo's quest for justice in the main plot. See, especially, T. B. Tomlinson, *A Study of Elizabethan and Jacobean Tragedy* (Cambridge: Cambridge Univ. Press, 1964), pp. 73-85; G. K. Hunter, "Ironies of Justice in *The Spanish Tragedy*," *RenD*, 8 (1965), rpt. in *Shakespeare's Contemporaries*, ed. Max Bluestone and Norman Rabkin, 2nd ed. (Englewood Cliffs, N. J.: Prentice-Hall, 1970), pp. 61-73; Arthur Freeman, *Thomas Kyd: A Study of Facts and Problems* (Oxford: Oxford Univ. Press, 1967), pp. 80-115; Ronald F. Broude, "Time, Truth, and Right in *The Spanish Tragedy*," *SP*, 68 (1971), 130-45. My discussion is guided by a similar conviction that the play has a thematic rather than narrative structure, although I would argue that Kyd treats the problem of justice as part of a larger problem of order.

[2] All quotations of the play are taken from the Revels edition by Philip Edwards (London: Methuen, 1959).

[3] "The Spanish Tragedy, or Babylon Revisited," *Essays on Shakespeare and the Elizabethan Drama in Honor of Hardin Craig*, ed. Richard Hosley (Columbia, Mo.: Univ. of Missouri Press, 1962), p. 26. Johnson observes that Isabella's destruction of the garden seems to prefigure Hieronimo's revenge, but he does not pursue this insight further.

[4] *Richard II*, III.iv.29-66. In his speeches the Gardener explicitly likens the plants to political forces in the state, making his well-trimmed garden a formal emblem of political order. Kyd is never so explicit.

[5] As Edwards, p. 43n., points out, there is some confusion about whether the arbor from which Horatio is hanged is an arch of trellis-work or a tree (during the play it is identified as both). His conjecture that it is the former is probably correct. According to Chambers, *The Elizabethan Stage* (Oxford: Clarendon Press, 1923), III, 55-56, leafy trellises or bowers provided ideal opportunities for the kind of eavesdropping that Horatio's murderers engage in.

[6] Aldo D. Scaglione, *Nature and Love in the Late Middle Ages* (Berkeley and Los Angeles: Univ. of California Press, 1963), pp. 64-65, points out that the enclosed garden was a conventional literary setting for courtly love trysts, as "a symbolic place of refuge from the morality of the church." In *The Spanish Tragedy*, Horatio and Bel-imperia seek refuge from the court rather than the church in Hieronimo's bower, but their use of the garden does suggest the clandestine, furtive quality of their love affair.

[7] For a discussion of the development of the garden as a literary symbol in Latin, medieval, and Renaissance literature, see A. Bartlett Giamatti, *The Earthly Paradise and the Renaissance Epic* (Princeton: Princeton Univ. Press, 1966). My remarks on the garden as a false paradise are largely indebted to his work.

[8] *The Language of Tragedy* (1947; rpt. Bloomington, Ind.: Indiana Univ. Press, 1966), pp. 52-53.

[9] The union of Mars and Venus was variously interpreted in the Renaissance, and it is admittedly difficult to tell which interpretation (if any in particular) Kyd had in mind here. A favorite subject of Italian painters, the conjunction of Mars and Venus symbolized the neoplatonic concept of *discordia concors*, the notion that harmony is born of the union of opposites (see Edgar Wind, *Pagan Mysteries of the Renaissance*, rev. ed., [New York: Norton, 1968], pp. 75ff.). On the other hand, the tendency to moralize Ovid was still very strong in sixteenth-century England, and the following couplet from the "Epistle" to Golding's translation of *Metamorphoses* (1567) seems relevant to Kyd's use of the Mars-Venus allusions:

The snares of Mars and Venus shew that tyme will bring too lyght
The secret sinnes that folk commit in corners or by nyght.
(II. 111-12)

Golding's emphasis on the clandestine, night-time character of this affair is similar to Kyd's portrayal of the Horatio-Bel-imperia tryst, and Golding, like Isabella, in II.iv.58-59, explicitly alludes to the "time, truth, and right" *topos* that Broude finds central to the play.

[10]*The Earthly Paradise*, p. 85.

[11]The use of the garden as a political metaphor was less general than a reader familiar with Shakespeare's history plays might think. Prior to the 1590s it was mainly employed by political satirists. On the development of the garden as political metaphor, see Peter Ure's introduction to the Arden edition of *Richard II* (Cambridge, Mass.: Harvard Univ. Press, 1956), pp. li-lvii.

[12]Johnson, pp. 25-27, finds echoes of Genesis, 11, Isaiah, 13, Jeremiah, 51, and Revelations, 18 in Isabella's language. In his essay Johnson is primarily concerned with the relevance of the Tower of Babel episode in Genesis to the play; not only did it inspire the device of the multilingual playlet, says Johnson, it also provided the rationale for Hieronimo's revenge: the Marshal becomes a Protestant avenger doing God's work. While Johnson's thesis is intriguing, his argument is not fully convincing, and we should not, in any case, ignore the other biblical sources. John's prophecy in Revelations is especially relevant to the conclusion of the play. In his prophecy Babylon is destroyed as a lesson to the corrupt kings of the earth, who are the horrified witnesses to the destruction; in *The Spanish Tragedy,* the King and Viceroy suffer in similar fashion. They are made to witness Hieronimo's revenge and are left behind to mourn as the dead abandon Spain-Babylon for Elysium.

[13]But there are dissenters. Broude, p. 143, and Ernest de Chickera, "Divine Justice and Private Revenge in *The Spanish Tragedy,*" *MLR,* 57 (1962), 230-32, both see the King's partiality toward his nephew as a sign of political corruption.

[14]Medieval and Renaissance political theorists universally denounced this practice. Erasmus' reasoning in chapter nine of *The Education of a Christian Prince* (1515) is exemplary: these marriages are motivated solely by political expedience and so violate the sacramental idea of marriage. Moreover, they usually fail to achieve their political objectives, and so are twice cursed.

[15]Edwards, p. lviii., holds that the subject of the King's ignorance "is best not inquired into. The plot demands it and the play shall have it." But surely it is significant in that it reflects the King's fatal neglect of internal affairs and of the interests of justice in his kingdom.

[16]Jonas A. Barish, in *"The Spanish Tragedy,* or the Pleasures and Perils of Rhetoric,"* Elizabethan Theatre,* Stratford-upon-Avon Studies, No. 9, ed. John Russell Brown and Bernard Harris (New York: St. Martin's, 1966), pp. 59-85, acutely observes that the play shows us "a breakdown of the links between rhetoric and reality" (p. 81). Hieronimo's cacophonous playlet, he notes, mirrors the "inner ethical chaos" of the Spanish court (p. 83).

[17]Hunter, for whom the play is "an allegory of perfect justice," calls our attention to the inscrutability of divine justice in it, asserting that Hieronimo's madness results from "the collision of his human sense of justice with the quite different processes of divine justice" (p. 71). Hieronimo only finds his way out of the dilemma, Hunter argues, when he abandons human justice.

Henry IV: From Satirist to Satiric Butt

Jo Ann Davis

"For now a time is come to mock at form"
2 Henry IV, IV.v.118

The changing role of Henry Bolingbroke provides a vehicle for describing the logical development of form in the second tetralogy. The play sequence moves from the tragedy of *Richard II*, where Henry is a satirist, to the *Henry IV* plays which are structured for maximum exposure of Henry as object of satire primarily by means of parody and caricature. In fact, it is Henry's failure as a satirist that produces the multiple plots of *Henry IV* Parts 1 and 2. If the tetralogy is viewed from this formal perspective, Falstaff and his world exist as a corollary to Henry's becoming a satiric butt. The scene is thus set for both the expulsion of the objects of the satire and the return to an ordered ideal society first described by Gaunt in *Richard II* and finally epitomized in the new King Henry V.[1]

Henry Bolingbroke's dramatic status in the plays has anomolous features. For one thing, he is the only major figure whose "story" does not constitute a play: Richard and Hal have separate plays named after them which they dominate in word and in deed. And although Shakespeare named the two middle plays after Henry, neither is Henry's "story": he appears very little in either, and popular opinion has given both plays to Falstaff. For another thing, Henry appears to be a changed man in the Henry plays. In *Richard II*, Henry is essentially taciturn and satiric; his presence dominates but his words do not: for example, in the deposition scene where his presence dominates, he speaks only about one line out of every ten. But as king in the Henry plays, he has become verbose, a butt for much satire: in *1 Henry IV*, I.i. and III.ii, he speaks seven out of every ten lines. This marked verbal contrast, consistent throughout, reinforces his transformation from satirist to satiric butt. His windy and rhetorical delivery in the Henry plays reinforces his transformation from the silent but efficient king, a producer and director of action, into a whining, suspicious *senex*, a stock *commedia dell' arte* character.

Generally the function of satire is to uphold the order of a civilized community, to promote the public good. Through his satire of ceremony,[2] Henry in *Richard II* exposes the hollowness and ineffectiveness of state rituals which are played out by rote and which provide a color for insincerity and intrigue. As satirist, however, Henry does not go beyond exposure and deflation. The corrective impulse is absent in him. Thus rather than using satiric weapons to change outmoded rituals or to correct corrupted ceremony, Henry maintains the form and ritual which he has already exposed to ridicule. By revealing Henry's limitations as a satirist, Shakespeare forces us to judge not only the weakened rituals of Richard's court but also the rule of power separated from meaningful state ritual epitomized in Henry's rule.

In *Richard II*, Henry first accomplishes this satire of ritual primarily through invective and verbal deflation in Act I, and he retains the ability to mock and expose in usually brief verbal slashes throughout the play. However, with his return to England, Henry begins to control the action and to stage scenes which expose to contempt and mockery the ritual and ceremony which governed Richard's court. Thus the design of the play makes Acts III, IV, and V satiric reflections as they parallel in form ceremonies which made up the pattern of the early acts of the play.

Once we are furnished with background information in I.ii—that the Lancastrians believe Richard guilty of his uncle Gloucester's death—we realize the extent to which Henry has used and satirized the ritual of trial by combat in scene i. Not able to challenge the King, Henry has challenged the King's friend and has indirectly accused the King of mismanaging money, undermining law, and suborning murder. The mode—pre-combat ceremony—has become a tool which Henry manipulates to excoriate the King.

In his first appearance after his unlawful return from banishment, Henry's terse response ironically directs attention to the cloying, sugared rhetoric of Northumberland's fulsome flattery, and, as in the deposition scene, demonstrates Henry's limited tolerance for the insincerity of ceremonious utterances. But Henry can court allies, and he goes on to promise young Percy, Ross, and Willoughby "recompense" in "fortune" and "treasury" when his own "fortune ripens." He woos York with blatant and overblown appeals to sentimentality, calling him "my father," and swearing to one and all that he returns to claim only "his own."

Henry here demonstrates his satiric contempt for mankind. He offers each what is of prime importance, promising fortune to the greedy and ambitious and extravagant familial sentiment to the sentimental York. Henry's vocabulary in the scene is permeated by the language of economics and litigation.

The form and ritual of allegiance is exposed and satirized as the basic motivation, gain, is paramount to any question of "right." Henry's satiric pandering
to ceremony and ritual scarcely glosses over his recognition of the base
motivations for allegiance.

The Flint Castle scene makes explicit both visually and verbally Henry's
contempt for ceremony and ritual. As satirist he exposes the powerlessness
and falsity of ritual separated from meaning. Learning that Richard is inside
Flint Castle, Henry orders Northumberland to observe the niceties of state
ritual and to report to Richard that

> Henry Bullingbroke
> On both his knees doth kiss King Richard's hand,
> And sends allegiance and true faith of heart
> To his most royal person; hither come
> Even at his feet to lay my arms and power.
>
> (III.iii.35-39)[3]

The form of ceremonious obedience is then exploded both by Henry's
provisos:

> Provided that my banishment repeal'd
> And lands restor'd again be freely granted.
>
> (40-41)

by Henry's threats:

> If not, I'll use the advantage of my power,
> And lay the summer's dust with show'rs of blood
>
> (42-43)

and by his visual reinforcement of those threats:

> Go signify as much, while here we march
> Upon the grassy carpet of this plain.
>
> (49-50)

The form is proper ritual; the reality is the marching army: ritual is overwhelmed, exposed and mocked by power. The crowning satiric touch of
contempt is Henry's order:

Let's march without the noise of threat'ning drum.

(51)

And like an anxious stage director Henry orders his men to report the audience reaction to the dominant satiric images he has arranged:

March on, and mark King Richard how he looks.

(61)

When Richard descends to the court, Henry burlesques the familiar ritual of hierarchial order; he kneels and orders his followers to "show fair duty to his Majesty" (188). Richard recognizes the satiric contempt implicit in the contrasting visual images:

Up, cousin, up, your heart is up, I know,
Thus high at least, although your knee be low.

(194-95)

With Henry now in effective control, the last two Acts of the play parody the earlier ones. Act IV mirrors Act I with satiric deflation run wild. We are prepared for this having witnessed the short legal shrift Henry gave Bushy and Green in III.i. Now the ritual of accusation and defense in the Bolingbroke/Mowbray confrontation of I.i. is here parodied and burlesqued until any semblance of meaningful ritual is held up to derision. The same crime, Gloucester's murder, is under contention; instead of Mowbray being accused, it is now Aumerle, with Richard named as co-conspirator. Henry, blatantly rigging the scene, satirizes the state ritual by exaggeration. The evidence is contrived, as Surrey demonstrates. But it is exaggeration moving toward burlesque that puts the knife into the heart of state ritual. At least nine gages are exchanged in a hurly-burly of accusations and defense. Ritual is reduced to absurdity as the stage is littered with gages; Shakespeare runs out of names for gage-throwers, resorting along the way to "another Lord"; and Aumerle even has to borrow a gage, having run out of them. Henry perfects the absurdity when he rules that the accused Aumerle must await the recall of the banished Mowbray, a signal inconvenience since Mowbray is dead.[4]

The comic tone of this encounter is the most devastating blow Bolingbroke could arrange for state ritual—for ritual, not believed in, not taken seriously, is especially vulnerable to derision. Here it is not only stripped of meaning but reduced to nihilistic absurdity, and power exults over the debased form of ritual.

Henry, in his process of *becoming* king, would rather dispense with ceremony and ritual altogether. He reduced it in the Bushy/Green execution scene and set it up for scorn in the multiple gage scene. Since the decision is foregone, Henry would now atrophy ritual by making the rapid leap from subject to king, from floor to throne without any trappings of ceremony. Accordingly, officious York simply announces that Richard yields his scepter to Henry, and Henry moves to sit on the throne.

But Henry now first begins to emerge as the object of satire as the Bishop of Carlisle interferes and lists Henry's crimes against the state and Richard, with the simplest form of satire: invective and curse. The least Carlisle asks for is that Richard be present, and the least is what Bolingbroke grants.

The ceremony of formal deposition is an unfamiliar one. Henry's power drive has led him to satirize in order to expose, but the absence of a new system or new ethic results in the confirmation that Henry doesn't want to *correct*, only to possess. His nihilistic and destructive satire of ritual demonstrates his greatest weakness: he does not have a substitute for the very forms he satirizes. When his own planned and unceremonious assumption of the throne is aborted, Henry is thwarted by his own limitation: without belief in rituals he cannot ad lib and invent one. Since for him there is no intrinsic meaning in ritual, he cannot imagine how one goes about deposing a king publicly and ritualistically. Thus the scene which he has so carefully managed and controlled up to now is stolen from him. In the arena of state ritual he is the one now deposed, no longer director and star. It is Richard who usurps direction and management of the scene in which he stars.[5] One simple indication is that when Richard is on stage, Henry delivers only eleven brief questions and statements entirely dependent upon Richard's dramatically determinant words and actions.

The direction of *events* is not changed—both Richard and Henry know this: Henry has the power; Henry will be king. But Richard's elaborate and ritualistic speeches tear away the hypocritical facade and satirize the idea that Henry's assumption is legitimate.

Henry's attempts to bring Richard to the point at hand are prosaic. Only when Richard calls for the glass, studies his face, and recognizes its transience as a power image does Henry attempt any statement not directly related to the business of deposition. But even Henry's satiric flouting of Richard's grief

> The shadow of your sorrow hath destroy'd
> The shadow of your face.
>
> (IV.i.292-93)

is elaborated by Richard and thus transformed for Richard's purposes:

> Say that again.
> The shadow of my sorrow! Ha, let's see.
> 'Tis very true, my grief lies all within,
> And these external [manners] of laments
> Are merely shadows to the unseen grief
> That swells with silence in the tortur'd soul.
> There lies the substance; and I thank thee, King,
> For thy great bounty, that not only giv'st
> Me cause to wail, but teachest me the way
> How to lament the cause.
>
> (293-302)

Henry, who by choice has been more director and producer than leading man, clearly has problems with his temperamental star's liberties with the script.

These events are capped with the triumphant role of Henry, reported by York, with people cheering him while they treat Richard with contempt and throw dust on him. Satirists frequently deal with their victims in like manner, exposing them to public ridicule and often physical abuse. Jonson in *Poetaster* has his satiric victim fed an emetic to make him throw up his hard words, Shakespeare in *Twelfth Night* has Malvolio shut up in a dark place, and Scala in *The Pedant* (1611) gives his victim a thrashing. This reported triumph parallels and inverts Henry's departure for banishment earlier; in this case it is Richard who is being driven out and flaunted. York in this scene has adopted Henry's attitude toward ritual and meaning, but he is not conscious of satire when he tells his wife

> To Bullingbroke are we sworn subjects *now,*
> Whose state and honor I for *aye* allow
>
> (V.ii.39-40, emphasis added)

and announces that he is pledge for Aumerle's

truth
And lasting fealty to the new-made king,

(44-45)

Obviously if sworn oaths were lasting and eternal, York would not now have a "new-made King."

Earlier in the play York epitomized the concerned and loving father; Henry pandered to York's sentimentalized view of paternity to enlist York's sympathy and aid. Now, however, the sham of ritual has undermined other forms of order in Henry's realm. A scene of comic hysteria follows York's discovery of Aumerle's "treason": father berating son, mother opposing father, lost boots, beaten servants, unanswered questions, and a pell-mell race out the door reduce potentially serious matters to burlesque, and York's absolute rejection of his son is submerged in knock-about comedy.[6]

Aumerle reaches Henry first and is granted a pardon even before he has explained his crime with the proviso that it be an intended crime and not a committed one. They are interrupted by York's frenzied banging on the door, demanding entrance, calling Aumerle traitor, and warning Henry to protect himself. Henry quickly draws his weapon only to be assured by the capitulating words and actions of Aumerle that he has nothing to fear. Relaxed, Henry re-asserts his control of the scene, admits York who falls into the room panting. York exposes the rebellion and Henry grants Aumerle pardon again, because of York's loyalty. Henry is then confronted with an unexpected quirk: the father rejects the King's pardon of his son, demanding Aumerle's death. Henry is prevented from replying by the third hysterical entrance as the Duchess of York arrives and pounds on the door, identifying herself: "a beggar begs that never begged before." Henry recognizes the burlesque of the scene and, taking up the jingling couplets, replies,

> Our scene is alt'red from a serious thing,
> And now chang'd to 'The Beggar and the King.'
> My dangerous cousin, let your mother in,
> I know she is come to pray for your foul sin.

(V.iii.79-82)

It is easy for Henry to recognize and identify the caricature of the scene, which parodies his own satiric kneeling to Richard at Flint Castle. Soon all three Yorks are kneeling and making their contradictory pleas. Three times Henry tells his aunt to rise, but she remains kneeling and the caterwauling surges on. Any seriousness in the scene having long collapsed, the verse continues in an epidemic of jingling rhyme:

> *Duch.* For ever will I walk upon my knees,
>   And never see day that the happy sees
>   (93-94)
> *Aum.* Unto my mother's prayers I bend my knee.
> *York.* Against them both my true joints bended be.
>   (97-98)

The visually and poetically ridiculous is stressed in York's contribution to the kneeling contest and his attempt to have Henry separate word and meaning by using French so he can later break his word.

> *York.* Speak it in French, King, say '*pardonne moy.*'
> *Duch.* Dost thou teach pardon pardon to destroy?
>   (119-20)

The comic extravagence is capped by the Duchess' exaggerated thanks, "a god on earth thou art" (136).

The final scene is almost atavistically ritualized. Henry, the King as earthly god, sits on England's throne as one after another of his followers, all anxious "to thrive in this new world" (IV.i.78), rush in to present him verbally with bloody sacrifices, the mangled corpses of his enemies. Henry is no longer the complete satirist attacking state ritual, and the world of the play shifts, taking on a new focus. The extravagance Henry as satirist employed in his devaluing state ritual returns to haunt him. And Henry's world of satires and burlesques begins now to generate a life of its own, mocking the mocker. Exton brings on stage the body of murdered Richard and explains, "From your own mouth, my lord, did I this deed" (V.vi.37). Whereas Richard had to deal with indirect accusation of murder in public, Henry is ironically forced to deal with his responsibility for murder directly in public, in the midst of other blood offerings he had been approvingly accepting.

Henry is caught in an old play he no longer directs. Like Richard who had to banish Mowbray, Henry banishes Exton, but he also publicly judges and announces sentence on himself: a ritualistic penitential voyage to the Holy Land. His gestures are empty of meaning, but he cannot abandon the form of ritual which was part of Richard's court. The world of the play takes its revenge on Henry by forcing him to adhere to the form which he as satirist had despised, and his pledge of a pilgrimage to Jerusalem, a ritualized expiation, is transformed in the succeeding plays into a reiterated joke awaiting the punch line.

In *Richard II*, Henry has comparatively few lines for a major character. His infrequency of utterance stands as a satiric counterpoint to the verbosity of Richard, for whom verbal expression and state ritual are inseparable. Henry, the silent king, focuses on the reality of power: even the drums of his great army are silent. In denying Richard as his King he must deny and satirize the ritual and ceremony which surround Richard as an outward expression of his supposed power. The satirist Henry has no soliloquy—his public expressions and his control of the play's action provide for him self-expression. The satirist needs no moments of introspection.

This is still the "old world"; no new Adam has emerged to unify ritual and meaning and thus to provide England with a viable replacement of meaningless ritual.

In the Henry plays Henry himself becomes the butt of satire and is thus never allowed to capture our emotions or our respect. Henry becomes not a flamboyant Richard but develops as *Senex,* the miserly, critical, and suspicious old man, parodied by Falstaff, whose greed and amorality are reflected throughout the kingdom. Prudence and economy in speech and action characterize Henry in *Richard II,* but in the Henry IV plays Henry has lost the ability to be economic of words or prudent in action, as his lengthy speeches and rash denunciations of Hal illustrate. His brevity of speech and sardonic manner in *Richard II* are changed into longwinded petulance and suspicion. Rather than satirizing state ritual, Henry tries to make his kingdom now conform to order, ritual, and ceremony, an impossible task since he himself has reduced ritual to meaninglessness.

Bolingbroke has disappeared into his role and lofty rhetoric; he now has little objective distance from himself or others. The plays' structure, repetitive imagery, and parallel characters force the reader to view Henry as satiric butt and prevent us from accepting his self-evaluation as a rightful—and long-suffering—ruler.

Henry's major scenes in Part I are confrontations: in I.iii. with Hotspur; in III.ii. with Hal; and in V.iv. with Douglas. He is no longer certain of control, and his personal weakness, epitomized in Hotspur's refusal to obey him and Douglas' beating him in single combat, reinforce the satire directed at him in the play. Like Falstaff condemning those who steal from him, Henry, the regicide and usurper, condemns those who would steal his land and power. Like the coward Falstaff who feigns death in order to live, Henry has many men counterfeit his appearance to draw off attacks that would be directed at him, causing Douglas to threaten to kill his whole wardrobe. The satiric scope of the play refuses to let the audience view Henry as noble or honorable by reducing him to the level of the unprincipled Falstaff. The rebels plot to steal the kingdom as the tavern crew plots to steal purses (and, in turn, to rob one another: I.ii.162-166 and III.i.97-119) as Henry has stolen the kingdom from Richard. All Henry's appeals to honor, right, privilege of office, and ceremonial recognition of place are satirized by the contrapuntal presence of rebels and tavern thieves. A satiric leveling process is dramatized, and the vital dramatic function of the tavern gang and the rebels is to expose Henry, to puncture his hypocrisy, to condemn his immoral action. Henry's moral outrage at the idea of rebellion directed against him is thus exploded by parody in Falstaff's moral indignation at having *his* pocket picked.

The verbal extravagance of Hotspur parallels that of Falstaff and both undercut and puncture the king's long-winded, self-serving rhetoric. These are the three big talkers of the play; none is a successful hero, and the King is no longer a sun god but a vile politician.

While the satire focused on these three brings the play world's morality to its knees, Hal begins to emerge as the man who can unite ritual and substance. He rejects the parts offered him by Falstaff, Henry, and Hotspur: he will not rob the exchequer for his friends; he will not shun the company of common men and make a sham of duty; he will not emulate Hotspur's idea of honor. Form separated from meaning is nihilistic. Hal satirizes false notions of reputation and honor by allowing Falstaff to take public credit for defeating Hotspur in single combat, while he seeks to merge the form and meaning of ritual in his private elegy and respectful ritual over his dead opponent's body.

By *2 Henry IV*, King Henry has been reduced to only three appearances, the first of which does not come until the middle of the play. Henry has ceased to be an important character in his own play; he exists as a reminder of the play world's old Adam, satirized and certainly overshadowed by those exaggerated parodies of his worst qualities, Falstaff and Shallow.

In his first appearance, Henry rails at the dull god sleep for eluding him. And he closes the scene with one of his frequent reminders of his intention to make a pilgrimage to Jerusalem (III.i.107-08). With appropirate gallows humor, the play delivers both to Henry in his final scene, when he is given permanent sleep in a palace room called Jerusalem chamber.

As satiric butt in the two Henry plays, Henry resembles the *senex iratus*, the irritable old man of Greek New Comedy, who remained an active dramatic figure in the Renaissance. Giacomo Oreglia's description of the Pantalone illustrates the similarities:

> The comic attributes of Pantalone arise above all from the contradictions of senility: he is very avaricious yet a lover of pomp and splendor, wily yet rash; slanderous and quarrelsome, subject to sudden explosions of fury and vehement outbursts of curses and invective . . . at times [he] even becomes the rival of his own son. . . . A hypocrite, . . . [he] symbolizes in the Commedia the contrast between the old and new generation.[7]

Henry's avarice is what causes Hotspur to renounce his allegiance to Henry in their dispute over who gets the "honorable spoil" (I.i.74). Henry himself and the rebels provide constant reminders of Henry's overweening lust for royal power, and Henry soldered followers to him by promising them monetary reward in Part I, on the expectation that his own treasury would be enlarged. Henry sees his son as his rival for the crown: in Part II, he falls asleep with the crown on his pillow and grows furious when he discovers that it is gone and Hal has taken it. His assumption that Hal wishes him dead reveals more about his own nature than about Hal's.

The *senex* never trusts his son and constantly complains about his son's ingratitude. In a Pantalone's complaint, the *senex* whines,

> Oh son . . . how have you repaid all that I have done for you, the sleepless nights you have caused me, the bezants I have paid for you, the labours I have undertaken for you? With what ingratitude you repay a father who has done so much for you! (p. 82).

Similarily, when Henry learns that Hal has taken the crown, he explodes with fury and vehemently attacks his sons, all sons:

> See, sons, what things you are!
> How quickly nature falls into revolt
> When gold becomes her object!
> For this the foolish over careful fathers
> Have broke their sleep with thoughts, their brains with care,
> Their bones with industry;

> For this they have engrossed and pil'd up
> The cank'red heaps of strange-achieved gold;
> For this they have been thoughtful to invest
> Their sons with arts and martial exercises;
> When like the bee tolling from every flower
> [The virtuous sweets],
> Our [thighs] pack'd with wax, our mouths with honey,
> We bring it to the hive, and like the bees,
> Are murd'red for our pains.
>
> (IV.v.64-78)

Henry follows this with a long, self-pitying speech to Hal in which with almost ghoulish relish he describes what England will be like when Hal is crowned. Because Henry is no longer a successful satirist and because all his descriptions of a disordered kingdom that mocks at form apply to his own reign, his satire blows back in his face.

Northrop Frye's description of the comedic form points out the necessary role of the *senex:* "the hero's society rebels against the society of the *senex* and triumphs, but the hero's society is a Saturnalia, a reversal of social standards which recalls a golden age in the past before the main action of the play begins."[8] Following this pattern, Hal stays at a distance from his father's society, absenting himself from court and refusing to sit on his father's Council (*1H4.* III.ii.33-35). Though he does not actively contend with his father for power, his father views him as an anxious rival. Hal does triumph, achieving the crown in a natural manner, and he does reverse the standards which have prevailed in his father's reign. Henry and Falstaff are removed. England's golden age, remembered by Gaunt in *Richard II*, is recalled. Hal becomes a father/king to his brothers and country and takes as his new father and advisor the morality figure, the Lord Chief Justice. A world of justice, a paternal ruler, and military victory against foreign enemies is assured.

Thus in these three plays Henry has moved from satirist to satiric butt, and he and the agents involved in his exposure are finally expelled from the play world allowing a truly new world and a new man, Henry V, to take over a world which reunites ritual and meaning, another "Eden, demi-paradise" (*R2.* II.i.42).

END NOTES

[1]The universally accepted chronology for the four plays reflects, in part, tacit critical assumptions that they are in various ways evolutionary as a group. There is a great deal of criticism which regards these plays as purposively integrated in both conscious and subconscious ways. See, for example, the most recent extensive treatment of both tetralogies, Moody E. Prior, *The Drama of Power* (Evanston, Ill.: Northwestern Univ. Press, 1973). Prior, on pp. 4-9, expresses caution about tetralogy groupings and proposes a five play sequence from *Richard III* to *Henry V*. "In these five plays every significant variant among the possibilities of sovereign power is represented" (p. 9). With regard to form, Prior tends to stress the "individual dramatic units." He regards Richard as the focus for Shakespeare's exploring a "new idea of tragedy" (p. 181); he also views the widespread preoccupation with Falstaff as producing misguided readings of *1 Henry IV* as satire (p. 209).

I am suggesting that focussing on Bolingbroke's changing role reveals a coherent and evolutionary development in formal design in the second tetralogy. I have found the following books particularly helpful in developing my thesis: E. M. W. Tillyard, *Shakespeare's History Plays* (1944; rpt. New York: Collier, 1962); C. L. Barber, *Shakespeare's Festive Comedy* (Princeton: Princeton Univ. Press, 1959); Alice L. Birney, *Satiric Catharsis in Shakespeare* (Berkeley, Cal.: Univ. of Cal. Press, 1973).

[2]Tillyard's treatment of *Richard III* deals extensively with the ceremonious aspects of the play; see pp. 280-299.

[3]My text is G. Blakemore Evans, ed., *The Riverside Shakespeare* (Boston: Houghton Mifflin Co., 1974).

[4]Shakespeare has reproduced the facts of this plethora of challenges from Holinshed who contains no hint of irony in his account. The relevant passage may be conveniently found in Richard Hosley, ed., *Shakespeare's Holinshed* (New York: Capricorn Books, 1968), p. 91. But Shakespeare superimposes on it the dramatic exchange on Norfolk's death (a death which Holinshed states as a bare fact two pages later). Henry's "Why, Bishop, is Norfolk dead?" (IV.i.101) may be delivered in a tone of either mock-innocent amazement or genuine surprise. The play does not provide specific information about Henry's state of knowledge here. Neither does Shakespeare tell us in I.i. that Bolingbroke has knowledge of Richard's complicity in Gloucester's murder, but the whole design of the play as well as of the scene stresses Henry's continuing knowledge and control. On those compelling grounds, I prefer mock-innocent amazement. In either case the ironic climax is egregious.

[4]Ann Righter, in *Shakespeare and the Idea of the Play* (London: Chatto and Windus, 1962), after discussion of the metaphor of the world as a stage, asserts that "Shakespeare seems to have been concerned with the play metaphor to a degree unusual even among his contemporaries" (p. 81). Richard III is of course a self-proclaimed actor and director, and Waldo F. McNeir, in "The Masks of Richard the Third," *SEL*, 11 (1971), 167-186, explores Richard III in that light. On *Richard II*, see Georges A. Bonnard, "The Actor in *Richard II*," *ShJ*, 87 (1952), 87-101, and Leonard Dean, "*Richard II*: The State and the Image of the Theater," *PMLA*, 67 (1952), 211-218.

[6]Waldo F. McNeir's treatment of this episode is illuminating: "The Comic Scenes in *Richard II*, V.ii. and iii.," *Neuphilologische Mitteilungen*, 73 (1972), 815-822.

[7]*The Commedia dell' Arte*, trans. Lovett F. Edwards (New York: Hill and Wang, 1968), 78, 80.

[8]*Anatomy of Criticism* (Princeton: Princeton Univ. Press, 1957), p. 171.

Dr. Johnson's Philurbanism

Arthur J. Weitzman

There may be community, said Imlac, of material possessions, but
there can never be community of love or esteem. (*Rasselas*, Chap. XII)

Dr. Johnson's often quoted and strenuous defences of his adopted city
must be read against a rising tide of criticism of London's economic growth.
London of the 1740's and 50's seemed to many people an oppressive giant,
compromised by dissipation, crime, and corruption. Fear of the magnetism of
the capitol is amusingly conveyed by Sterne in *Tristram Shandy*. My Father
[Walter Shandy] proposed to appoint a judge at every entrance to the city
and to send each traveler back to where he came from if he could not give a
good reason for going to London: "By this means I shall take care, that my
metropolis totter'd not thro' its own weight;—that the head be no longer too
big for the body" (I, 18). Walpole's regime blurred, if not obscured, the
Augustan vision of a society dedicated to urbane pursuits of intellectual conversation, artistic patronage, reason, satire, raillery, skepticism and decorum.
These were thought to be endangered by a court corrupted by its dependence
on and propinquity to the great emporium in the City. So Pope argued in *The
Dunciad*, mock celebration of Smithfield muses brought to the ear of Kings.
Dismayed by an establishment hardened and apparently unresponsive even to
the hammer blows of his 30's satires, Pope warned with profound contempt
that the apocalypse was upon them. Pope's later poems, not to mention his
flight from London to Twickenham, already a fashionable suburb to those escaping the harshness of city life, reveal a gathering anti-urban momentum
which would culminate in rejection of the city by Cowper, Wordsworth and
the romantics of the nineteenth century. By the middle of the eighteenth
century a chasm had opened between the urbanists and anti-urbanists. Two
systems of thought and outlook were already in competition.

Dr. Johnson, whose love of London hardly needs documentation, appears
ambivalent on the question of London's growth. With chameleon-like
virtuosity, he expressed both the anti-urbanists' complaint in his Juvenalian
imitation *London* and later with no less perspicacity the ideals of those in

favor of the city's continued domination of the nation. In a well-known remark to Boswell, he offered this paean to the city: "why, Sir, you find no man, at all intellectual, who is willing to leave London. No, Sir, when a man is tired of London, he is tired of life; for there is in London all that life can afford."[1] Yet in his poem on *London*, he developed a persuasive rationale for the sensitive to quit a metropolis polluted by foreign vanities, superfluous luxury, money-grubbing courtiers, an arrogant nobility and crime in the streets. This seeming inconsistency has often been noticed but never fully explained. Critics have traditionally maintained that Johnson, the lover of London, was the recipient of a handsome pension and a lionized writer invited on terms of equality with the great and wealthy. Young Johnson the satirist was poor and newcomer to an inhospitable city. His attack on the city—so the argument runs—is merely the borrowed voice and attitude of Juvenal adapted to English circumstances; the evils of London are exaggerated in order to convey the shocking effect requisite for savage anger. Recently Howard Weinbrot has asserted Johnson's sincerity but attributed the weakness of the poem to his inability to achieve aesthetic distance between the speaker and subject. The voice of attack is too shrill and sweeping in condemnation; Thales appears insolent and a bit of a crank.[2] Criticism, however, seems to have missed Johnson's evolving attitude toward commerce and the urban milieu in which he found himself. I am proposing that he did have a change of heart toward the city partly due to the literary recognition he received in his later years and partly due to his sophisticated appreciation of what the city meant in national life. His favorable comments were often reactions to the mounting attacks on urban life that mark his era.

I

The assault on London was subsumed in the controversy over luxury. It began with Mandeville's brittle thesis that private vices make for public benefits; that is, a desire for luxury (which Mandeville equated with vice) is economically beneficial in that it encourages industry and trade and makes possible a favorable balance of payments. Traditional moralists reacted with predictable fury to Mandeville's bold theory of economic development, overturning by the way the aims of this science, which had been directed toward thrift, saving and careful regulation of resources. In the spate of refutations that followed Mandeville's publications,[3] the city of London became a target synonymous with luxury, which was thought to be destroying the moral fibre and integrity of the nation. One gets a strong whiff of this in the satires of Swift, Pope and the novels of Fielding.

Later a number of city-haters, mostly clergymen, bristled with pessimistic conclusions about the course of English society. Their argument was that by encouraging finery and ornament merely for show, or as Veblen terms it, conspicuous consumption, urban society fosters extravagance and debauchery, decreasing men's capacity for hard work and seducing the citizenry away from public service and sacrifice. The desire for luxury also creates artificial needs, but since only a few can enjoy luxuries and provide for large families, there develops among the poor a fear of marriage and procreation. The more children one has to support the fewer the luxuries. Hence the great evil to the pessimists of the age; declining population.[4] In contrast, frugal simplicity of taste and manners "regulate[s] the luxurious fancies, and restrain[s] the fruitless indulgencies of a people" to quote one clergyman's diatribe against commerce and the city.[5] Restrained living encourages procreation. This polemicist warns of the spread of luxury to remote corners of the nation; "the original and real source of [luxury] is always some enormous and destructive city."[6] The same Christian divine opined that luxury and cities were evil since they tended to drive up the wages of laborers. Even so objective an analyst as Arthur Young, the famous agriculturist, complained of the pernicious effect of the city in raising the price of labor in the country. Economists like Young often assumed that "the debauched life of [London's] inhabitants, occasion [laborers] to be more idle than in the country."[7] An unconscious "hard" primitivism of a life of self-denial, keeping close to the soil or shop and inuring the individual to hard labor, was the dominant attitude up to mid-century. ("Hard" primitivism should be contrasted with what might be called "soft," which under the influence of sentimentality formed the attitude that people living a rural life were more benevolent and gentler than city people. William Cowper's *The Task* is probably the best expression of this gentle and kindly primitivism.) It was, however, hard primitivism which fit neatly into the Mercantilist outlook. "Politicians," Young exhorted, "are so clear in their opinion, that low prices of labour are of the utmost importance to all trading states; that I must be allowed to express my amazement, at the legislature's suffering the capitol to increase in the prodigious manner it has done of late."[8]

One of the most popular of jeremiads of this period expressive of hard primitivism was John Brown's *Estimate of the Manners and Principles of the Times* (1757); it went through seven editions in two years. His charge of cultural decline appealed to those well-heeled people who felt guilty about sudden national affluence, and like some prophets of doom in our own day he warned England of "rolling to the Brink of a Precipice that must destroy us" (p. 15). Foreshadowing Spengler's gloomy prophecies, his argument was more subtle than other attacks on London's growth. He admitted the gains of trade to the national wealth, at least in the early stages of development, but in the last phase of commerce the town becomes a den of temptation, a bower of bliss, enticing rich youths to pursue pleasure and making them useless to serve society. In this tertiary stage of the disease, "the Contention for *Gain*, which had begun in *Town*, spreads itself by Degrees into the Country" (p. 110). The city and its values have in his opinion a disastrous effect on the arts, which are in precipitous decline. Men of fashion in their pursuit of idle amusement no longer read books, he reported. On the other hand agricultural life encourages the arts to flourish. Martial bravery and war-like virtues, cultivated in the country, produce good soldiers able to defend the nation. But like other hard primitivists, Brown betrayed a fatal contradiction which Mandeville's shrewder analysis revealed. Rigorists like Brown attacked luxury and the city, but expected England to compete with France and other Continental powers on an equal footing. His solution to the growth of luxury is mere wishful thinking: "Commerce and Wealth be not discouraged in their *Growth*; but checked and *controuled* in their *Effects*" (p. 217). Mandeville showed they were inseparable; the desire for luxury is the spur to commerce, as every advertising executive knows, not its undesirable side effect.

Across the aisle were the urbanists, mainly those apologists of commerce or overseas expansion, whigs, merchants, rentiers of every stripe, for whom London was merely a money machine or a convenient marriage market. Their urbanism offered little hope to the less fortunate. Here, for example, is Mandeville's prescription for social justice: "To make the Society Happy and People Easy under the meanest Circumstances, it is requisite that great numbers of them should be Ignorant as well as Poor" ("An Essay on Charity and Charity-Schools"). Needless to say, this is not the sort of reasoning Johnson could sympathize with.

In 1738, when the poem *London* was written and published, Johnson had resided in the city for one year. In the manner of an archetypal myth, Boswell remarks that Johnson sought "his fortune in London, the great field of genius and exertion, where talents of every kind have the fullest scope, and the highest encouragement" (*Life*, I, 101). The reality was very different as the poet was quick to observe from first hand experience:

> This mournful truth is ev'ry where confess'd,
> SLOW RISES WORTH, BY POVERTY DEPRESS'D:

> But here more slow, where all are slaves to gold,
> Where looks are merchandise, and smiles are sold.   (ll. 176-79)

Johnson's *London,* however, is not a personal poem at all, but a satire, like Pope's *One Thousand Seven Hundred and Thirty-Eight,* on Walpole's government on the one hand and the growth of luxury on the other. These targets appear synonymous, yet the blurring of the two causes a confusion in Johnson's poem, echoing the confusion of the rhetoric against cities fashionable in mid-eighteenth century.

At the heart of the poem is the hard primitivism of anti-urban propaganda. Johnson contrasts vain and vice-ridden London, the scene of Walpole's and his minions' exploits, with the rustic ideal exemplified by Scotland or Ireland. He summons a mythic past from a distant and austere age, "Alfred's golden reign," as a foil to corruption. The contrast is analogous to Juvenal's treatment, which invoked a distant Roman past and rustic life to condemn contemporary Roman vice. Both Umbricius and Thales (the speakers respectively of Juvenal's poem and Johnson's imitation) show a preference for native and earthy simplicity to foreign sophistication, urging a patriotic insularity to combat national hesitation and complacency. However, Johnson's version is marred by an inconsistency that smacks of political opportunism. At one point he expresses the view of a back-bench Little Englander, and at another the frustration of the imperialist who seeks to teach France and Spain a lesson. This confusion runs through the poem. London is a den of vice, where "the fell attorney prowls for prey," the rich "raise palaces, and manors buy, / Collect a tax, or farm a lottery"; "rustick grandeur" is now "lost in thoughtless ease," "the warrior dwindled to a beau." On the other hand, Thales recalls England's past glories under Elizabeth when

> her cross [was] triumphant on the main,
> The guard of commerce, and the dread of Spain,
> Ere masquerades debauch'd excise oppress'd,
> Or English honour grew a standing jest.   (ll. 27-30)

As Donald Greene has shown, Johnson is merely echoing whig-opposition polemics; Walpole has not been aggressive enough with Spain over the indignities of Jenkins' ear, nor extended British trade with proper militancy.[9] The poet pursues two inconsistent ideals, return to the simple life of bucolic innocence and "rustick grandeur," and contrarily revenge for the honour of English seamen and protection and enlargement of British trade abroad. The hard primitivism advocated by Johnson and the anti-urbanists cannot be squared with a policy of continuing economic growth and influence abroad. This helps to explain perhaps Johnson's schizophrenic pronouncements on trade. "Depend upon it," he once said, "this rage of trade will destroy itself" (*Life,* V, 231). Yet at another time in response to someone's expressed fear the English trade was in decline, Johnson riposted, "Never fear, Sir. Our commerce is in a very good state. . . . " (*Life,* II, 357).[10]

The years following Johnson's outburst against the government, a decade in which he saw Walpole fall and the opposition Whigs take over, may have been sufficiently sobering to one of his undogmatic temperament. His attitude toward the city changed during what James Clifford calls the "obscure middle years."[11] The stinging rebuke delivered by the poet gave way to the defence of the city by the essayist. By the time Johnson wrote *The Rambler, The Idler* and *The Adventurer* in the 1750's he had developed a rationale for his strong love of his adopted city and a tempered understanding of commerce. Not that he mellowed, becoming less rebellious to established government, but he matured intellectually. He discarded prejudice and simple emotional reactions when they conflicted with his enlarged views. And in spite of all that has been said of Johnson's dour outlook on life, his philurbanism, as I call it, represents a more hopeful vein in his writings than his critics and biographers have so far mined. What was the nature of this defence of the city?

The London in which he settled was finally accepted and then respected by Johnson as essentially a center of commerce. Trade made possible the wealth and breadth of the city. He had no hankering for any other urban arrangement; no earthly reflection of the City of God, or royal city like St. Petersburg or garden city had any appeal to him. In the eighteenth century there was a good deal of speculation about possible forms cities should take. An inchoate town planning movement had begun, an offshoot of an Enlightened thinking. Johnson rejected or perhaps neglected planned development in favor of growth based on commercial need. For him the charm of London lay in its inexhaustible variety and complexity of streets and buildings, which were to the rationalists of the age a gothic mixture: "It is not in the showy evolution of buildings, but in the multiplicity of human habitations which are crowded together, that the wonderful immensity of London consists" (*Life,* I, 422). For an adequate understanding of the pullulating life of London, one "must survey the innumerable little lanes and courts" *(Ibid.).* In his many habitations, he always remained in the hurly-burly of town life generally around Fleet Street, which was then as now a focus of commercial activity. Not only did Johnson accept the complexity of the city's topography, he saw it as a means of bringing diverse people together. The xenophobia of his poem *London*, in which he attacks French re^f gees and manners, is apparently epudiated in *Rasselas*, when Imlac describes the inhabitants of Cairo, an Eastern analogue to London: "This, said Imlac to the Prince, is the place where travellers and merchants assemble from all the corners of the earth. You will here find men of every character, and every occupation. Commerce is here honourable . . . . " (Chap. XVI). To Johnson the success of the British emporium was due to its heterogeneity, and everything we know of the history of London of this period marks it as a melting pot offering economic opportunities,[12] foreshadowing in kind, if not in scope, New York City 60 and 70 years ago.

This philurbanism is nowhere so fully developed as in *Adventurer No. 67*,[13] Johnson's systematic answer to the city detractors of his day. This essay is remarkable in that Johnson anticipates in part the urban theories of modern sociologists like Max Weber, George Simmel, the Chicago school of urban studies of Robert Park, Earnest Burgess, Louis Wirth and more recently Harvey Cox.[14] In his defense of the city, Johnson assimilated Mandeville's analysis while avoiding the unpleasant conclusion that vice is necessary for economic development. Moreover, where Mandeville saw the purpose of wealth and economic growth to feed, clothe and shelter the population and protect society from foreign conquest, Johnson perceived other positive attributes to be gained in the commercial metropolis: "leisure for intellectual pleasures, and . . . the happiness of reason and reflection." It is true, Johnson admits, that the prosperity of the city, the springs of trade rest upon the desire for the superfluities of life: "custom, curiosity, or wantonness, supplies every art with patrons, and finds purchasers for every manufacture." He mentions with wry exaggeration "thousands and myriads raised to dignity, by no other merit than that of contributing to supply their neighbours with the means of sucking smoke through a tube of clay." But the pursuit of "modish trifles" gives the multitudes work and they are "preserved from idleness, and consequently from want." This is so far orthodox Mandeville. However, in his tone, more than anything else, Johnson avoids the rigorist position of finding all luxury and pleasure vicious.[15] By the choice of tobacco, then considered an innocent pleasure, Johnson makes luxury appear harmless. In this essay he employs a persona slightly astringent but withal tolerant; the rhetoric is subtly ironic with an agreeable lubricity in the phrasing that keeps his manner cool while systematically deflating the primitivists and rural reformers.

The commercial city has virtues not apparent at first glance. The unity of society is enhanced by linking together "the great and the mean," he suggests in the essay from *The Adventurer*; there is a "secret concatenation of society." Each contributes his part, and in a moment of benevolence, Johnson claims that "no man is without some quality, by the due application of which he might deserve well of the world." Urban exploitation of various skills is beneficial for it produces "arts of every kind," and "the wants of man may be immediately supplied." Johnson is addressing himself to one of the oldest and most persistent anti-urban complaints, that cities produce alienation or to use Durkheim's word *anomie,* a social void. Not so, claims Dr. Johnson; the work of each for society leaves him "with the pleasing consciousness of having contributed something to the happiness of life." Is this happiness an illusion, which Swift detected as *"the Possession of being well deceived;* the Serene Peaceful State of being a Fool among Knaves"? *(A Tale of a Tub,* Sect. IX). Perhaps. But for Johnson there is the inevitable alternative to a commercial city; a feudal society in which the serf or farm laborer is at the mercy of his master. In response to Boswell's fear of the breakdown of traditional subordination, Johnson retorted, "No man now depends upon the Lord of a Manour, when he can send to another country, and fetch provisions. The shoe-black at the entry of my court does not depend on me. I can deprive him but of a penny a day, which he hopes somebody else will bring him; and that penny I must carry to another shoe-black, so the trade suffers nothing" *(Life,* III, 262). In a large city, institutions remain intact in spite of individual caprice or failure. Men's fortunes are removed from one person's will. Society affords the individual more security. The social cohesion of the Middle Ages held no attractions to the eighteenth-century man of London. Feudal life and clan-like solidarity are gladly exchanged for "the plenty and ease of a great city."

Johnson deflates, moreover, the notion of the self-sufficient savage. The ease by which the city dweller filled his needs, it was felt by anti-urbanists, took "away from our native abilities . . . We are so accustomed to give and receive assistance, that each of us singly can do little for himself," Johnson paraphrases the primitivist's argument. Luxury and specialization soften men of city nurture. In a polished society a man "may lie stretched upon a couch, and see all the treasures of all the elements poured down before him." In reply to such a point of view, Johnson admits the validity of the argument but appeals to something better to defeat it. The virtue of self-reliance (the ability to endure) in a primitive state is superseded by the virtue of mutual aid in society. Primitive life makes man resourceful, but it cannot make him secure, and he thus cannot be happy, which is Johnson's test of the ultimate purpose of human existence. The city dweller (better described as the civilized man) has been exempted from the power of chance. In a primitive society all energy is devoted to preserving one's life; in an urban society "to receive and to communicate assistance constitutes the happiness of human life." The doctrine of *meum* and *tuum* thus posed no barrier to Johnson. He saw the possibility of community based on material possessions not because the innate goodness of man mitigated his greed for property, but because of the nature of urban society. Johnson envisioned a commercial metropolis in which individuals are induced to specialize in trades and callings to provide for one another, as well as produce luxuries admittedly for a few. Out of this conurbation with its conflicting and complementary vocations, desires and tastes come the undeniable benefits of "arts" in the broadest sense, leisure and beyond that the unity of society based on human interdependence.

II

In the light of Johnson's pro-urban theory as expressed in *Adventure No. 67* and his scattered remarks in Boswell's biography, we may also see the relevance of his geographical interests. I have already touched on *Rasselas,* in which Cairo becomes the school of life for the young prince and his party. It is only in the large commercial city that the full variety of human existence may be experienced. Cairenes may not always be happy, but as the hermit's choice demonstrates, city life is better than fruitless isolation in a remote cave. In addition, *A Journey to the Western Islands of Scotland* becomes significant when examined from the prospect of the mid-century debate over town and country. Whatever purposes Johnson initially had in undertaking this tour with Boswell to a primitive world as distant culturally as "Borneo or Sumatra," the Londoner's imagination seized on the economic and sociological implications of Highland Scotland. One must recall that just prior to Johnson's trip north in 1773, fashionable London was being regaled with uncritical accounts of a paradise in Tahiti by the naturalist Joseph Banks and Captain Cook, who had returned only two years previously from the South Pacific. John Hawkesworth, Johnson's friend, was preparing for the press "luscious descriptions" of the innocent and free life led by the Tahitians, which were based on Cook's and Banks' journals. These reports strengthened the myth of the noble savage then at the height of its vogue. Johnson reacted with his usual skepticism to such tales, and in the *Journey*, he slyly deflated the idea of primitive splendor under cover of an objective narrative of his travels in the hinterlands of Scotland.[16]

He observed in the islands thinly scattered communities eking out a precarious sustenance from an inhospitable land. Whole villages were preparing or contemplating emigration to America. The refrain of a doomed culture occurs frequently in his account. The clan chieftains had "gradually degenerate[d] from patriarchal rulers to rapacious landlords." With mischievous rhetoric Johnson demolishes the widespread belief that people untouched by luxury and urban temptations are more beautiful, healthier and live longer. "To expand the human face to its full perfection, it seems necessary that the mind should co-operate by placidness of content, or consciousness of superiority."[17] Highlanders are neither exempt from ordinary ill health nor the ravages of time: "I found no instance here of extraordinary longevity," says Johnson bluntly. Their having little to work upon makes them appear "habitually idle," one of the worst conditions in which a man could find himself by Johnson's standards. Not living in a society "extensively diversified with trades," the people of remote Scotland "endure many inconveniences, which a little attention would easily relieve." Johnson provides a portrait of a decadent culture without enterprise or self-help, the people listless, their leaders unable to offer an alternative. Nor has Johnson much sympathy with the warrior image of the traditional highlander: "A man, who places honour only in successful violence, is a very troublesome and pernicious animal in time of peace; and that the martial character cannot prevail in a whole people, but by the diminution of all other virtues . . . The strong must flourish by force, and the weak subsist by stratagem" *(A Journey,* p. 94).

The people of the islands as Johnson reported with sorrow were in general discontent and emigrating from the land. A combination of landlord rapacity and lack of opportunities was forcing them out. How different is his description of Aberdeen, comprising an old part "in decay, having been situated in times when commerce was yet unstudied" and an emerging city:

> New Aberdeen has all the bustle of prosperous trade, and all the shew of increasing opulence . . . The houses are large and lofty, and the streets spacious and clean. They build almost wholly with the granite used in the new pavement of the streets of London, which is well known not to want hardness, yet they shape it easily. It is beautiful and must be very lasting.[18] *(A Journey,* p. 14)

Johnson here plays his major chord to balance the elegiac theme of the doomed Highland and feudal culture. A new city based on trade arises in splendor adjacent to the ancient episcopal city now declining. So also the affirmative coda as the book ends, Johnson's depiction of a progressive college in Edinburgh dedicated to teaching the deaf and dumb. He found "smiling countenances and sparkling eyes, delighted with the hope of new ideas." This college must have been to him the flower of city culture, for of all people and sights he was treated to in the Scottish capitol, this was the one experience he memorialized, because it was deeply, if unconsciously, felt. A school like this in the Highlands was inconceivable in the context of Johnson's observations of general decay. In the interweaving of these two themes of old and new, feudal and commercial societies, Johnson clearly celebrates the latter as the best hope for Scotland, even as he recognizes the fading beauty of the former.

III

Notwithstanding Johnson's confidence in the urban way of life, he did not flinch from clear-eyed perception of the ugly side of London. He was on equal terms with the respectable and the outcast. How often has it been pointed out that Johnson took compassion on the casualties of a competitive society and gave shelter to a menagerie of unfortunates. He understood enough about prostitution to write a vivid and touching account in *Rambler No. 171*: "No place," he declared "but a populous city can afford opportunities for open prostitution." Vice and terror also made up the fabric of urban life. Boswell reported an attempted mugging of Johnson by four robbers. The robust man of letters kept them at bay until the watch came up (*Life,* II, 299). Of a young man's first introduction to the town, Johnson wrote:

> When he first settled in London, he was so much bewildered in the enormous extent of the town, so confounded by incessant noise, and crowds, and hurry, and so terrified by rural narratives of the arts of sharpers, the rudeness of the populace, malignity of porters, and treachery of coachmen, that he was afraid to go beyond the door without an attendant, and imagined his life in danger if he was obliged to pass the streets at night in any vehicle but his mother's chair. *(Rambler No. 195)*

This young man, once acclimated to the city, joins with others in pursuit of mindless pleasure at the coffee houses "where he met wits, heirs, and fops, airy, ignorant, and thoughtless as himself." And like the Mohocks of a previous generation, this group decides to prowl the town at night. They begin their escapade as a claque at the theater, but are transformed into a dangerous mob after being forcibly ejected from their seats. Out in the streets they "dispersed a rabble of drunkards less daring than themselves, then rolled two watchmen in the kennel, and broke the windows of a tavern." Finally the night's frolic is brought to a violent close in a pitched battle between these young bloods and a group of chairmen defending their property. In the end the young wastrel is rusticated for two years under the care of a French tutor. In the course of this realistic narrative, Johnson exposes the vicious life led by a small group within the leisure class, whose activities range from the merely foolish in foppish dress, clowning in coffee houses and masquerades to the dangerous street brawls that occurred in London.

A disheartening social superiority assumed by the wealthy was also a target of the moralist. In the guise of a young woman looking for a servant's place, he contributes a letter to *The Rambler* (No. 12) showing how difficult it is for someone without connections to get a decent job. A country-bred girl has been given a superior education but by force of circumstances must support herself as a domestic. She is obliged to take all sorts of abuse from haughty and capricious London ladies who invariably find fault with her demeanor, which is not humble enough. The letter exhibits the mortification felt in the cold and stratified world of London society. Behind the girl's desperate search is the fear of ending up in the streets as a beggar or prostitute. "Preserve me from bad courses," she prays. Johnson characteristically avoids the abyss, and at the last moment a kindly lady comes to the girl's aid. Most people are callous or cruel, Johnson implies here, but there is always help for the virtuous even in the impersonal city.

The extent of poverty in the capital and the effects of uncertain employment were well known to him. He thought the numbers of people dying from hunger or disease occasioned by hunger were underestimated:

> This happens only in so large a place as London, where people are not known. What we are told about the great sums got by begging is not true: the trade is overstocked. And, you may depend upon it, there are many who cannot get work. A particular kind of manufacture fails: those who have been used to work at it, can, for some time, work at nothing else.

> You meet a man begging; you charge him with idleness: he
> says, "I am willing to labour. Will you give me work?"—"I
> cannot."—"Why, then you have no right to charge me with
> idleness." (*Life*, III, 401)

Moral superiority of rich and secure people was justly despised by Johnson.

He also recognized a familiar form of sham or "front" put on to give a false impression, possible only in a large impersonal city. However, with characteristic tolerance, he saw these expedients as a means of bettering oneself: "There is no place," Johnson told Boswell, "where economy can be so well practised as in London. More can be had here for the money, even by ladies, than any where else. You cannot play tricks with your fortune n a small place; you must make an uniform appearance. Here a lady may nave well-furnished apartments, and elegant dress without any meat in her kitchen" (*Life*, III, 378). He perceived a certain malaise, a lack of community will. During the Gordon riots in 1780, he witnessed the rioters plundering Old Bailey: "They did their work at leisure in full security, without sentinels, without trepidation, as men lawfully employed in full day. Such is the cowardice of a commercial place" (*Life*, III, 429).

One could go on enumerating instances of Johnson's recognition of some of the ugly features of the commercial metropolis. Do they vitiate his urban theory as expounded here? Can he confidently assert against the testimony of his own experience the benefits of a large city? Isn't he rationalizing his own psychological dependencies on the city which afforded him the opportunities he so happily seized? To some extent all theory, as Freudians are quick to remind us, is a form of rationalization. This is no less true of Johnson than of any other, but however much an intellectual defence may be psychological rationalization, its persuasive value must be measured by its ability to penetrate and explain reality. In the middle of the eighteenth century, rural reformers claimed that England was in decline, population was decreasing and the blame lay with the unrestricted growth of trade in London. But the anti-urbanists as I have implied offered a muddled explanation of this so-called decline and were caught in two conflicting aims, the desire to remain an essentially rural economy with court, country and town in nice balance, and the desire to compete with other European powers and extend England's sphere of influence. In actual fact, England was not experiencing a population decrease; England's population almost doubled in the eighteenth century.[19] As Macaulay put it, the fear reflected "the contemporary fit of national depression."[20] The prophecies of doom were really forms of polemic

mounted by traditionalists afraid of changes brought about by new tech-
nology and rising expectations. In his first treatment of the city in *London*,
Johnson echoed the charges of these rural traditionalists. Later, however, he
recognized the folly of intransigence, and the claims of the rural reformers
were patently absurd to him. He clearly saw and on the whole welcomed
London's commercial domination of the nation. In his maturer writings, he
attempted to work out a theory which would reconcile this assertive business
world and its fearful consequences with the ancient urban ideal of the cultivation of arts and leisure. The emporium of London was the crucible of the
nation. New ideas, new people, inventiveness and dynamic competition would
form the texture of society, creating the conditions for a stimulating way of
life, if not a happy one; no utopia, but a community which offered hope to
every range of human talent. It was against the anti-urban campaign that we
see Johnson developing this theory. The hope afforded by the city had to be
balanced against its evils. Johnson chose to look at its promise, but he did not
ignore the many shortcomings of his daily experience. In this I believe he
proved to be more accurate and gave his generation more hope than the anti-
urbanists who saw only evil in the expansion of London.

END NOTES

[1] James Boswell, *Life of Johnson*, ed. G. B. Hill and L. F. Powell (Oxford: Clarendon Press, 1964), III, 178—hereafter cited as *Life*.

[2] "London and the Proper Grounds of Satiric Failure," in *The Formal Strain* (Chicago: Univ. Of Chicago Press, 1969), pp. 165-91.

[3] See F. B. Kaye, "The Influence of Bernard Mandeville," *SP*, 19 (1922), 83-108.

[4] See D. V. Glass, "The Population Controversy in Eighteenth-Century England. Part I, the Background," *Population Studies*, 6 (1952), 69-91.

[5] William Bell, *A Dissertation on Populousness and Trade* (1756), p. 5.

[6] *Ibid.*, p. 15.

[7] *Tour through the Southern Countries of England and Wales*, 2nd ed. (1769), p. 325.

[8] *Ibid.*, p. 326.

[9] *The Politics of Samuel Johnson* (New Haven: Yale Univ. Press, 1960), pp. 82-92.

[10] These contradictions were reconciled by John H. Middendorf, "Johnson on Wealth and Commerce," in *Johnson, Boswell and Their Circle* (Oxford: Clarendon Press, 1965), pp. 47-64.

[11] "Some Problems of Johnson's Obscure Middle Years," in *Johnson, Boswell and Their Circle*, pp. 99-110.

[12] M. Dorothy George, *London Life in the Eighteenth Century* (New York: Harper and Row, 1964), chaps. 3 and 6.

[13] The question of this essay's attribution was settled by L. F. Powell, "Johnson's Part in *The Adventurer*," *RES*, 3 (1927), 420-29.

[14] For a good overview of the development of modern urban theory see Don Martindale, "Prefatory Remarks: the Theory of the City," in *The City* by Max Weber (Glencoe, Ill: Free Press, 1958), pp. 9-62; Harvey Cox, *The Secular City*, rev. ed. (New York: MacMillan, 1969).

[15] Johnson admitted being influenced by Mandeville, but he expressed serious reservations concerning the latter's economic theories (*Life*, III, 291-93).

[16] My view is in fundamentals at variance with Jeffrey Hart, "Johnson's *A Journey to the Western Islands*: History as Art," *EIC*, 10 (1960), 44-59. His analysis was answered by D. J. Greene, "Johnsonian Critics," *EIC*, 10 (1960), 476-80.

[17] *A Journey to the Western Islands of Scotland*, ed. M. Lascelles (New Haven: Yale Univ. Press, 1971), p. 84. Hereafter cited as *A Journey*.

[18] Professor Hart, *op. cit.*, p. 47, senses "considerable bitterness" in this paragraph and doubt on the durability of the new city. With no less sensitivity, I hope, I detect Johnson's open approval of the renewal of the city.

[19] The population of England from 1695 to 1801 increased from approximately five and a half million to 9,168,000: T. S. Ashton, *An Economic History of England: The Eighteenth Century* (London: Methuen, 1959), p. 2.

[20] "Essay on Pitt."

Panentheism in The Prelude

Keith A. Gould

Among Wordsworth scholars, few topics have generated more discussion than the topic of Wordsworth's God. Some students, such as Hoxie N. Fairchild, have systematically analyzed Wordsworth's religion, tracing his evolution from Protestantism to Godwinism to pantheism to stoicism to High Anglicanism.[1] Others have despaired at the futility of systematizing an essentially unsystematic thinker; R. D. Havens, for example, feels that "Any study of Wordsworth's religion must inevitably come to the conclusion that no formulation of his beliefs is possible."[2] Even among those who consider the poet's creed coherent, there is little agreement. Some see Wordsworth as a slightly disguised pantheist, others as a disguised Christian. These extremes seem illustrative of a general tendency in Wordsworth scholarship. One group finds Wordsworth essentially a naturalist in the tradition of the eighteenth-century Enlightenment and traces in him tendencies of Hartley and other naturalistic philosophers; another group considers his mysticism predominant over his naturalism and emphasizes his suprasensuous links with Spinoza, Kant, and Boehme.

Most readers, however, think that Wordsworth's religion falls somewhere between the extremes of pantheism and theism. They feel that his attitudes shifted as he grew older, and that the bold naturalism of his early years mellowed as he underwent personal tragedy, until in later years he became an orthodox Anglican. It is true that the early poetry seems more naturalistic and the later poetry more spiritualistic, but I think it impossible to pinpoint radical religious changes in such a complex thinker. I find it unlikely, for example, that Wordsworth's shift from naturalism to theism, if such a shift exists, can be traced to February 5, 1805, the day the cold waters off Portland Bill closed over the *Earl of Abergavenny* and Wordsworth's brother, John. Rather, I see Wordsworth's alternate explorations of naturalism and theism as a rudimentary development of the doctrine we now call panentheism.

I do not claim a coherent philosophic system for Wordsworth, if by that one means a system marked by consistency and discursive logical analysis. Though a philosophic poet, Wordsworth was no philosopher; he was bound by no rules of analytic reason. Often he distanced himself artistically by creating personae who explored opposing philosophic views. In some poems he presented philosophic themes in a comic setting; in others he treated them seriously. Occasionally he used a philosophic view as an unobtrusive premise behind a narrative; at other times he advanced the view seriously through a narrator. Nor, behind the devices, was he consistent. Throughout his life he remained open-minded and exploratory. But I do feel that in his major poetry, especially in the 1850 revision of *The Prelude,* Wordsworth leaned strongly toward panentheism.

Panentheism is not a new doctrine. Its emergence can be traced through such diverse thinkers as Plato, Schelling, Fechner, Whitehead, and Buber. But because the doctrine remains relatively unknown, I will leave Wordsworth briefly and summarize the basic tenets of the philosophy. In this discussion I will rely chiefly on the writings of Charles Hartshorne, whom I consider not only the foremost living process philosopher but the champion spokesman of panentheism.

Panentheism (to give a preliminary definition) ascribes to God qualities which normally are denied him. The panentheist agrees with classical theists that God is absolute, independent, permanent, immutable, and impassive; however, the panentheist denies that these are his only, or even his most important, qualities. Rather, in some aspects of his nature God can indeed be relative, dependent, temporal, mutable, and passive.[3]

But, we may reasonably ask, how can God be both permanent and changing? How can he be both independent and dependent? Panentheism seems to contain insuperable paradoxes. Hartshorne contends, however, that the paradoxes occur not in panentheism but in the classical theism of Judaism, Christianity, and Islam. And indeed, theism does seem to contain paradoxes. For example, we are told that God is totally independent in every respect, yet that God desires that we lead lives glorifying him. But a totally independent God would insofar be totally indifferent, would have no need of our worship. We are told that God is absolute, but that he loves his creation. Now love is the ultimate relation; not only is the lover one who understands and tries to help, he is "the one who takes unto himself the varying joys and sorrows of others, and whose own happiness is capable of alteration thereby."[4] Thus one cannot love without in some way being sympathetic toward the loved one. A God who truly loved, then, would not be absolute in every degree but must somehow be relative.

We are told that God is good and that he is behind all acts. But then, we surmise, he must be the cause of all wickedness and all suffering. Surely a

God who causes suffering cannot be good. And to theologians who contend that human tragedy and suffering have an ultimate divine purpose not immediately obvious to imperfect human intelligence, we might defer, but still wonder about the suffering of animals. It would seem that either divine power or divine goodness must be limited (*MVG,* p. xv). Finally, we are told that God is immutable and that he is all-knowing. If he is all-knowing, then surely he "knows" his changing creation. Unless we assert that there is no such thing as "change," we must assume that God, in order to know the changes in the universe, somehow must "change" with them. So either he is all-knowing or he is immutable: he cannot be both.

Hartshorne feels that these paradoxes in traditional theism are caused by man's fondness for oversimplification. In considering ultimate contraries such as the one and the many, permanence and change, or being and becoming, we tend to decide in each case which of the contraries is good or admirable, then we attribute it (in some supremely excellent form) to God. The contrasting term is then denied completely to deity.[5] Thus, for example, we might decide that God is permanent, and therefore we might deny him mutability. But Hartshorne would have us question such a one-sided assertion. For one thing, if we ascribed to God only one side of a contrary, then reality would consist of God and something else. God then would not be all-inclusive, since he would not contain the "something else."

However, if we subscribe to Morris Cohen's "Law of Polarity," ultimate contraries become correlatives, mutually interdependent. According to Cohen, nothing can be wholly delineated by viewing only one side of the ultimate contraries. Thus nothing can be described adequately in terms of simplicity, being, or actuality; instead the description must include the contrary aspects of complexity, becoming, or potentiality (*PSG,* p. 2). Both theism and pantheism seem to follow the doctrine of the "invidious nature of categorical contrasts" in which one pole of a contrary is seen as more excellent than the other. Both, that is, deny Cohen's Law of Polarity to God (*PSG,* p. 2). Classical theism sees the supreme being as eternal but denies temporality; it sees him as independent, as knowing but not including the world, and thus denies him any dependence. Pantheism sees deity as relative, containing all relative or interdependent items (that is, containing the world), but denies any wholly absolute or independent aspect to God (*TDR,* p. 89). Both theism and pantheism, by refusing to admit God's dipolar nature, thus are truncated doctrines because they deny Cohen's law.

It might seem that Hartshorne has denounced theism and pantheism only to substitute a system more paradoxical, but he is careful to eliminate contradictions in panentheism by positing two main aspects in the essence of God, to one of which the one pole supremely applies, to the other the other (*PSG,* p. 4). An analogy might be useful here. A person really has two aspects, an aspect of identity and an aspect of novelty. He is a new, different person every moment, in that he changes with his differing environment, his varying moods, his physiological adjustments. But, as we know, his identity does not change. A Charles Hartshorne today will recognizably be the same person to-morrow or next week. And there is no paradox here: change is a combination of identity and difference (*MVG,* p. 109). In the same way, God can change in some aspects of his nature, but still remain absolute and permanent.

Like most analogies, this is useful only to a point; the uniquely human predilection for viewing God as a person, though a supremely perfect person, can lead to misleading notions about man's importance in the universe. But the analogy does help eliminate seeming contradictions in panentheism, for if we posit a two-sided God we can ascribe to his abstract aspect (his "charac-ter," if you will) such qualities as absoluteness, permanence, or impassivity; to his other side we can ascribe such qualities as relativity, temporality, pas-sivity (*PSG,* p. 4).

It is important, however, that we negate from either aspect of God any nonsupreme form of either pole, any mediocre unity or complexity, activity or passivity, self-sufficiency or dependence. Because God is the supreme form of either pole, of course he would contain these nonsupreme forms in his supreme reality; however, he would not include them in his essence, but only in his accidents. This point cannot be overemphasized, for it explains how God can contain mediocrity—the negative, nonsupreme quality of "wicked-ness," for example—in his reality, without containing any defect of wicked-ness in his essential character. Just as a building need not be small because its parts are, so God need not be wicked because wickedness is included among his accidents (*PSG,* p. 4).

The revolutionary conclusion that God, through his relative aspect, can share the feelings of his world helps resolve the old theological dilemma con-cerning God's role in the tragedy and suffering deeply woven into life. Ac-cording to panentheism, "divinity is not the privilege of escaping all sufferings but the exactly contrary one of sharing them all" (*MVG,* p. xvi). No longer need we worry about a deity contriving all our woes. As Hartshorne observes, the details of events just happen: they are not contrived, planned, or divinely decreed. Now we can be reassured by the knowledge that when we encounter tragedy, God shares that tragedy. When we mourn, God mourns; when we suffer, God suffers. As Alfred North Whitehead says, "God is the great

companion—the fellow sufferer who understands."[6] (Significantly, the
Christian idea of a suffering deity, symbolized by the Cross, achieves technical metaphysical expression through panentheism.) But we must remember
that suffering contrasts with joy. If the one saddens, the other delights us. If
God grieves with our sorrows, he equally rejoices with our joys.

The panentheistic God, then, is a two-sided God. In his abstractness, God
is absolute, eternal, and independent. In his concreteness, which includes the
abstract qualities just as a man includes his character, God is the supere-
minent case of relativity, temporality, and dependence. He is a God participating directly in his creation. He is a sympathetic, sensitive God deriving
value from all things. For every diversity, there is a diversity of relationships
in him. Through his infinite sensitivity, he registers relationships to the last
and least item of events. And because he is qualified and conditioned by these
social relations, God is eminently personal and social, the supreme case of
personality. Most important, by being related to all things in a sympathetic
union surpassing all human sympathy, he genuinely becomes what classical
theism could postulate only through paradox: a God of love.

Given this rudimentary outline of panentheism, we can return to Wordsworth and see how the doctrine illuminates his poetry. I find panentheism
everywhere in Wordsworth, in poems as diverse as "The Old Cumberland
Beggar," "Tintern Abbey," the "Immortality Ode," "Hart-Leap Well," "It
is a Beauteous Evening," "Loud is the Vale," and *The Excursion.* But because
The Prelude contains the fullest treatment of Wordsworth's developing
panentheism, I will focus on that poem. Many of my *Prelude* thoughts
originated in talks with my friend and former teacher, Maurice B. Cramer,
and I gladly acknowledge his influence on my *Prelude* reading.

Not only does *The Prelude* trace the growth of a poet's mind; on a deeper
level, it traces the growth of Wordsworth's conception of God. The poem
presents special problems for analysis, since the process of bit-by-bit grad-
ualism through which the mind develops is not presented chronologically.
We must take care to distinguish the experiences of the youthful persona
from those of the mature narrator who has experienced the consummate
vision on Mt. Snowdon. But if read carefully, the poem does reveal an
awakening panentheism.

I do not confine Wordsworth's panentheism to *The Prelude* of 1805. De
Selincourt has been troubled by Wordsworth's revisions of *The Prelude* of
1850, contending that not only did the poet add "pietistic embroidery" to
"lull the eyes of the heresy hunters," he "Christianized" some passages so
that they "give a new colour to his work and are foreign to its original

spirit."[7] No one would deny that the 1850 poem contains Christian language, but many such passages can also be called panentheistic. In fact, the 1850 *Prelude* contains some of Wordsworth's strongest panentheism.

In focusing on Wordsworth's *Prelude* God, I disagree with scholars who have concluded that God plays no major role in the poem. M. H. Abrams takes this stance in his recent study *Natural Supernaturalism:*

> My concern isn't with the valid autobiographical question: "What was Wordsworth's creed—pantheist, panentheist, Christian?" in the sense of "What propositions about God would Wordsworth have been prepared to assert outside the poem?" With respect to the conceptual scheme of *The Prelude*, the relevant question is: "What role does God play within the poem itself?" To answer this question it is not enough to list the passages in which reference is made to God; for the essential matter is, "What does God do in the poem?" And to this the answer is patently, "Nothing of consequence."[8]

Abrams' book is perhaps the most valuable study of the Romantic tendency to "naturalize the supernatural and humanize the divine" yet to appear, but I find a deafening silence where God should illuminate his discussion of *The Prelude.*

A rudimentary awareness of God is evident in Book I, when the narrator discusses several boyhood experiences, times when the "ministry of fear" operated on him. Surely the woodcock-stealing, egg-stealing, and boat-stealing episodes in Book I partake of the numinous, at least to some degree. After robbing woodcock snares set by others, the youth often would be admonished by nature:

> I heard among the solitary hills
> Low breathings coming after me, and sounds
> Of undistinguishable motion, steps
> Almost as silent as the turf they trod.
>   (I. 329-32.)

Similarly, after ransacking raven nests, the boy received strange messages from nature:

With what strange utterance did the loud dry wind
Blow through my ears! the sky seem'd not a sky
Of earth, and with what motion mov'd the clouds!

(I. 348-50.)

Finally, the boat-stealing incident on Ullswater reveals the same pattern of admonishment:

I dipp'd my oars into the silent Lake,
And, as I rose upon the stroke, my Boat
Went heaving through the water, like a Swan;
When from behind that craggy Steep, till then
The bound of the horizon, a huge Cliff,
As if with voluntary power instinct,
Uprear'd its head. I struck, and struck again,
And, growing still in stature, the huge Cliff
Rose up between me and the stars, and still,
With measur'd motion, like a living thing,
Strode after me.

(I. 402-12.)

Each of these episodes, essentially unchanged in the 1850 *Prelude*, seems to hint at animism. Surely if the being or beings striding after the boy is God (or "gods" in nature) he is not the complete panentheistic God who loves and participates in his universe while simultaneously remaining apart from it. But such passages can be explained if we see in *The Prelude* a developing awareness of God; here the narrator presents the boy who is just beginning to intuit the immanent God who is present everywhere in his creation. The youth has not yet stepped beyond the notion of "God in all things" to the sense of a unified, transcendent God behind them. He moves from senses to emotion (fear), then on to the realm of ethics (guilt). He has intimations of his place in the dynamic, active universe. In other words, such experiences are rudimentary God experiences, characterized by fear and awe because often first intimations of God are of his mystery, inscrutability, and power.

Immediately after the boat-stealing episode, we are given another perspective. The focus shifts from the boy's rudimentary God experiences to the mature narrator's judgment of such experiences. In a brief, admirably condensed panentheistic statement, the narrator sees such events as leading to a God both immanent and transcendent:

> Wisdom and Spirit of the universe!
> Thou Soul that art the Eternity of Thought!
> That giv'st to forms and images a breath
> And everlasting motion! not in vain,
> By day or star-light thus from my first dawn
> Of Childhood didst Thou intertwine for me
> The passions that build up our human Soul,
> Not with the mean and vulgar works of Man,
> But with high objects, with enduring things.
>
> (I. 428-36.)

Through precise word choice, Wordsworth here carefully distinguishes between God's immanence and his transcendence. "Wisdom" is a quality which Hartshorne ascribes to the absolute, immutable, transcendent God. It is a trait of God's paramount character (what Coleridge would call his "ipseity"), that which would not change though conditions changed. "Spirit" seems to refer to God's relativity (what Coleridge would call his "alterity"): it is that aspect which goes forth from him into all things in the universe, that which gives everlasting motion or dynamism to all things. "Soul," the "Eternity of Thought," brings us back to the unchanging God who has a distinct personality. "Soul" in its transcendent absoluteness creates eternal process; through its "spirit," which is the relative soul in action or motion, it is able to give "to forms and images a breath / And everlasting motion"—that is, to give motion to forms so that they can exist, apprehend, and have the potentiality of being apprehended.

The well-known "Sentiment of Being" passage in Book II also suggests panentheism. The narrator tells of times in his youth when he was becoming increasingly aware of "the great social principle of life":

> . . . I was only then
> Contented when with bliss ineffable
> I felt the sentiment of Being spread
> O'er all that moves, and all that seemeth still,
> O'er all, that, lost beyond the reach of thought
> And human knowledge, to the human eye
> Invisible, yet liveth to the heart,
> O'er all that leaps, and runs, and shouts, and sings,
> Or beats the gladsome air, o'er all that glides
> Beneath the wave, yea, in the wave itself

And mighty depth of waters.

(II. 418-28.)

The narrator seems to be speaking of a faculty within the human soul which can "feel" a universal being which permeates everything in nature, and this knowledge brings him joy:

> Wonder not
> If such my transports were; for in all things
> I saw one life, and felt that it was joy.
> One song they sang, and it was audible,
> Most audible then when the fleshly ear,
> O'ercome by grosser prelude of that strain,
> Forgot its functions, and slept undisturb'd.

(II. 428-34.)

Such passages suggest panentheism, although God's immanence is emphasized more than his transcendence. But Wordsworth's later revision of the closing lines contains indubitable panentheism:

> Wonder not
> If high the transport, great the joy I felt,
> Communing in this sort through earth and heaven
> With every form of creature, as it looked
> Towards the Uncreated with a countenance
> Of adoration, with an eye of love.
> One song they sang, and it was audible,
> Most audible, then, when the fleshly ear,
> O'ercome by humblest prelude of that strain,
> Forgot her functions, and slept undisturbed.

(1850; II. 409-18.)

The youth who had sensed a universal being which existed in the chain from lower to high*er* levels has now become a youth who senses this sentiment of being from lower to the high*est*—to the "Uncreated." The song of joy has become a song of joyous worship and of love. All creatures look toward the Uncreated with a "countenance / Of adoration, with an eye of love." Wordsworth does not yet give us Hartshorne's complete panentheism which involves loving reciprocation between God and his universe, perhaps because at this stage in his development the youth has not discovered that the love is mutual; however, the revised passage strongly suggests a panpsychic universe bound together into aesthetic unity by the consciousness of mutual love between the created and the "Uncreated."

R. D. Havens does not consider such events God-experiences, saying that Wordsworth seems rarely "in his communing with nature to have been conscious of a Divine Person." Havens feels that Wordsworth "seldom interpreted what happened to him at these times as directly connected with the Deity," and adds: "He was intensely conscious of one life in all things, but this life he seems to have thought of as an impersonal force, not as God."[9] But Wordsworth did equate this interior life from which we draw our powers with God, as is evidenced from unpublished lines connected with the "Sentiment of Being" passage. Wordsworth speaks of the one interior life "In which all beings love with God, themselves / Are God, existing in the mighty whole."[10] And Helen Darbishire has found a manuscript passage (unnoticed by de Selincourt) which develops the point still more:

> Such consciousnesses seemed but accidents
> Relapses from the one interior life
> Which is in all things, from that unity
> In which all beings live with God, are lost
> In god and nature, in one mighty whole
> As undistinguishable as the cloudless east
> At noon is from the cloudless west when all
> The hemisphere is one cerulean blue.[11]

As *The Prelude* progresses, the youth's "God-consciousness" continues to develop. By Book III, he is becoming more and more aware of God in his transcendent, immutable aspect:

> I look'd for universal things; perused
> The common countenance of earth and heaven;
> And, turning the mind in upon itself,
> Pored, watch'd, expected, listen'd; spread my thoughts
> And spread them with a wider creeping; felt
> Incumbences more awful, visitings
> Of the Upholder of the tranquil Soul,
> Which underneath all passion lives secure
> A steadfast life.
>
> (II. 110-18.)

Experiences verging on the mystical, trance-like moods of religious ecstasy in which the "light of sense" goes out and the youth becomes a "living soul" conscious of merging with the "one life in all things," become common. A typical passage occurs in Book IV:

> Gently did my soul
> Put off her veil, and, self-transmuted, stood
> Naked as in the presence of her God.
> As on I walked, a comfort seem'd to touch
> A heart that had not been disconsolate,
> Strength came where weakness was not known to be,
> At least not felt; and restoration came,
> Like an intruder, knocking at the door
> Of unacknowledg'd weariness.
>
> (IV. 140-48.)

Such experiences led Wordsworth to his celebration of the God-apprehending power of the imagination. Later in Book VI the narrator tells of the disappointment he had felt when, as a youth fourteen years before, he and a companion had crossed the Alps without realizing it. After pondering the experience, the narrator recognizes that beyond all disappointing worldly goals lies the human soul's transcendent goal:

> Imagination! lifting up itself
> Before the eye and progress of my Song
> Like an unfather'd vapour; here that Power,
> In all the might of its endowments, came
> Athwart me; I was lost as in a cloud,
> Halted, without a struggle to break through.
> And now recovering, to my Soul I say
> I recognize thy glory; in such strength
> Of usurpation, in such visitings
> Of awful promise, when the light of sense
> Goes out in flashes that have shewn to us
> The invisible world, doth Greatness make abode.
> There harbours whether we be young or old.
> Our destiny, our nature, and our home
> Is with infinitude, and only there.
>
> (VI. 525-39.)

Such a conclusion seems to suggest the Christian concept of the Heaven-bound soul, but it also is in accord with the panentheistic concept of a God who takes all human existence into his divine existence.

Immediately after this passage occurs the well-known Gondo Gorge incident, in which the narrator recognizes a panentheistic God:

> The immeasurable height
> Of woods decaying, never to be decay'd,
> The stationary blasts of water-falls,
> And every where along the hollow rent
> Winds thwarting winds, bewilder'd and forlorn,
> The torrents shooting from the clear blue sky,
> The rocks that mutter'd close upon our ears,
> Black drizzling crags that spake by the way-side
> As if a voice were in them, the sick sight
> And giddy prospect of the raving stream,
> The unfetter'd clouds, and region of the Heavens,
> Tumult and peace, the darkness and the light
> Were all like workings of one mind, the features
> Of the same face, blossoms upon one tree,
> Characters of the great Apocalypse,
> The types and symbols of Eternity,
> Of first and last, and midst, and without end.
>
> (VI. 556-72.)

Havens says of this passage, "Here we have the conviction of the unity underlying all phenomena and of the external world as a revelation of the Deity, but no feeling of the presence of God."[12] But surely he is wrong. Here we have not only the "presence of God," we have Wordsworth's most extended treatment (up to this point) of *The Prelude* God. The permanence, peace, and silence of God in his absoluteness underlie the change, agitation, and sound of God in his relativity. That Wordsworth is speaking of God is evident from the language of the passage. Behind all the process, the agitation, is unity: all the varied aspects of the scene are

> . . . like workings of one mind, the features
> Of the same face, blossoms upon one tree,
> Characters of the great Apocalypse,
> The types and symbols of Eternity,
> Of first and last, and midst, and without end.
>
> (VI. 568-72.)

The Miltonic echo of the last line ("On Earth join all ye Creatures to extol / Him first, him last, him midst, and without end" *Paradise Lost,* V.164-65) also supports the contention that God is present at Gondo Gorge.

This God is not the consummate panentheistic God, however. Although he appears in his contrary aspects of absoluteness and relativity, he is still somewhat terrifying and unapproachable. We are given an expression of God's infinite energy both for destruction and creation, but he is still far from Hartshorne's God who is sympathetically dependent on his universe, who loves, enjoys, and suffers with his world. The youth leans toward panentheism, but at this point, almost exactly halfway through *The Prelude,* he has not completed his panentheistic vision.

Not until the narrator has turned his attention from nature to the world of men and traced the youth's residence in London, his growing awareness of the suffering and agony of mankind, his experiences in France and agonizing disillusionment after the Revolution, and his eventual restoration to faith through the ministry of nature, through his "spots of time," and through his loved ones, are we given his complete vision of the panentheistic God. The vision occurs on a mountaintop, the traditional place for definitive visions.

For the nocturnal ascent of Mount Snowdon, the youthful Wordsworth and his companion, Robert Jones, hired an old shepherd to guide them through the mist to the mountain's summit, where they planned to watch the sunrise. The ascent was uneventful; except when the shepherd's dog gleefully cornered a hedgehog, the three men trudged separately up the mist-covered path, each lost in his own thoughts. Wordsworth walked in the lead, his head down, when suddenly he stepped through fog into bright moonlight illuminating a remarkable scene:

> . . . on the shore
> I found myself of a huge sea of mist,
> Which, meek and silent, rested at my feet:
> A hundred hills their dusky backs upheaved
> All over this still Ocean, and beyond,
> Far, far beyond, the vapours shot themselves,
> In headlands, tongues, and promontory shapes,
> Into the Sea, the real Sea, that seem'd
> To dwindle, and give up its majesty,
> Unsurp'd upon as far as sight could reach.
> Meanwhile, the Moon look'd down upon this shew
> In single glory, and we stood, the mist

Touching our very feet; and from the shore
At distance not the third part of a mile
Was a blue chasm; a fracture in the vapour,
A deep and gloomy breathing-place through which
Mounted the roar of waters, torrents, streams
Innumerable, roaring with one voice.
The universal spectacle throughout
Was shaped for admiration and delight,
Grand in itself alone, but in that breach
Through which the homeless voice of waters rose,
That dark deep thoroughfare had Nature lodg'd
The Soul, the Imagination of the whole.

(XIII.42-65.)

As in Gondo Gorge, the scene is one of tumult and peace, darkness and light, sound and silence, the one and the many. The roar of waters meets the silence of the heavens. There is complete interaction: clear air meets mist, moonlight meets the darkness of the chasm; sound blends with muffled silence; the ocean of mist blends with the real ocean far away; hills sticking through the mist blend with real islands in the distance. And dominating all is the blue chasm, that "deep and gloomy breathing-place" through which roar the sounds from the valley below.

The narrator calls this roar of waters rising through the chasm to the silent moon a symbol of the creative imagination:

A meditation rose in me that night
Upon the lonely Mountain when the scene
Had pass'd away, and it appear'd to me
The perfect image of a mighty Mind,
Of one that feeds upon infinity,
That is exalted by an underpresence,
The sense of God, or whatsoe'er is dim
Or vast in its own being, above all
One function of such mind had Nature there
Exhibited by putting forth, and that
With circumstance most awful and sublime,
That domination which she oftentimes
Exerts upon the outward face of things,
So moulds them, and endues, abstracts, combines,

>Or by abrupt and unhabitual influence
>Doth make one object so impress itself
>Upon all others, and pervade them so
>That even the grossest minds must see and hear
>And cannot chuse but feel.
>
>   (XIII. 66-84.)

As many readers have noted, this "mighty Mind" which "feeds upon Infinity" and is "exalted by an underpresence, / The sense of God," seems to be the mind of man; the roar through the chasm seems a perfect image of the human creative imagination at work. Later lines in the 1805 Snowdon meditation corroborate this reading, for Wordsworth says that Nature's power

>   . . . is the express
>Resemblance, in the fulness of its strength
>Made visible, a genuine Counterpart
>And Brother of the glorious faculty
>Which higher minds bear with them as their own.
>
>   (XIII. 86-90.)

Through their ability to "build up greatest things / From least suggestions," these minds are "made thereby more apt / To hold communion with the invisible world"[13]—presumably, with the world of God.

Such a passage hardly establishes Wordsworth's panentheism, especially since it comes at the climax of his greatest work. Rather, the poet's focus seems to be not on the consummate God but on traces of God's immanence in man. It is true that throughout *The Prelude* the narrator has considered man's creative imagination Godlike. In Book III he says,

>   Of Genius, Power,
>Creation and Divinity itself
>I have been speaking, for my theme has been
>What pass'd within me.
>
>   (III. 171-74.)

In Book X we learn that "the Godhead which is ours / Can never utterly be charm'd or still'd,"[14] and late in Book XIII we are told that

> God and Man divided, as they ought,
> Between them the great system of the world
> Where Man is sphered, and which God animates.
>
> (XIII. 266-68.)

Though panentheism does include immanent divinity, any view which focuses on God's immanence without admitting his simultaneous transcendence, as Wordsworth seems to do in the 1805 Snowdon episode, is not panentheistic. This dilemma threatens to undermine my entire reading of God's role in *The Prelude.*

But I contend that Wordsworth himself sensed that his limited focus in the 1805 Snowdon was inconsistent with the thematic pattern he had been developing earlier, for the 1850 passage is completely revised and leaves a different impression from that created by the earlier text—an impression back toward panentheism. In the vision, for example, the focus shifts from the chasm, the symbol of tremendous creative process, to the interpenetration of the whole scene, and especially to the moon:

> . . . as I looked up,
> The Moon hung naked in a firmament
> Of azure without cloud, and at my feet
> Rested a silent sea of hoary mist.
> A hundred hills their dusky backs upheaved
> All over this still ocean; and beyond,
> Far, far beyond, the solid vapours stretched,
> In headlands, tongues, and promontory shapes,
> Into the main Atlantic, that appeared
> To dwindle, and give up his majesty,
> Usurped upon far as the sight could reach.
> Not so the ethereal vault; encroachment none
> Was there, nor loss; only the inferior stars
> Had disappeared, or shed a fainter light
> In the clear presence of the full-orbed Moon,
> Who, from her sovereign elevation, gazed
> Upon the billowy ocean, as it lay
> All meek and silent, save that through a rift—
> Not distant from the shore whereon we stood,
> A fixed, abysmal, gloomy, breathing-place—
> Mounted the roar of waters, torrents, streams

Innumerable, roaring with one voice!
Heard over earth and sea, and, in that hour,
For so it seemed, felt by the starry heavens.

(1850; XIV. 39-62.)

The changes are subtle but significant. The previous sentence, "Meanwhile, the Moon look'd down upon this shew / In single glory," has been expanded to

. . . only the inferior stars
Had disappeared, or shed a fainter light
In the clear presence of the full-orbed Moon,
Who, from her sovereign elevation, gazed
Upon the billowy ocean.

(1850; XIV. 51-55.)

In Book V. the narrator had used "sovereign" to adumbrate a panentheistic God:

In progress through this Verse, my mind hath look'd
Upon the speaking face of earth and heaven
As her prime Teacher, intercourse with man
Establish'd by the sovereign Intellect,
Who through that bodily Image hath diffus'd
A soul divine which we participate,
A deathless spirit.

(V. 11-17.)

Milton uses "sovereign" ("sovran") in connection with God's will, and perhaps this is another of many Miltonic echoes in *The Prelude*. Also, the shift in emphasis from the chasm to the whole scene dominated by the moon is significant, since Wordsworth often saw the moon as a symbol of God or of religion.

Other changes between the 1805 and 1850 lines are equally revealing. The earlier ten lines devoted to the chasm where "Nature lodg'd / The Soul, the Imagination of the whole" have been cut to six, with a new image added in the last two: " . . . and, in that hour, / For so it seemed, felt by the starry heavens." Such evidence suggests that Wordsworth has shifted from man's mind to God's mind. More support for such a conclusion is supplied by 1850 revisions in the meditation which follows the vision:

> When into air had partially dissolved
> That vision, given to spirits of the night
> And three chance human wanderers, in calm thought
> Reflected, it appeared to me the type
> Of a majestic intellect, its acts
> And its possessions, what it has and craves,
> What in itself it is, and would become.
> There I beheld the emblem of a mind
> That feeds upon infinity, that broods
> Over the dark abyss, intent to hear
> Its voices issuing forth to silent light
> In one continuous stream; a mind sustained
> By recognitions of transcendent power,
> In sense conducting to ideal form,
> In soul of more than mortal privilege.
>
> (1850; XIV. 63-77.)

The change from a "mighty Mind" to a "majestic intellect" seems a change toward God; man's mind can be "mighty," but only God's could be "majestic." The Miltonic echo in the phrase

> . . . a mind
> That feeds upon infinity, that broods
> Over the dark abyss

is also significant, since God in *Paradise Lost* "Dove-like satst brooding on the vast abyss" (I.21).

Other phrases in the 1850 meditation also are panentheistic. In the line " . . . its acts / And its possessions, what it has and craves, / What in itself it is, and would become," Wordsworth distinguishes carefully between God's absolute and his relative qualities. "Acts" seems to refer to God's relativity, his sympathetic actions and reactions with his universe. "Possessions" also suggests relativity; God "possesses" all existences by taking them into his divine existence and retaining them forever in his memory. But "possessions" also could be God's immutability, his absoluteness. "What it has" could imply the absolute being of God, or it could again refer to his memory. "And craves" suggests the relative panentheistic God who loves and delights in the novelty and variety of his universe, who divinely appreciates any individual act of creativity or of love. "What it is" suggests God's "ipseity," his independent, immutable essence, his actuality. "And would become" suggests the relative God's "alterity," his capacity to change with his ever-changing universe, his ability to be the "self-surpassing surpasser of all things."

In the 1850 Snowdon vision and meditation, then, we have not only the previous glorification of man's God-like mind, but the glorification of God's mind. In fact, the narrator symbolically journeys into God's mind; his vision (11. 40-63) is of the divine imagination in operation. Like Hartshorne's God "whose datum is the universe," (*TDR*, p. 77) the Snowdon God takes all currents of existence into his existence. He imaginatively transforms all the multeity, all the roaring confusion of every act in the universe, into unity: through the

> . . . fixed, abysmal, gloomy breathing-place—
> Mounted the roar of waters, torrents, streams
> Innumerable, roaring with one voice!
>
> (1850; XIV. 58-60.)

God's imagination, which is sovereign and removed from the unified confusion rising to it, performs the divine miraculous act of internalizing external objects. The result is divine social interaction, divine "feeling of feeling": the multeity is "felt by the starry heavens."

The Snowdon episode contains Wordsworth's most complete expression of panentheism. That the 1850 revision of the episode seems more panentheistic than the earlier passage suggests that Wordsworth not only retained but strengthened his panentheism as he grew older. I find it significant that *The Prelude* closes with the word "divine," for the entire movement of the poem, culminating in the Snowdon meditation, has been toward "The feeling of life endless, the great thought / By which we live, Infinity and God" (XIII. 183-84). Wordsworth's wife called *The Prelude* "The Growth of a Poet's Mind," but I think "The Growth of a Poet's God" would have been an appropriate title, for such it seems.

Full analysis of the possible sources of Wordsworth's panentheism is beyond the scope of this study. He may have approached rudimentary echoes of the anima mundi after reading Cudworth's *True Intellectual System of the Universe* (1678), a volume in his library.[15] From his two volumes of Boehme, he may have adopted the notions of nature as the images produced by God's imagination and of the intimate merging of the imaginative mind with its object.[16] Though he did not know Schelling, he may have learned through conversations with Coleridge of Schelling's view that the world is God's affirmative self-realization,[17] that "God leads human nature through no other course than that through which his own nature must pass," and that "Participation in everything blind, dark, and suffering of God's nature is necessary in order to raise him to highest consciousness."[18]

But there is little doubt that Wordsworth's poetry displays a developing, coherent panentheism. At times, especially in early passages, he emphasized God's immanence and relativity; at others, especially in later passages, he emphasized God's transcendence and absoluteness. But in his greatest poetry—"Tintern Abbey," the "Immortality Ode," "Hart-Leap Well," and especially The Gondo Gorge and Snowdon passages of the 1850 *Prelude*, Wordsworth's God is a panentheistic God who sympathetically participates in his universe while simultaneously remaining independent from it.

END NOTES

[1]*Religious Trends in English Poetry* (New York: Columbia Univ. Press, 1949), Vol. III, pp. 138-262.

[2]*The Mind of a Poet* (Baltimore: Johns Hopkins Univ. Press, 1941), p. 197. Hereafter cited as Havens.

[3]Charles Hartshorne, *The Divine Relativity* (New Haven: Yale Univ. Press, 1948), p. ix. Hereafter cited in the text as *TDR*.

[4]Charles Hartshorne, *Man's Vision of God* (Chicago: Univ. of Chicago Press, 1941), p. 111. Hereafter cited in the text as *MVG*.

[5]Charles Hartshorne, *Philosophers Speak of God* (Chicago: Univ. of Chicago Press, 1953), p. 1. Hereafter cited in the text as *PSG*.

[6]*Process and Reality* (New York: The Free Press, 1969), p. 532.

[7]Ernest de Selincourt, ed. *The Prelude, or Growth of a Poet's Mind,* 2nd ed. (1926; rev. Helen Darbishire. London: Oxford Univ. Press, 1960), pp. lxxi-lxxii. Hereafter line numbers cited in the text; all quotations are from the 1805 version unless otherwise noted.

[8]*Natural Supernaturalism* (New York: Norton, 1971), p. 90. Hereafter cited as Abrams.

[9]Havens, p. 174.

[10]*The Prelude,* "Notes," p. 622.

[11]*The Prelude,* "Notes," p. 525.

[12]Havens, p. 183.

[13]*XIII.* 98-105.

[14]*X.* 171-72.

[15]Havens, p. 190.

[16]N. P. Stallknecht, *Strange Seas of Thought* (Bloomington: Indiana Univ. Press, 1958), pp. 43-45.

[17]E. D. Hirsch, Jr., *Wordsworth and Schelling* (New Haven: Yale Univ. Press, 1960), p. 34.

[18]Schelling, *The Ages of the World,* quoted in Abrams, p. 190.

Structure and Unity in The White Doe of Rylstone

John G. Rudy

The White Doe of Rylstone has been praised for its music and its diction, for its imaginative power and its dynamic spirituality. But I believe it has never received the attention it deserves as a truly precise and coherent narrative work. From the time of the poem's composition, readers have complained that the cantos which tell the story of the Norton Rebellion—what Wordsworth called "the mere business parts" of his narrative—are broken, tedious, and ill-adapted to the parts about Emily and the doe. Lamb remarked that "the principal characters do nothing." Coleridge, who was afraid the poem might be viewed as an imitation of Walter Scott, valued only those passages dealing with Emily. "The whole of the rest," said Coleridge, "and the delivering up of the family by Francis, I never ceased to find, not only comparatively heavy, but to me quite obscure as to Francis' motives." When *The White Doe* appeared in 1815, seven years after its completion, *The Quarterly Review* stated flatly that the narrative possessed little interest and that "the story is told, as it were, in scraps."[1] Later critics, together with recent scholars, seem only to acquiesce in these early judgments. Mary Moorman, for example, compares Wordsworth to Scott in her discussion of the poem and argues that "Scott could certainly outdo him in 'the business parts' of a narrative poem with a medieval theme."[2]

Wordsworth, however, believed that a comparison of *The White Doe* with Scott's romances was inconsiderate and unrewarding. The action of *The White Doe,* he explained in a Fenwick note to the poem, bears no resemblance to Scott's narrative procedures: "Sir Walter pursued the customary and very natural course of conducting an action, presenting various turns of fortune, to some outstanding point on which the mind might rest as a termination or catastrophe. The course I attempted to pursue is entirely different. Everything that is attempted by the principal personages in 'The White Doe' fails, so far as its object is external and substantial. So far as it is moral and spiritual it succeeds."[3] If I am reading this note correctly, Wordsworth here is not rejecting traditional narrative forms, nor is he minimizing the importance of the Norton story as it appears in the poem. Rather, he is indicating that the plot of *The White Doe* is mainly one of moral and spiritual development, and not simply a development of incident.

To be sure, Wordsworth was uneasy about the narrative portion of his poem and told Justice Coleridge, in 1836, that "he should devote much labor to perfecting the execution of it in the mere business parts . . . . "[4] But the changes introduced into the text the following year were stylistic and did not involve structure. Wordsworth was convinced that the poem's narrative architecture was entirely a matter of spiritual action. " 'The White Doe' starts from a high point of imagination," he declared in a famous letter to Wrangham, "and comes round, through various wanderings of that faculty, to a still higher—nothing less than the Apotheosis of the Animal . . . . And as the Poem thus begins and ends with pure and lofty Imagination, every motive and impetus that actuates the persons introduced is from the same source; a kindred spirit pervades, and is intended to harmonise, the whole" (*P.W.*, III, p. 547). Imagination, then, is the major theme of *The White Doe* and is also the salient organizing principle upon which the poem is constructed.

But I think Wordsworth's comment on imagination as a unifying and spiritualizing device, though certainly valid, can be overemphasized by critics of the poem.[5] The reader is tempted, as it were, to ignore some of the more basic, perhaps more common aspects of narrative style in the verse itself and to dismiss the conduct of physical action in the story of the Norton Rebellion as a mere fragmented sequence of mundane events only faintly connected with the spiritual thrust of the poem as a whole. A better course, I believe, is to read the poem in response to the implications of its title, which is in two parts. The subtitle, "The Fate of the Nortons," underscores the importance of historical event and particular detail in the work and balances the more remote, more spiritual implications of the first heading. By insisting on two titles, Wordsworth suggests, perhaps unknowingly, that *The White Doe* posits a tension between the realm of the spirit and the everyday world of historical affairs and that the main function of the poem is "to harmonise the whole." An examination of the complex network of discordant and contradictory elements in the poem will, I believe, reveal that *The White Doe* derives both its structure and its power from the tension between given extremes and that the poem's aesthetic effect resides primarily in its heroine's ability to balance and to reconcile these extremes.

The movement of images and events in Canto I provides a good example of how this process of tension and balance works throughout *The White Doe*. The poet begins his narrative with a picture of a group of brightly arrayed people coming to Bolton Priory for Sunday Services:

> The sun shines bright; the fields are gay
> With people in their best array
> Of stole and doublet, hood and scarf,
> Along the banks of crystal Wharf,
> Through the Vale retired and lowly,
> Trooping to that summons holy.   (3-8)

The visual images in the first stanza are bright; the mood is joyous and gay. But juxtaposed to this cheerful scene is the vision in the next stanza of the Priory itself, which "Too harshly hath been doomed to taste / The bitterness of wrong and waste" (19-20). The ruined Priory, "That sumptuous Pile" (18), surrounds the chapel to which the worshippers are going and bears mute testimony to a history of violence and human misery. The mood is no longer cheerful. The visual imagery describes a wasteland, and the passage produces a general sense of discord and disharmony.

Furthermore, the image of a Mass occurring within a structure whose courts have been "ravaged" (21) and whose fabric has been "shattered" (25) conveys a sense of irony that is extended shortly afterward in the lines that describe the sounds of the Mass and the sounds of nature:

> A moment ends the fervent din,
> And all is hushed, without and within;
> For though the priest, more tranquilly,
> Recites the holy liturgy,
> The only voice which you can hear
> Is the river murmuring near.   (43-48)

Just as the visual images in the first two stanzas depicted a contrast between the gaiety of the Sunday worshippers and the somber atmosphere of the Priory ravaged by past struggles and by time, so the sounds conveyed in lines forty-three through forty-eight indicate an ironic contrast between the noise, "the fervent din," of the congregation and the peaceful voice of nature in "the river murmuring near." In so far as it has a voice, nature appears to be more intelligible and, by extension, more meaningful than the high festival in the chapel.

To some extent, however, the contrasting elements in both passages are resolved. The vision of the tiny chapel in the heart of the ruined Priory arrests the poet's depiction of the wasteland, and in the stanza that contrasts the congregation's fervent din with the river's peaceful voice, the narrative is suspended in order to permit the entrance of the white doe:

> Comes gliding in with lovely gleam,
> Comes gliding in serene and slow,
> Soft and silent as a dream,
> A solitary Doe!   (55-58)

The doe moves quietly, effortlessly, supported in her dreamlike mission of peace by the assonances and alliterations of the verse itself. The syllables vary downward from eight in line fifty-five to six in line fifty-eight, compelling the reader to move more slowly, and finally to stop. A truly harmonious vision, contraries of sight and sound disappear, and the narrative, for a brief moment, is at a seeming standstill.

This method of tension and balance between contrasting elements, together with partial resolutions of the extremes depicted, forms a pattern of discord and synthesis employed by Wordsworth throughout the poem. It is especially evident in those lines which actually attempt to define the white doe. After the entrance of the doe in stanza four, the narrative shifts to a description of the animal:

> White she is as lily of June,
> And beauteous as the silver moon
> When out of sight the clouds are driven
> And she is left alone in heaven;
> Or like a ship some gentle day
> In sunshine sailing far away,
> A glittering ship, that hath the plain
> Of ocean for her own domain.   (59-66)

Wordsworth compares the doe first to a lily, then to the moon, and finally to a ship. Like the lily, the doe's color distinguishes her from her natural surroundings; yet it is a familiar color in nature. But in so far as the lily is of the earth and the moon is of the heavens, Wordsworth suggests that the doe is also both natural and supernatural. She is in nature, fitting into its organic wholeness as completely as any lily. Yet, through comparison with the moon, she acquires an aura of pure ethereal spirituality that forwards and enhances the implications of the quality of perfect harmony she achieves with regard to her natural surroundings.[6]

A similar dialectic is at work in the lines that compare the doe to a ship "that hath the plain / Of ocean for her own domain." Just as images of earth and heaven come together in descriptions of the doe's whiteness, so contrary concepts of possession merge in the ship simile. The sea surrounds her and dwarfs her; yet the sea is her possession, her domain. To the poet, then, the doe represents whatever it is that unifies, combines, impregnates, and inter-animates with all things in the universe. She resolves the tensions between the particular and the general, between earth and heaven, and society and nature, between noise and silence, and land and sea, and between desolation and vernal splendor. She is both the object of the poet's imaginative attention and the impulse that provokes that attention.

In his letter to Wrangham, Wordsworth explained these seeming paradoxes in his apprehension of the objects and symbols in *The White Doe* when he declared: "Throughout, objects (the Banner, for instance) derive their in-fluence, not from properties inherent in themselves, not from what they *are* actually in themselves, but from such as are *bestowed* upon them by the minds of those who are conversant with or affected by those objects" (*P.W.,* III, p. 547). For Wordsworth, the white doe is both the symbol of the imagi-native faculty at work on reality and the product of that faculty. Thus he writes at one point:

> The presence of this wandering Doe
> Fills many a damp obscure recess
> With lustre of a saintly show;
> And, reappearing, she no less
> Sheds on the flowers that round her blow
> A more than sunny liveliness.   (100-05)

The doe's interanimation with her surroundings gives life to nature and is representative of the way in which imagination acts on objects to create a sense of order and meaning that transforms the organic world into a new universe.

After these lines of imaginative reconciliation, the narrative descends back into a depiction of discordant elements in the everyday world of particular, historical affairs. The poet describes the congregation's insecure and super-stitious reactions to the doe by focusing first on a little boy who sees the creature and who is curious about her identity:

> Bright was the Creature, as in dreams
> The Boy had seen her, yea, more bright;
> But is she truly what she seems?
> He asks with insecure delight,

> Asks of himself, and doubts,—and still
> The doubt returns against his will.   (192-97)

The boy senses intuitively something beautiful and meaningful in the doe, but, like the rest of the congregation, his consciousness is divided and incomplete. Imaginative apprehension of the animal is blocked by fear and superstition. The minds of the people who view the doe are not adequately prepared to accept the creature as a natural and spiritual impulse that can lead them to a new sense of reality:

> If, undeceived, my skill can trace
> The characters of every face,
> There lack not strange delusion here,
> Conjecture vague, and idle fear,
> And superstitious fancies strong,
> Which do the gentle Creature wrong.   (211-16)

Wordsworth then enumerates some of the myths involving the doe and indicates, especially through the scholar, who believes the animal to be the fairy godmother of the alchemist Lord Clifford, how these superstitions create an atmosphere of discord and disharmony. At the end of his discourse on the doe, the scholar says: "And all is now disquieted— / And peace is none, for living or dead!" (306-07). Diametrically opposed to the scholar, however, the poet answers:

> But look again at the radiant Doe!
> What quiet watch she seems to keep,
> Alone, beside that grassy heap!
> Why mention other thoughts unmeet
> For vision so composed and sweet?   (309-13)

Once again Wordsworth has set up a contrast. The scholar's vision of the doe is opposed to the poet's vision, and tension mounts as images of discord and disharmony offset the atmosphere of tranquillity and harmony surrounding the animal. And once again Wordsworth introduces something that partially relieves, or that suspends, the tension. He addresses the harp, a traditional symbol of poetry, and explains that "we have been full long beguiled / By vague thoughts, lured by fancies wild" (324-25). To resolve the tensions produced by contrasting visions of the doe, and to correct the superstitions that "do the gentle Creature wrong," Wordswroth says that he has been commanded "To chant, in strains of heavenly glory, / A tale of tears, a mortal story!" (335-36).

Significantly, the poet indicates at this point that he is going to tell "a mortal story." Although the poem, as Wordsworth explained in his notes and letters, begins and ends with imagination, and even though imagination constitutes its major theme, the story of the rebellion and its failure is absolutely necessary to his purpose in *The White Doe.* In most of Wordsworth's poetry, imagination works through human experience. The "mortal story" here provides the framework for the human experience upon which the theme of imagination builds. "The Fate of the Nortons" is important not only because it dramatizes the insurrection, but also because it conveys the growth and development of Emily Norton's consciousness. More precisely, it is a story about the growth and effect of the imaginative faculty in a specific group of historical individuals. Thus, the "mortal story" has a definite historical flavor that will counterbalance the superstitions of the congregation by underscoring the reality of imagination in the common everyday world of fact and incident.

In order to achieve a sense of immediate reality, the poet leads us into a web of discordant and contradictory events held together by the dialectic tensions which exist between and within the major figures in the tale. The three leading characters are Emily, her brother Francis, and her father Richard Norton. Together, they form a complex tri-partite structure that enhances a world of cross-purposes and divided attentions. The unifying object, or symbol, in the story is the banner which Emily makes for her father's campaign. Dramatic tension is constructed upon the reactions of Francis and Richard to the banner and to the cause it represents. For instance, describing the father's response to the banner, the poet writes:

> Her Father did with joy behold,—
> Exulting in its imagery;
> A Banner, fashioned to fulfill
> Too perfectly his headstrong will. (350-53)

Not only is the banner emblematic of the father's relatively noble endeavor to release Mary, queen of Scotland from prison and to restore the Catholic religion to England, it also symbolizes his vanity and his stubborn will. The lines suggest that Richard is a divided soul and that he does not act entirely with reason. His loyalty to his faith and to his country is counterbalanced,

to some extent tarnished, by his vanity. Similarly, Francis's loyalties are
divided. He wants no part of the revolution and tells Richard:

> A just and gracious queen have we,
> A pure religion, and the claim
> Of peace on our humanity. (386-88)

Yet Francis loves his father and feels the need to express his loyalty to his
family. Qualifying his position with regard to the revolutionaries, he confesses
to Emily:

> With theirs my efforts cannot blend,
> I cannot for such cause contend;
> Their aims I utterly forswear;
> But I in body will be there. (507-10)

This quality of self-division within each figure is mirrored outwardly in the
rupture that occurs between the two when Francis tries to dissuade his father
from the campaign and encounters Richard's anger. Richard views the
insurrection in terms of martial splendor and religious glory. Francis is the
very embodiment of despair and can only utter a prophesy of doom. To his
sister he declares: "Hope nothing, I repeat; for we / Are doomed to perish
utterly" (532-33). The tension between father and son mounts throughout
Canto II until, at the end of Canto III, in lines of truly penetrating irony,
Richard curses Francis:

> Thou Enemy, my bane and blight!
> Oh! bold to fight the Coward's fight
> Against all good . . . . (924-26)

Here, as in Canto I, divided consciousness begets illusion and misapprehen-
sion. The gentle Francis, who deeply loves his family and who is certainly
brave enough to challenge his father's dream of revolutionary glory, is
branded an enemy and a coward.

In the opening lines to Canto IV, however, the narrative shifts back to
Rylstone Hall. The vision of peace and of quiet harmony at Rylstone interrupts the narrative and suspends momentarily the mounting sense of discord
in the temporal affairs of Richard and Francis Norton. But even here there is
an undercurrent of dissonance. The white doe enters and approaches the

pensive Emily, who awaits news of the fighting. But Emily does not respond to the animal. Like her brother and her father, Emily is also divided within. She desires to follow Francis in his endeavor to dissuade Richard from his mad campaign; yet she is committed to obey her brother's command that she remain at home:

> *Her duty is to stand and wait;*
> In resignation to abide
> The shock, AND FINALLY SECURE
> O'ER PAIN AND GRIEF A TRIUMPH PURE. (1069-72)

These lines are significant, of course, in so far as they announce the theme of triumph over grief and suffering. But the hope they convey at this time does not erase the quality of self-division that inhibits the maid's capacity to accept the doe and all the worlds of peace and unity contained within an imaginative apprehension of the creature. By the end of Canto IV, we are left only with the vague promise that Emily will transcend her present sufferings. Like the child in Canto I, Emily, at this point in the story, is incomplete.

Through Cantos V and VI, the narrative moves along a downward course. Richard Norton is captured and executed. But before he dies, he blesses Francis and asks him to bear the banner to Bolton Priory, "To wither in the sun and breeze / 'Mid those decaying sanctities" (1294-95). Honoring his father's last wish, Francis secures the banner and attempts to steal off with it. Father and son have achieved a reconciliation, and Francis, perhaps for the first time in the story, appears to be acting with singleness of purpose. But here, too, there is a deep current of irony and dissonance stemming from divided attentions. Even as he flees toward Bolton Priory, pursued by Bowes and his men, Francis suspects his motives in attempting to make off with the banner. He seems really to want nothing to do with it, but he feels constrained to express some kind of loyalty to his father's ideal.[7] As a result of this inward conflict, he acts without reason and, as the poet suggests, brings his own life into danger:

> Such conflict long did he maintain,
> Nor liberty nor rest could gain:
> His own life into danger brought
> By this sad burden—even that thought,
> Exciting self-suspicion strong,
> Swayed the brave man to his wrong. (1406-11)

Unable to convince his pursuers that he is not part of the rebel forces, Francis draws suspicion to himself and is captured and killed.

With the death of Francis, the physical action of the poem comes to an end. Through death, discordant activities and tensions are suspended. Emily wanders off, crushed by sorrow and despair, and her brother's prophesy of decay and desolation becomes an actuality:

> 'Tis done;—despoil and desolation
> O'er Rylstone's fair domain have blown;
> Pools, terraces, and walks are sown
> With weeds; the bowers are overthrown,
> Or have given way to slow mutation,
> While, in their ancient habitation
> The Norton name hath been unknown. (1568-74)

This, I believe, is the point at which Scott would have ended the poem. But for Wordsworth, it is simply one more step, one more partial resolution, in the process of tension and balance that has been evolving steadily throughout *The White Doe*. Emily survives the shock, as the poet promised, and returns to her father's ruined home. She has managed to accept the tragic consequences of the past and, though deeply saddened by her experiences, displays a heroic fortitude that enables her to rise above the divisive qualities of hatred, despair, and cynicism:

> The mighty sorrow hath been borne,
> And she is thoroughly forlorn:
> Her soul doth in itself stand fast,
> Sustained by memory of the past
> And strength of Reason; held above
> The infirmities of mortal love;
> Undaunted, lofty, calm, and stable,
> And awfully impenetrable. (1621-28)

Reason, together with remembrance of things past, aids Emily in her attempt to reconcile the discordant and conflicting faculties of her consciousness. She has seen her father and her brother divided against each other. She has seen her world laid waste through armed allegiance to conflicting theologies. Yet she has also witnessed the partial reconciliation of these conflicts. Her father and her brother were brought together again at the point of death, and a new peace has settled over the land. In the midst of discord and disharmony, there exist patterns of unity and sources of renewal available to man in the present life. By accepting the past, with all its sorrows, with its myriad juxtapositions of darkness and light, of tumult and folly, Emily transcends her sufferings and is complete. She is now prepared for imaginative encounters with reality and stands on the threshold of a new world. In Chapter XIV of *Biographia Literaria,* Coleridge explores the importance of this unity among the human faculties in his attempt to define exactly what it is that the artist achieves ideally in his work:

> The poet, described in *ideal* perfection, brings the whole soul of man into activity, with the subordination of its faculties to each other, according to their relative worth and dignity. He diffuses a tone, and spirit of unity, that blends, and (as it were) *fuses,* each into each, by that synthetic and magical power, to which we have exclusively appropriated the name of imagination. This power, first put in action by the will and understanding, and retained under their irremissive, though gentle and unnoticed, controul . . . reveals itself in the balance or reconciliation of opposite or discordant qualities . . . . [8]

By suggesting that the imagination is, ideally, subordinate to the faculties of will and understanding, Coleridge, I believe, voices what Wordsworth has been laboring to demonstrate throughout *The White Doe*—that aesthetic experience is the result, not of a specific faculty, but of the whole human consciousness. Indeed, as we move through the poem, we will see that the imagination in moments of great vision ceases to exist as a separate entity. It joins with other processes, both external and internal, and becomes part of a total way of seeing. The redemptive energies of this visionary process grow out of what can best be described, then, as a collection of shared experiences. The imagination, though certainly the most important faculty in the consciousness, and the one that Wordsworth claimed to be celebrating in the poem, is not displayed as a totally creative and autonomous power. Nor does it serve a solipsistic mind that endeavors to create out of nothing or to invest with life what is otherwise thought to be dead. Rather, it is made to participate in, and thus redeem, what the poet, through his powers of reason and understanding, through years of study and contemplation, believes to exist and to be vital to the spiritual well-being of the race.

Emily, when she confronts the past without rejecting any of its features, becomes for Wordsworth the dramatic embodiment of the artist himself in his moments of greatest insight and creativity. She has met the crisis head-on, and she has made her choice. It is not to a specific set of images, nor to a particular concept, but to the very process of imagination, with its winding, obstacle-endowed courses, that she has given herself. There have been moments of doubt and vexation in the past; there will be dark moments in the future. But faith in the natural rhythms of imaginative enterprise and in the mind's continuing ability to incorporate its dark moods into the totality of poetic experience brings strength and courage and an outward-moving willingness to risk the unknown and to encounter all that the future holds. Through suffering, Emily acquires the vantage point of the philosophic mind and realizes that there is yet something constant in the universe.

The white doe is the focus of this constant. Earlier in the poem, the doe was a symbol of the unifying and transforming powers of the imagination. She now becomes a living reminder that nature is instinct with spirit and process. Her return to Emily declares the presence of ultimate harmonies available to man in the realm of common experience. Step-by-step, Emily allows the doe to enter her consciousness and to aid her in the process by which sorrow and loss give way to joy and spiritual fulfillment. Time stops. Change and mutability are viewed as necessary conditions of the temporal world, as conditions not simply to be endured in the feeble hope for something better to come, but as operations to be accepted in the knowledge that there is diffused throughout the universe a spirit of pure and immutable love:

> But here her Brother's words have failed;
> Here hath a milder doom prevailed;
> That she, of him and all bereft,
> Hath yet this faithful Partner left;
> This one Associate that disproves
> His words, remains for her, and loves. (1785-90)

In this redeeming spirit of love, and with the aid of her own imagination, Emily moves within herself to encounter a new and joyous awareness of the world around her. And like the doe, she merges with her surroundings, allowing nature to minister to her soul until she is at peace with herself and content with her lot:

> Her own thoughts loved she; and could bend

> A dear look to her lowly Friend;
> There stopped; her thirst was satisfied
> With what this innocent spring supplied. (1854-57)

Emily, in effect, has merged with the divine spirit of nature represented by and contained within the doe and has become one with the God who created her and all things in the universe:

> From fair to fairer; day by day
> A more divine and loftier way!
> Even such this blessed Pilgrim trod;
> By sorrow lifted towards her God. (1848-51)

Emily has achieved what her father and her brother could not achieve, except perhaps at the point of death, and what the scholar, with all his knowledge of local history, could not perceive in the gentle visitations of the doe—an unmediated union with the given. This, I believe, is the higher point of imagination that Wordsworth mentioned in his note to the poem. It is not a state of being in which the poetic mind creates a new reality, or in which the individual seeks to inhabit a world apart from nature. It is, rather, a state of imaginative perception which enables the participant to inhabit already existing forms and processes in the belief that earthly matter contains spiritual potentialities sufficient for the aspiring mind of man. The faculty that Wordsworth celebrates in this poem is a power of habitation, not an apocalyptic or completely transcendental energy that would drive man away from nature and into a realm of pure ethereal spirituality. Emily does not betray nature for heaven. She reconciles the temporal and the eternal, the human and the divine, the natural and the spiritual, not by joining the two realms of being in a mere covenantal unity that really bespeaks their eternal separation, but by applying to nature the energies of her own imagination in such a way as to perceive and then to share in the interpenetration of the spiritual in the mundane.

Emily's role in her correspondence with the doe, then, is not merely one of spiritual transcendence through passive renunciation of temporal existence. Emily not only receives impulses of a divine origin, she adds to the spirit of love within the doe. What she adds is her own experience of wholeness and of oneness with reality, her own ability to reconcile discordant qualities in herself as well as in the world around her. Similarly, the doe must not be viewed only as a symbol of the imagination. She is also a natural vehicle through which God and man correspond. The supernatural attributes with which the creature is endowed only enhance the reality of its eternal nature. The doe, like the God that inhabits it, survives through countless generations to serve as testimony to the immortality of man's imagination. And insofar as she has merged with the doe, Emily becomes eternal.[9]

Thus, the poem comes full-circle, reconciling the discordant elements depicted in Canto I. The availability of eternal peace in the realm of human experience resolves the tensions of the temporal world, and the poem ends with an apostrophe to the doe and a message to all mankind: " 'Thou, thou art not a Child of Time, / But Daughter of the Eternal Prime' " (1909-10)! But the truth of this lesson in appearances, like the conduct of physical action in the story of the Norton Rebellion, is contingent upon states of being, not upon laws which are commonly believed to be entirely separate from human consciousness. Indeed, Wordsworth meant exactly what he said when he explained that action fails "so far as its object is external and substantial." He did not mean to imply that the narrative as a whole is weak and ill-adjusted. If anything, *The White Doe of Rylstone* is one of the most carefully constructed poems Wordsworth ever wrote. This, I think, is why he did not, perhaps could not, alter the "business parts" of his narrative. As it stands, structure of incident plays to reflection and metaphor in such a way as to make a series of resolutions in the moral plot. Emily's ascent to beatific peace of mind is the culminating action in this sequence of resolutions. Had Wordsworth packed the poem with details of the fighting, had he involved Emily more directly in the actions of Richard and Francis Norton, he would only have succeeded in clouding the central truth upon which the narrative is constructed—that the real struggles of life occur not on battlefields, but in the mind itself.

END NOTES

[1]The statements by Lamb, Coleridge, and *The Quarterly Review* are reprinted in Alice P. Comparetti's critical edition of *The White Doe of Rylstone* (Ithaca: Cornell Univ. Press, 1940), pp. 248, 261, 254. For discussion of Wordsworth's revisions between 1808 and 1815, see Comparetti, pp. 38-41.

[2]Mary Moorman, *William Wordsworth: A Biography. The Later Years, 1803-1850* (Oxford: Clarendon Press, 1965), p. 113. See also Helen Darbishire, *The Poet Wordsworth* (Oxford: Clarendon Press, 1950), p. 155. The fullest collection of criticism to 1940 is Comparetti's edition, pp. 247-88.

[3]Ernest DeSelincourt and Helen Darbishire, eds., *The Poetical Works of William Wordsworth,* III, 2nd ed. (Oxford: Clarendon Press, 1954), p. 543. Hereafter cited as *P.W.*

[4]Christopher Wordsworth, *Memoirs of William Wordsworth, Poet-Laureate, D.C.L.* (London: Moxon, 1851), II, p. 313. See also DeSelincourt's note, *P.W.*, III, p. 548.

[5]Recent critical discussions explore in greater depth than those of the past the role imagination plays in the spiritualization of the doe and in Emily's ascent to beatific peace of mind. See especially Martin Price, "Imagination in *The White Doe of Rylstone,*" *PQ*, 33 (1954), 189-99; Ellen D. Leyburn, "Radiance in *The White Doe of Rylstone,*" *SP*, 47 (1950), 629-33; and Geoffrey H. Hartman, *Wordsworth's Poetry, 1787-1814* (New Haven: Yale Univ. Press, 1964), pp. 324-31, 405-07. Price, whose essay marks a truly penetrating study of the doe's "mode of being," shows how *The White Doe* is essentially a poem about the imagination: "The qualities of the Doe which make her mysterious and provocative in the first canto are given a largely natural explanation in the ensuing narrative. The result is not an explaining away but a deepening of the Doe's influence." Leyburn reaffirms the centrality of the doe in the poem's total structure and connects Wordsworth's descriptions of the animal and her surroundings with concepts of imaginative power. Hartman acknowledges his debt to Price and goes on to show how Wordsworth was here attempting to define the progress from a Catholic to a Protestant mode of imaginative participation. But while these studies illuminate Wordsworth's theory of imagination, they fail to link that theory with a central stylistic principle that runs throughout the narrative and that affects the poem's imagery, tone, rhythm, and structure of incident. Consequently, for many readers, *The White Doe* loses its appeal as a narrative work and becomes instead a progress poem in the tradition of *Lyrical Ballads.* "*The White Doe* is still a lyrical ballad," says Hartman. "Its interest does not derive, even in part, from the report of heroic event or 'moving accident,' and this despite the fact that it tells of a Catholic insurrection in the time of Elizabeth and that it describes the strange apparition of the doe."

[6]Florence Marsh, in *Wordsworth's Imagery: A Study in Poetic Vision* (New Haven: Yale Univ. Press, 1952), pp. 62-63, complains that the doe is more supernatural than natural and that "her overspiritualization makes her seem an arbitrary, not a natural, symbol." Marsh raises a point of view this paper is attempting to correct.

[7]The death of Francis is a complex matter. I do not mean to oversimplify his motives in securing the banner, nor am I suggesting that the banner is a hostile symbol. A good discussion of Francis as stoical hero appears in Elizabeth Geen, "The Concept of Grace in Wordsworth's Poetry," *PMLA,* 58 (1943), 701-04. See also Jane Worthington |Smyser|, *Wordsworth's Reading of Roman Prose* (New Haven: Yale Univ. Press, 1946), pp. 69-71; and John F. Danby, *The Simple Wordsworth: Studies in the Poems 1797-1807* (London: Routledge, 1960), pp. 134-35.

[8]Elizabeth Schneider, ed., *Samuel Taylor Coleridge: Selected Poetry and Prose,* 2nd ed. (San Francisco: Rinehart, 1971), p. 290. The poetic theories of Wordsworth and Coleridge are, of course, far more complex and divergent than my comparison here implies. But I do not think their ideas are so different as to invite entirely separate considerations. An especially useful study of the subordinate, yet crucial role that imagination plays in the developing religious thought of Wordsworth and Coleridge is James D. Boulger's "Coleridge on Imagination Revisited," *WC,* 4, i (Winter, 1973), 13-24.

[9]I think critics continue to misinterpret the nature and intent of Emily's relationship with the doe. Geoffrey Durrant, for example, in *William Wordsworth* (London: Cambridge Univ. Press, 1969), p. 14, argues that Wordsworth was here attempting a metamorphosis in the manner of Ovid and concludes: "The experiment was not successful, but the poem serves to remind us of Wordsworth's resourcefulness." Hartman is more explicit. He feels that Emily's transcendence is linked with Anglican thought and that Wordsworth, fearful of apocalyptic separation from the realm of elemental form, was here imposing restraints on the imagination: "Under the pressure of these many restraints, Wordsworth's mind has little chance to fall in love with or explore its own impressions" (*Wordsworth's Poetry,* p. 330). I am inclined, however, to subordinate Hartman's concern with the level of orthodoxy in Emily's ascent to imaginative life. What is important is that Emily's association with the doe allows her freedom of thought and feeling within continually evolving patterns of renewal present in the workings of nature; it brings her peace of mind and union with the given.

Irony Without Positive Norms: Robert Browning's "In a Year"

Robert J. Cornet

An interesting and moving poem in itself, Browning's "In a Year" illuminates an important area in the poetics and rhetoric of irony: the possibility of irony created without reference to positive norms. The usual theoretical discussions of irony formally define that mode as the contrast and juxtaposition of appearance and reality. This usually means that we discover the false appearance by means of a positive, affirmed reality, the relationship of the two being that of conclusion to premise: in order to know what something is *not* we need to know what it is.[1] As prevalent as this view is in contemporary theory, at least one earlier theorist has dissented from it: Søren Kierkegaard. In *The Concept of Irony, With Constant Reference to Socrates,* he defines irony as "infinite absolute negativity:"

> . . . it negates by virtue of a higher which is not. Irony establishes nothing, for that which is to be established lies behind it. . . . As the ironist does not have the new within his power, it might be asked how he destroys the old, and to this it must be answered: he destroys the given actuality by the given actuality itself.[2]

Though his definition sounds like a slogan for philosophical nihilism, it implies a formal principle that need not be linked with that philosophical position. Irony may suggest the existence of a positive norm, but it need not posit that norm as a necessary premise in its logical structure. It may operate by a strictly negative dialectic, by strict self-contradiction.[3]

"In a Year" is such a negative irony. In it the speaker, the woman in a failed love affair, offers a causal analysis of that failure, not only with the apparent formal intent of finding the cause of, and overcoming, loss, but also with the ethical intent of attenuating her own responsibility for the loss. From her analysis we learn, though she will not face this, that the means she used to hold love led to love's loss. Formally put, the denial of the consequent (love), denies the antecedent (her acts). She also so structures her primary hypothesis for future action, an attempt to overcome separation, that she commits the fallacy of assuming that if she denies the antecedent she will deny the consequent: alive she has no hope, dead she will. Further, the means of denial she chooses is in the same class, the mutable, as the means she originally used in her failed attempt to hold love; thus, her unsuccess is guaranteed with logical inevitability. Because these recognitions occur in the audience and not in the speaker we judge her to be an unreliable speaker, the object of Browning's irony. We may conclude, then, that the speaker is responsible for the failure because she offers the wrong kind of love. But if that is what we conclude, that positive *conclusion* cannot also be the poem's positive standard, the *premise* for that conclusion. We come to that conclusion by means of the poem's negations. We may recognize, through the poem's formal, causal structure, what love is *not*. But we will not learn, nor need we assume, what love *is*.

The poem opens with a statement of finality:

Never any more,
　　While I live,
Need I hope to see his face
　　As before.
Once his love grown chill,
　　Mine may strive:
Bitterly we re-embrace,
　　Single still.

(11. 1-8)

Ostensibly, the stanza is merely descriptive of a present condition which seems irremediable. Whatever love existed between the two no longer exists as mutual affection. They may re-embrace as a physical fact, but they do so as two separate persons. They are "single still." And the speaker places the blame for this condition on her lover. On the face of it, there seems little chance or hope of this condition being overcome. Too, there is little explicit indication that the speaker actively entertains such a hope. But lines 2, 3, 4, and 6 might possibly work counter to this hypothetical meaning of the stanza. The apparent flat statement of fact in the first half of the stanza could conceivably contain within it something like an "argument" based on conditional logic. The speaker has no hope of seeing her lover under the condition of her living. If she changes those conditions, i.e., dies, then she might hope "to see his face / As before." Put in more formal terms, the lines may implicitly contain the suggestion that the speaker may wish to deny the consequent by denying the antecedent—which, of course, is logically invalid. That implication is somewhat supported by the suggestion in line 6 that the speaker might, in some fashion, try to overcome this unhappy state: his love has grown chill, but "Mine may strive." Because, however, the elaboration that follows the colon of that line insists on the separation, one's initial hypothesis for the statement is probably that she means her love can strive, but it does very little good.

Stanza II begins to define the speech as an informal causal analysis of this loss of love:

> Was it something said,
>   Something done,
> Vexed him? Was it touch of hand,
>   Turn of head?
> Strange! that very way
>   Love begun:
> I as little understand
>   Love's decay.
>
> (ll. 9-16)

In setting out the general causal categories, she settles on two possibilities: something said or something done. Since these are possibilities that could have "vexed him," then we must assume that they are her "saying" and her "doing." At this point it seems that she can entertain the notion that she is somehow partly responsible for this loss of love. But as she elaborates on the possibilities, the sense of responsibility, or blame, is attenuated by her selection of detail. If it were something so slight as "touch of hand" or "turn of head," something so seemingly incidental, then it would be hard to "charge her" (or for her to charge herself) with some serious ethical breach. The second half of the stanza confirms this attenuating motif: the speaker sees such a possibility of the cause of loss as essentially mysterious, as strange as the beginning of love, possibly beyond the realm of human responsibility. Neither case is susceptible to understanding, or rather, her understanding. There is more "strange" here, though, than what the speaker explicitly cites. One wonders if it is significant that in the attenuating elaboration of lines 11 and 12 it is not speech but action that is particularized as the cause of love's decay, and that then is cited as also the initiator of love. The implication would seem to be that in the beginning of love was its ending (which would be ironic if nothing more), and that the sign of this beginning and ending was some kind of *physical* act, not speech. Equally curious, though consonant with this complex of physically tangible events, is the description of the loss of love as "love's *decay*" (my italics), a word whose usual context is some natural, physical process of deterioration.

The third stanza carries forward the causal investigation and is apparently based on the speaker's identification of the "way" of love's beginning and ending since it presents her account of love's good start:

> When I sewed or drew,
>   I recall
> How he looked as if I sung,
>   —Sweetly too.
> If I spoke a word,
>   First of all
> Up his cheek the colour sprung,
>   Then he heard.
>   (ll. 17-24)

Probably the most striking characteristic of this picture is its ingratiating "sweetness" and tenderness. The implicit sexuality is sublimated and domesticated. That she no longer experiences this loveliness is, indeed, sad and bitter. But if she is attempting to find the cause of that sad loss in the genesis of love, then this pretty picture would seem to leave us in the mystery, the "strange" that she settles on in stanza II. Why love should arise (and then be lost) is undiscovered and seemingly undiscoverable here. But perhaps the very focus of the stanza makes that discovery, and its corollary (loss), impossible at this point, since it defines the nature of not *her* love, but his. It is conceivable that, despite her rhetoric of attenuation, which this stanza tacitly carries out, the cause of "love's decay" must be sought not solely (or possibly at all) in him, but in her. The very loveliness of this stanza shifts attention away from the speaker's initial question in stanza II of her own responsibility in the affair. Her actions are not directed at him in any immediate way, as, for instance, a "touch of hand" would be. The explicit signs of love are made to reside in him, in his gentility.

There is also another, apparently minor, incommensurability between this stanza and the preceding. There, she offers two hypotheses for love's decay, saying or acting, and then settles on action: touch of hand or turn of head; and these, in turn, are cited as love's cause. With the description of love's beginning in stanza III, we see that there was, indeed, doing and saying, but neither as literally and flatly sensory as stanza II might lead us to expect. What "sensual" activity the lines describe becomes transformed; it is given more than a literal physical import. Stanza III is really somewhat remarkable for its very lack of tactile sensation; there is no "touch of hand" here. The locus of this nonliteral rendering of experience is not the speaker, but her lover who perceives act as song, a form of speech, and speech through act, "the colour *sprung*" (my italics). In these chiasmatic metamorphoses the literal act and speech become more significant, are given a kind of indeterminate "poetical" value that lifts them beyond the mundane. To be sure, the dominant effect of this presentation of her lover's metamorphosing is pathos at the recollection of what she has lost, but beneath that pretty pathos this minor contrast between the two stanzas suggests, perhaps, a contrast between the two persons, a contrast that may not work in the speaker's favor.

Stanza IV continues her delineation of love's good beginning with further description of her lover's actions and then a declaration concerning her own condition, but in language that avoids the specificity of the picture of her lover:

> Sitting by my side,
> At my feet,
> So he breathed but air I breathed,
> Satisfied!
> I, too, at love's brim
> Touched the sweet:
> I would die if death bequeathed
> Sweet to him.
>
> (ll. 25-32)

Her lover's actions in the first quatrain establish a mutuality and proximity of the two without introducing any actual "touch." As with the previous stanza the picture is fairly innocent and "idealized." Here, the lover is said to be "satisfied" in his love, not by gratification of any physical appetite, but merely by sharing the same breath as the speaker. Because this is a description of the initial stages of a love affair, leading to some crucial moment, I don't think it necessary or desirable to regard this rather ethereal picture as normative for love's full career, and thus as an implicit resolving norm for the whole poem. We know that this is what the speaker has lost; we may learn, even if she doesn't, why she lost it; but I don't think we learn by what positive means she could have kept and developed it. Thus, the strategy of the poem is essentially negation.

The second half of the stanza, the speaker's first statement about her role as lover and not just love object, ostensibly confirms the mutuality evoked by the previous descriptions, and should seal the two as a justly matched love pair. But this quatrain evokes nearly as many contrasts as similarities to the first quatrain of the stanza. In the first quatrain we find an explicit description of a lover's actions; in the second we find a very pretty metaphoric declaration, but one whose literal tenor, her actions, is suppressed. In the first quatrain the literally sensual is greatly sublimated; in the second, the metaphor is quite directly sensual. In the first quatrain, the sign of mutuality is in breath, or, it would be safe to say, in life; in the second, the claim of mutuality finds its vehicle in death. It is this last contrast that is probably most curious. To express this stage of mutual love the speaker uses the sensual metaphor of drinking some sweet liquid, or rather, being about to drink it— at "love's brim." touching the *"sweet."* The restraint of "touch" contrasts rather sharply with the extremity of declaration found in the next two lines. In these final two lines of the stanza the elaboration of the idea of mutuality repeats the quality "sweet," but this time as something offered by death, or rather, "bequeathed," a word whose usual context is jurisprudence and the disposition of property. Here, that context hardly seems relevant. But after we encounter stanzas VI and VII it may retrospectively appear quite ironically apt. At any rate, for the speaker, both death and love share this same sensual quality. Why she should thus unify these two realms, while her lover finds the unity of their love in breath, is, here, most "strange."

But, of course, the quatrain's ostensible purpose is preparation for her imperative call for speech that opens stanza V:

> "Speak, I love thee best!"
>   He exclaimed:
> "Let thy love my own foretell!"
>   I confessed:
> "Clasp my heart on thine
>   Now unblamed,
> Since upon thy soul as well
>   Hangeth mine!"
>   (11. 33-40)

After two stanzas that follow generally from the "action" motif (the action described being primarily the lover's), we now encounter a stanza that follows from the "speech" motif. And, in this rehearsal of the genesis of love, it is the climatic stanza. That action has led to this speech. Furthermore, the ostensible sense of the stanza would seem to confirm the mutuality of love tacitly declared by the preceding action, would make their "loves" mirror one another (1. 35).

This ostensible sense seems much like the psyche-epipsyche concept[4] that is often taken as the positive norm underlying a fair amount of Browning's other love poetry, but it is the contention of this essay that this poem lacks such a positive norm. If the psyche-epipsyche norm were fully embodied in this stanza, then it would offer a "definition" of love, through elaboration of a positive content, that would account for the lasting union of the two lovers, now become one, and would account for "true" love. If we saw that these two lovers presently under consideration violated this normative statement, then we would find that the speaker is unreliable for claiming that she has something that she does not have, that she falsely asserts she fits a category that she does not fit. But, the irony of this poem is not that the mutuality claimed by this stanza is later denied, that it represents some norm violated by the speaker, but that it is a quite accurate statement and prediction. What happens is that as the poem proceeds, as the "love" in this love affair advances beyond its first ethereal beginnings, it receives definition. As it is defined, through the *speaker's actions*—it is revealed as something that leads to its own decay, the condition which the speaker finds intolerable. We, then, find what "true" love is *not*, not what "true" love *is*. And this discovery is made not by reference to any positive standard, but through the revelation of the contradictions implicit in this kind of love. Even if we take true and lasting love as the standard, for this poem it remains a contentless "good." Thus, the strategy of the poem is analogous to the irony that Kierkegaard attributes to Socrates, the "infinite absolute negativity" that "negates by virtue of a higher which is not."[5] That higher may exist and may be positively defined in other Browning poems, but it does not exist as a positive norm for and *in* this *particular* poem. If one were writing as essay on Browning's theory of love in general, reference to that defined higher might be appropriate here, though only if a poem in which it occurred were juxtaposed to this one. But it is not appropriate to a discussion of the strategy of particular poems that do not contain it.

Although the speeches of stanza V seem pretty straightforward in their insistence on a mutuality of love, they are not without a certain ambiguity which works against the sense and tone of romantic, "noble" union. The woman begins with a command and a claim: "Speak, I love thee best!" On the face of it this probably means that she declares her love and preference for him above all others, and would like to hear a sincerely reciprocal speech from him. There is a certain urgency to the line which can be credited to the strength of her feeling, but which also causes some curiosity. Why is this and her next short speech an imperative, not, say, an entreaty? Impressionistic readers might wonder if there is some reason that she must, in effect, "force" the issue. That impression could have some foundation in the ambiguity of the syntax, whereby the declaration also becomes the content of the imperative. This suggests that in addition to the ostensible meaning, the line might also imply two other meanings. First, there is the possibility that the use of the imperative is to be read as evidence that she alone *asserts* the commonality of their experience on little evidence; i.e., she has misread, somehow, his tender, speechless actions of stanzas III and IV. She says she loves and now she commands him to say that he does too. The reciprocity she desires must be ordered or it would not come at all. Second, the line may be wholly imperative. "I love thee best!" is strictly the object of "speak." Under this construction of the utterance, what looks like a cry *of* love is really a cry *for* love. The second reading will probably seem less likely than the first. But it may not seem so in retrospect when we find how little this speech tells us *about* her love, and when we find how desperate the speaker is *to be* loved.

At any rate, the answer she gets is not exactly at one with her command. Nor is the answer likely to resolve any of the ambiguities of her speech. All we can really say is that it ostensibly carries out the mutuality-mirror theme: "Let thy love my own foretell!" It is nearly impossible to make any certain character inferences from the man's response. It is conceivable he does not say, "I love you," because he wishes to equivocate: she really has misread his tenderness. But it is also possible that his response means roughly what it says: "my love matches your love; I really do love you." If the line doesn't indicate anything certain about the characters themselves at this point, it does indicate a good deal about the logic of the poem. The ambiguity leaves the meaning of love in this affair indeterminate. Further, his response places the responsibility for the definition of that love on the speaker, not the lover. Her love will "foretell" or predict his love. That is, the manner and meaning of her love will define his love. The implicit future orientation of the line is no accident. Because his speech points to the future and bases his love on hers, about which we know little, love's nature is kept essentially indeterminate. This would not be the case if it were *his* love fortelling *her* love since we would infer that we had been presented the characteristics of his love in stanzas III and IV. As we discover its nature defined by her actions in the second half of the poem, we should also "understand/Love's decay."

The ostensible sense of the last quatrain of stanza V, her confession that follows his shifting of "responsibility" back to her, completes the mutuality theme of the first half of the poem. A causal reading of the lines would probably yield something like: "let's unite our hearts as our souls are united"; a causal reading, somewhat erroneously, might even make the lines a description of the merging of the two that one tends to look for in Browning's love poems. But the lines are not description. Her second speech, here, as her first, is a command: take my heart. Thus we again run into a potential, though muted, paradox of sorts—the forced gift. Too, though she uses the romantic term "heart," which usually is taken to signify some relationship beyond the mere physical and thus would make this assertion consonant with the somewhat ethereal description of the lover's behavior in stanzas III and IV, the clause that catch term is embedded in could also suggest a less idealized request. He is to "*Clasp* my heart *on* thine" (my italics). That is, the actual consequence of this command may show that "clasp" is not used metaphorically at all, but is used quite literally to mean "physically embrace me so that in the juxtaposition my heart will be *on* yours." That literal, and physically erotic, meaning is countered (disguised might be more accurate) by the etherealizing language of the rest of the stanza. "Heart" seems to retain most of its metaphoric meaning as the seat of the emotions since it is something that can be blamed or "unblamed" in the next line. One wonders, though, why that should be an issue at this point, and, too, just whose heart it is that is "Now unblamed." One's first assumption is that it is his heart that is now blameless. Thus, she might be saying something like, "it's OK to embrace me, now, because we've declared our love." But, of course, that causal condition is far from certain as we have already seen. Thus, the command "Clasp my heart" would remain largely a physically erotic, willful command. Syntactically, the modification could apply to her heart (though unwittingly so) and be possibly predictive: she is "Now unblamed," but may not be in the future. Finally, this love affair is made a matter of the soul. The speaker issues her command/offer of her heart "Since upon thy soul as well/Hangeth mine." What this declaration means at this point seems pretty open. Does it mean that she *claims* her soul is somehow united with his; if so, the relationship of soul and soul is "spatially" curious to say the least since hers hangs upon his, evoking a sense of the external and perhaps parasitical. Or, does it mean that she claims that the *condition* of her soul *depends* on his, which in turn is the reason he ought to accept, or rather, clasp her heart. If so, there is a kind of circularity here in the relation of love and souls that keeps coming back to the speaker as its ultimate cause. To anticipate for clarification, her love will define his love; his love, as defined by hers, apparently will be taken as an index of his soul; his soul somehow defines, sets, causes the condition of her soul. The process begins and ends with her.

Following the climactic confession that marks the crisis of the genesis of love, the speaker returns, in stanza VI, to speculation on the decay of love, and begins to draw inferences apparently from the evidence that just has been laid before herself and us. In so doing, she also initiates the second phase of a structural cycle in which the middle eight stanzas form two parallel series of four stanzas each. (The first and last stanzas of the poem act as "present tense" frames for the argument.) Stanzas II and VI contain rhetorical questions that set the terms of speculation on responsibility. The next two stanzas in each series (III-IV and VII-VIII) describe *action* of the two lovers, in series A, primarily his action at the beginning of love, in series B, primarily her action during the career of love. The final stanza in each series presents *speech,* in series A, primarily reported speech, in series B, his hypothetical speech, a speech invented by her. As we shall see, the implicit contrast in this parallelism, the order provided by the poet, will work to her disadvantage as she continues to attempt a rhetoric of attenuation.

Stanza VI begins with a reiteration of the speech-action motives, again with a progressive narrowing to action as the locus of most concern:

> Was it wrong to own,
> > Being truth?
> Why should all the giving prove
> > His alone?
> I had wealth and ease,
> > Beauty, youth:
> Since my lover gave me love,
> > I gave these.

> (ll. 41-48)

The first half of the stanza apparently points back to the preceding stanza and refers to the "declaration" that opens that stanza and the imperative gift of her heart. Her question is, then, whether that speech (an emphasis that, at least momentarily, shifts attention from *action* as cause) and offer were somehow the cause of her present unhappiness, cause of the decay of love. Since both speech and gift were made by her, if the answer to her first question were yes, then she would be responsible for her love's demise. The grounds of her fault would be social decorum in this formulation, thus shifting attention from the more substantive issue of what she offered. Since her analysis of the fault matches the more obvious suspicions raised by stanza V (that she forced matters), she here meets those suspicions head on. She also makes a fairly effective effort of allaying them by using the rhetorical question. Since that device functions to enlist the audience in the services of the speaker's argument, we are rhetorically seduced into saying she really did no wrong.[6] Too, the content of this quatrain is given, by the speaker, the salutary qualities of "truth" and "reciprocal gift." Since all we know of that "truth" and "reciprocal gift" is that her "love" and "heart" are concerned, and since we must assume at this point that these latter terms have the favorable connotations we usually associate with romantic poems, we have no grounds for "answering" the question in any other way than to attenuate or even negate the speaker's responsibility in this mysterious demise of love. Her strategy here thus echoes that of stanza II. The second half of the stanza, though, should begin to work clearly against her attempts at attenuation, and should thus begin to confirm the suspicions aroused by the counterpointing tension of the first half of the poem. "Heart" and "love" move away from the idealizing and ethereal context of stanzas III, IV, and apparently, V, to a quite physical context. To match the gift of her lover's love, she presents "wealth and ease,/Beauty, youth." If love for her is equivalent to and defined by these mutable qualities, then we may begin to see why, indeed, it can "decay." With this recognition, one might also re-examine the potentially ambiguous language that opened the stanza to see if the speaker's linguistic tactics work against her rhetorical strategy. In the first line of the stanza the speaker uses the term "to own." Obviously, she means it in the sense of "to acknowledge" or "admit" or "confess." But it may also indicate ownership or possession. Hence, there may exist here something like a displaced oxymoron whereby the offer of a gift is also, or actually, a form of possession. Since the dominant member of the pair, possessor and possessed, is the possessor, this paradox would seem to be yet another pointer marking the speaker as the dominant character in this affair, the one who has chief responsibility for it. Certain ambiguities of the third and fourth lines of stanza VI also seem to work counter to her purposes. Rather than using the relatively neutral existential verb, "be," the speaker uses "prove." With the word "prove" notions of testing and trying are introduced into the line and poem. Hence, there exists the implication that the giving will be a test of something of hers: her "truth," her "gift," her "love," and perhaps her "self."

Similar ambiguities are manifested in stanza VII:

> That was all I meant,
> —To be just
> And the passion I had raised,
> To content.
> Since he chose to change
> Gold for dust,
> If I gave him what he praised
> Was it strange?
>
> (11. 49-56)

The ostensible function of the first quatrain is to offer a self-defense based on the notion of justice: all she meant to do was behave justly; hence, how can she be blamed? But because the key conceptual term of the first two lines is "meant" the stanza also operates as implicit self-definition by the speaker. Thus, if we take her syntax at its "word," *all she* meant was the antecedent of "that": wealth, beauty, youth and ease. In this counterpointed sense of the stanza, then, "to be just" yields the sense of "to be *exact.*" The speaker is wholly and exactly bound by the mutable. The counterpointed sense of the next two lines is less complex, since, as the lines stand, the speaker seems to admit some responsibility for the course of the love affair: she raised the passion. Yet, since this is in the context of a defense on the basis of justice, a category which, if she fit it, would attenuate her *personal* responsibility and error, one suspects that she means here not a willful engendering of passion, but a kind of inevitable consequence of her being her, something for which she is *not* responsible. It is merely her lover's response to her. It is something on his head. But, since in the parallel stanzas of series A her lover's response is characterized by sublimated passion, not completely erotic or sensual, and since her use of the word "passion" follows her narrative of the presentation of her gift (stanzas V and VI), her general pose of innocence seems quite suspect. In stanza IV he was "satisfied" by breathing the air she breathed; now the speaker says it was passion she had raised to content in their year together. In a way more telling than she seems to wish to admit, it is a passion that she truly has "raised."

The effort to shift responsibility for their affair *wholly* to him is made quite explicit in the second quatrain of the stanza. (That he probably also has, or may have, a blameworthy heart does not negate her blame; thus the ambiguity of modification in line 38 is borne out by these events.) In lines 52-54, her very effort to shift the "blame" also contrapuntally continues the definition of her love as part of the mutable world and as ultimately worthless. She says that he has chosen to change "Gold for dust." Obviously, her intent is to impeach his judgement, but in so doing she also impeaches her own value. Since the general theme of the last three stanzas has been reciprocal giving and receiving of something, the way seems to be prepared for generating a pun on "change/Gold." That is, "change" also carries a sense of commercial transaction (a concept made explicit in the next stanza) in which something is exchanged for something else. Here, then, the exchange is "Gold for dust." He offers gold, he receives dust; in the preceding stanza he offers love, he receives from her wealth and ease, beauty and youth. The counterpointed sense of the poem more and more seems to make the locus of love's decay primarily in her, not in him. This, of course, does not make him an injured innocent. Her love does ironically "fortell" his; but the process begins with her. The stanza concludes with another rhetorical question by means of which the speaker again attempts to have her audience make her argument for her. In this instance, one is to agree that the speaker acted in no unique manner. She did what any other young lady would have done and, in effect, had little choice to do otherwise. Since the counterpointed meaning of the poem to this point tacitly challenges her assumption of innocence, the audience might actually find the strangeness in the fact that the speaker finds her behavior in the affair not strange at all. Conversely, the thing that she finds non-mysterious might, in fact, unravel the mystery. The decay of love is quite likely implicit in her "non-strange" gift.

Despite the causal constructions of the last several stanzas (a probable syntactic irony in itself), the speaker is apparently no nearer a recognition of the reason for love's decay than she was at the beginning of the poem. With stanza VIII she abandons her specific causal analysis and begins to speculate on ways to rekindle love, to "strive," as stanza I prefigured, to overcome the intolerable condition of re-embracing "single still":

> Would he loved me yet,
>   On and on,
> While I found some way undreamed
>   —Paid my debt!
> Gave more life and more,
>   Till, all gone,
> He should smile "She never seemed ·
>   Mine before."

(ll. 57-64)

In the first quatrain of the stanza the speaker voices her desire to have her
lover's love, "On and on," to overcome its end, and she once again places
this *gain* in terms of a transaction whereby she gives something for what she
will get. His love for her would put her in "debt," a term that confirms the
legal-commercial implications of earlier terms. As ironic as the term itself is,
the major irony is the movement of the stanza itself between the two
quatrains. That is, line 59, "While I found some way undreamed," sets up
the expectation that the speaker will attempt to answer the wished for love
in some way hitherto unconsidered by her. Since what she gave before was
mutable and (as a consequence) the love was mutable, we might reasonably
expect this new gift to transcend the limitation of mutability. But with the
second quatrain comes the discovery that no such transcendence has
occurred. Rather, the mutable gift motif has been carried to its logical
extreme: she will give him all her life, so that she ends up giving him her
death. She would give "more life" (again her offer avoids the exact matching
of his, i.e., "love") and still "more,/Till, all gone,/He should smile 'She never
seemed/Mine before'." In an echo of her declaration of stanza IV (when she
had been *sharing breath* with him), she now wills her own death to *have* his
love. She will do this in order that he may say she never seemed his before,
though what he has, of course, is a corpse. From the desire for love as union
(stanza V), we have come to love as the final separation: he loving and she
dead. Her logic, whose validity is subject to the critique outlined for stanza
I, demands that in order to overcome love's decay she must will her own.
With a vengeance, death bequeaths his sweet to him.

That the means that *she* chooses provides an essentially illusory overcoming of singleness and decay of love is fairly clear from the speech she
invents for her lover in stanza IX, a speech that is ironically contrasted to
its parallel in stanza V where the man speaks a correspondence and equivalence of their loves:

> "What, she felt the while,
>   Must I think?
> Love's so different with us men!"
>   He should smile:
> "Dying for my sake—
>   White and pink!
> Can't we touch these bubbles then
>   But they break?"
>   (11. 65-72)

The scene that she creates with this invented speech is apparently that of her lover musing over her dead body. But rather than giving him lines that express his great personal loss, the speaker invents a speech that emphasizes their very lack of union. The speech is not without a certain ambiguity, but in this case the ambiguities lead to the same conclusion. Her attempt to win his love has not been successful. What she offers does not produce what she desires. The first reading of lines 65-67 would express this reversal since they would be taken as meaning that the man was surprised that she felt at all since he did not. The second reading also emphasizes the disunity between the two. The separation under this construction is first implied in the initial two lines of the stanza when the man is supposed to say that her feelings were a mystery to him (an observation that may not be wholly non-ironic), and made to declare that the love in the two is not at all alike. The scenario invented by the speaker of the poem to *overcome* their singleness, their separateness, ends up confirming it. In his final attributed speech of the stanza (its second quatrain) the man also defeats the speaker's intent in dying for him. Rather than seeing it as a gift to pay the debt of love, he seems to regard it as a pretty piece of flattery. For him, she has been a delicate toy, a "bubble," as though an effervescence at "love's brim," that breaks at a mere touch.

Because the hypothetical speech attributed to the man in this last stanza portrays him as a fairly callous and insensitive character who can equate the speaker's death with the breaking of a bubble, the stanza also functions as part of the speaker's attenuating rhetoric. It is the man in the case who is made the "monster" and who, because of his insensitivity and (perhaps) sensuality, is made the root cause of "love's decay." But this attenuation is also illusory since it is based on a scenario of the speaker's own invention. What she gets, by her own logic, follows from the kind of gift she offers. It is *her* plan that leads to this hypothetical conclusion. She offers the mutable and she gets the mutable. In that way the man's actual statement of stanza V, that her love foretells his love, is more accurate than the hypothetical statement of stanza IX. Since she offers that which passes away (historically, the wealth, ease, beauty, youth, and passion of the actual affair; hypothetically, the "life" of this scenario), she gets from him the equivalent.

The last stanza of the poem, X, returns the action to the present with an address to her lover followed by an aside to herself:

> Dear, the pang is brief,
>> Do thy part,
> Have thy pleasure! How perplexed

Grows belief!
Well, this cold clay clod
Was man's heart:
Crumble it, and what comes next?
Is it God?   (ll. 73-80)

The tension between her rhetoric of attenuation and the irony of her causing her own failure is maintained in the first three lines. After having rehearsed in the middle stanzas her inability to overcome the singleness, the loss of love, and having blamed that failure on him, her speech in the initial lines of this stanza voices that offer once again, and in such a manner as to *accuse* him of something. There seems to be more than just a touch of the self-willed martyr in those lines: the long-suffering one willing to undergo one more brief "pang" while suffering him to have his inevitable pleasure. Yet, in so doing (as the last quatrain implies) she is no nearer rekindling love. The offer itself, as the middle eight stanzas have shown, defeats her fundamental wish.

The last portion of that stanza—from "How perplexed" on—apparently is an aside to herself. The general theme of this last portion is her confusion of belief. Though the logical and narrative connections of this last portion are not very explicit, the speaker seems to be expressing her sense of betrayal, and her confusion of belief in the fact of that betrayal. Attempts at greater specificity are difficult primarily because of the ambiguity of the phrase "man's heart." Does she mean it in the sense of "the heart in a man," i.e., his heart? Or does she mean it in the sense of "heart that belonged to a man," i.e., her heart? If she means the latter, then we would probably construe the final quatrain as meaning something like: "I gave my heart to him and now it is a cold clod. When it is crumbled (apparently by the man as he has his pleasure), I will die and face God." This gives the poem a nicely pathetic ending. But it also gives the poem an ending that is empty of the irony we have found all through the rest of the piece. If she means the former, then we could construe that quatrain as meaning something like: "His heart is a cold clod now, and has thus betrayed my belief in him. Crumble it and what else will crumble? Is it God? Can I believe in Him?" This reading has the advantage of emphasizing the issue of faith in a broader sense, which is consistent with her earlier insistence (stanza V) that the condition of her soul depended on his heart. But it has three disadvantages: 1. it eliminates her death as the climax of the poem; 2. it turns on a doubtful linguistic equivalence of "Crumble" and "comes" in line 79; and 3. it, too, is not very ironic.

I think we can preserve the best of these two constructions, quite legitimately, if we do *not* try to resolve the ambiguity of "man's heart." We can preserve both the death and the doubt. In this construction, the speaker is, in effect, blaming the presence of a "cold clay clod" in herself on the "cold clay clod" in her lover. His heart is cold (cf. 1.5) because it has betrayed her, and her heart, which she had given him (in stanza V) is cold because it has been betrayed. Thus, the ambiguity ironically enacts a union of their hearts, not the kind she desired, yet a union nonetheless. But the irony cuts deeper than this. For, as we have already seen, the condition of his heart is a consequence of *her* mode of love and her heart. Thus, the ultimate cause of her heart being turned to "clay" is herself. In this way, the "clay" of this stanza echoes the "dust" of her gift in stanza VII: both terms define her. When this "clay" of her heart crumbles to the "dust" from which it came, it will be a self-made faithless heart that dies. Hence, her last two questions this time are not rhetorical. At death God will come next, but because of her self-induced perplexity of belief, that "fact" is here expressed as a doubting question. She has thus put her soul in mortal danger, the mortal danger of despairing doubt and nascent disbelief. With this final turn in the poem, her drama of *self*-destruction rises from simply romantic pathos to something very like moral tragedy.

END NOTES

[1]See A. R. Thompson, *The Dry Mock* (Berkeley: Univ. of California Press, 1948); Garnett Sedgwick, *Of Irony* (Toronto: Univ. of Toronto Press, 1935); Kenneth Burke, *A Grammar of Motives* (New York: Prentice Hall, 1945); Bert O. States, *Irony and Drama* (Ithaca: Cornell Univ. Press, 1971); Wayne Booth, *The Rhetoric of Fiction* (Chicago: Univ. of Chicago Press, 1961), and *A Rhetoric of Irony* (Chicago: Univ. of Chicago Press, 1974). Though in his recent book Booth seems to have moderated some of his theoretical positions on the impossibility of true negative irony, his long discussion of Beckett's nihilism (pp. 257-67) implies that he believes that under the negativism there "really" is an affirmative-positive norm.

[2]tr. Lee M. Capel (Bloomington, Indiana: Indiana Univ. Press, 1968), pp. 278-79.

[3]For a more extensive discussion of this issue see Robert J. Cornet, "The Structures of Unreality in Browning's *Men and Women*," diss. Pennsylvania State University, 1972, pp. 58-95.

[4]The psyche-epipsyche idea is probably derived from Plato's *Symposium*. It is a more pleasant version of Aristophanes' contention that proper lovers are two halves of a former whole whose happiness is determined by recovering that particular whole.

[5]Kierkegaard, p. 278.

[6]The use of "we" may be somewhat misleading. Her argument is directed at herself. But the rhetoric that disguises her unreliability from herself can also disguise it from her audience.

"A Death in the Desert": The Gospel According to Robert Browning

Donna G. Fricke

A great deal of scholarship has been devoted to redesigning Robert Browning's theology using such key poems as *Christmas-Eve* and *Easter-Day*, "Bishop Blougram's Apology," "Saul," "Karshish," "Cleon," *The Ring and the Book*, "A Death in the Desert," and numerous others. The scholarly task is certainly warranted, for there is little doubt that both Robert and Elizabeth Barrett Browning were more than passively interested in religion. Both poets frequently discussed religion in letters,[1] and both poets wrote numerous poems treating of various themes in religion.

The particular poem in question in this paper, "A Death in the Desert," is of central importance to scholars because Browning is answering certain nineteenth-century Higher Critics and clarifying his own position in contemporary biblical controversies. It seems, however, that the consensus judgment on the poem is "Browning's skill was only that of a brilliant amateur."[2] Some helpful scholarship to bring the reader to date on this consensus includes Mrs. M. G. Glazebrook's early and somewhat dated essay (1895), "A Death in the Desert" (Berdoe's *Browning Studies*, pp. 225-36) which contends that his poem is a rebuttal of the nineteenth-century Higher Critics such as Strauss, Baur, and Renan. Browning is said to be arguing against the importance of original events and for the central importance of faith.

Perhaps the most scholarly study on the subject is William O. Raymond's "Browning and Higher Criticism," (*PMLA*, 44 [1929], 590-621) in which "A Death in the Desert" is deemed Browning's "most elaborate and closely reasoned apologia for Christianity . . . " (603). DeVane (*Browning Handbook*, p. 264) writes of "A Death in the Desert" that "A number of critics at the time noticed that Browning was attempting to reply to Strauss and Renan in his poem . . . " and he concludes that C. H. Herford "has given the best judgment upon the poem" (quoted in part above, p. 264). Herford's judgment:

> To attack Strauss through the mouth of the dying apostle was
> a smart pamphleteering device; but it gave his otherwise noble
> verse a disagreeable twang of theological disputation, and did

no manner of harm to Strauss, who had to be met on other
ground and with other weapons,—the weapons of history and
comparative religion—in which Browning's skill was only that
of a brilliant amateur.

And finally, one should consult Boyd Litzinger's *Time's Revenge: Browning's Reputation as a Thinker: 1889-1962* (Knoxville: Univ. of Tennessee Press, 1964) for a thorough examination of Browning's alternating favor and disfavor as a religious thinker. Mr. Litzinger's conclusion may exemplify the enigma of scholarship on Browning's importance as a religious thinker: "The final evaluation of Browning's stature as a thinker is yet to be done" (p. 167). Now, over a decade and many Browning books later, Litzinger's pronouncement still holds true.

I trust that the modern Browning scholar will not accept Herford as the best judgment of the poem, for one glaring omission remains: a study of the poem qua poem. And I hope that modern scholars will accept Mr. Litzinger's challenge. Doubtlessly the poem has been thoroughly worked for meaning, but the conclusions of this method leave a great deal to be desired, for Browning's meaning in "A Death in the Desert" is interwoven with form and internal design. He is, on the contrary, meeting the Higher Critics on their own ground by using the "weapons of history and comparative religion," and it will be the purpose of this paper to demonstrate his careful mind, his achievement as a thinker, and the revelation of the basis of his own theology.

It is not necessary to determine whether Browning is answering Strauss's *Das Leben Jesu* (1835) or Renan's *La Vie de Jesus* (1863) or the entire school of Higher Criticism. It is known that he was thoroughly conversant on the subject of Higher Criticism and that he had read the theologians involved in the movement.[3] He was more than a theological Fellow Traveler, although he did not align himself or limit himself to one particular theology exclusively. One might conclude that he was definitely a Protestant, however, and closest in his own theology to the Presbyterians and Congregationalists. That is, the theological focus is emphatically Christocentric with structural dependence on the Doctrine of Love and the central role of the Scriptures. Compare Calvin:

> Just as old or bleary-eyed men and those with weak vision,
> if you thrust before them a most beautiful volume, even if
> they recognize it to be some sort of writing, yet can scarcely
> construe two words, but with the aid of spectacles will begin

to read distinctly; so Scripture, gathering up the otherwise confused knowledge of God in our minds, having dispersed our dullness, clearly shows us the true God.

(Institutes I, 6, i.)

I am not asserting that Browning was a strict Calvinist, only that he seems to be very familiar with Calvin's theological methodology and many of his literary analogies. He argues with many of Calvin's methods, such as the above optical analogy, and his final emphasis is also Calvin's; after examining the entire shell of theology, the final focus is on the core which is faith.

Of course there can be no conclusion to an argument on theology when the final focus is one of faith, for faith cannot be argued rationally. But Browning is not arguing faith in "A Death in the Desert," although it is a central theme in the poem as shall be demonstrated. Rather, he is recreating poetically the very process of Higher Criticism and demonstrating that Higher Criticism can be used by the traditional theologian as well as by the new theologian. "A Death in the Desert," is, then, more than the admirable defeat of a "brilliant amateur." The process of the poem and its conclusions neutralize the conclusions of certain Higher Critics such as Renan and Strauss by imitating their methodology. Browning too might have historical doubts about certain "facts," but he demonstrates that there is one seed of theology which is timeless and indestructible and that is the power of a faith in the Docrtine of Love which he personally finds in belief in God in Christ.

It is not my purpose to demonstrate that Browning "wins" the hypothetical argument with the conclusions of the Higher Critics, nor that his personal, and note that I say "personal," belief or faith is the final answer to all theological debates. I only wish to demonstrate that Browning has met the Higher Critics on their own ground and has used effectively their own weapons against them. He certainly neutralizes many of their theses, however, and proves himself an able and perceptive theological thinker and an admirable poet of ideas in "A Death in the Desert."

Basically, the focus of the hypothetical argument in the poem involves methods of biblical criticism. The term "criticism" as used here comes from the Greek *kritikos* meaning "literary expert," "able to judge" or "critical." Textual Criticism or Lower Criticism as it became known in the nineteenth century involved the collection and study of ancient manuscripts in order to determine, as closely as possible, the original texts of biblical writings. This process grew as the Church grew and can be said to have its beginning in the second century when the first arguments began as to which texts were authentic, which were forged, which were really divinely inspired, and which were figments of someone's over-active imagination.

The Higher Criticism movement of the nineteenth century went a step beyond Lower Criticism. These new critics wanted to reach conclusions, make judgments on the findings of Lower Criticism. From this grew such movements as the quest for the historical Jesus and the Johnnean controversy. That is, what was the real Jesus-the-man like; was he really divine; did his apostle John write the Fourth Gospel; if so, why was its content so different from the other synoptic gospels; did the same man write The Revelation? ad infinitum.

Some of the conclusions drawn by such Higher Critics as Strauss and Renan were that Jesus was more historical myth than historical fact and that the Fourth Gospel, if written at all by John, was rewritten by men after John who filled it with their own imagination and Greek philosophy. Renan went even further in his *L'Eglise* (1879) to suggest that the Fourth Gospel may have been written by Cerinthus, a Gnostic, and a central figure in Browning's poem. This view was first held by second-century Alogi.

The basic argument is actually far more complex than this brief synopsis indicates, but a demonstration through the poem may further clarify the debate and enlighten the reader about Browning's obviously thorough knowledge of the theological controversy.

"A Death in the Desert" may be divided into three main sections which do not run in linear sequence. The first section consists of three bracketed groups which represent commentary and explanation by the present owner of the Greek parchment supposed of Pamphylax the Antiochene: the first group, 11. 1-12, is a bibliographic description of the roll; the second group, 11. 82-104, is the paraphrase of a gloss on the parchment roll by a former reader, Theotypas; and the third group, 11. 665-88, is a directly quoted gloss by a reader of the parchment who had also read Cerinthus (a Gnostic heretic and supposedly a contemporary of John). The second section of the poem, 11. 13-70, 643-64, is the frame for the third section of the poem; it is the commentary and setting-of-the-scene for John's dramatic monologue by the supposed Pamphylax the Antiochene as told to Phoebas. And the third section of the poem is John's self-sufficient dramatic monologue in a cave in the desert near Ephesus just before his death, 11. 71-642.

Each of the three sections is absolutely essential to the total unity and purpose of the poem. This will be demonstrated as each section is viewed in explicative order, but first, a brief summary. The first section (written by the present owner of the roll) describes in bibliographic detail an ancient manuscript. It includes marginal glosses which are frequently found on manuscripts and which are often invaluable to the biblical historian as well as annoying, for they were often transcribed into the original text by later automaton-type scribes. It represents one time-sequence which is apparently pre-Constantine (before 306) because the writer still fears persecution. And, finally, it offers Browning as Poet an opportunity in the description of the Cerinthus-read gloss to make a judgment based on faith against conclusions of the Higher Critics.

The second section (that of the supposed manuscript of Pamphylax) describes the hypothetical circumstances of John's dramatic monologue and uses the same method of historical reconstruction that Renan uses in composing his *The Life of Jesus.* That is, he takes a particular historical tradition (that John lived to at least 100 A.D. and died in a cave near Ephesus), uses part of John's gospels for validity, and a contemporary environmental description of Asia Minor and reconstructs a final chapter in *The Life of John.* This section also presents the opportunity to dramatize the tradition of relating orally, depending on someone else to write about the event.

The third section, John's monologue, offers the poet a means for theorizing about John just as the Higher Critics theorized about him. It enables Browning to bridge time by demonstrating that John's contemporaries Cerinthus and the Ebionites were hypothesizing about the Christ's humanity just as were his nineteenth-century contemporaries, and that the answer to charges then as now was one of the power of the will to have faith in the Doctrine of Love through the belief in God in Christ. Critical comments on the poem itself expand this outline.

The first paragraph of the poem (the owner's bibliographic description of the parchment roll) establishes Browning's knowledge of biblical scholarship. Biblical palaeography was getting its start as a serious science in the nineteenth century, and many important discoveries were made during Browning's lifetime, although the most important work in the field is certainly twentieth-century (the 1931 Beatty discovery of papyri in Egypt and the 1945 discovery of the Essene library, miscalled "Dead Sea Scrolls"). But note Browning's apparent knowledge of the young science and biblical geography in the first paragraph alone. Parchment did not replace papyrus as a common writing material until the fourth century A.D. (this manuscript must have been written before 300) except in certain sections of Asia Minor where it was used as early as the second century in Pergamum (now Bergama).[4] Browning might have the reader assume that Phoebas or some scribe wrote down Pamphylax's story for him in Greek and as was customary "numbered" the columns with the Greek alphabet so that later scribes could follow easily the numerical order (from *Epsilon* to *Mu*). The reader is told, then, by the paleographer that this is a partial manuscript obtained through inheritance, and that it is preserved in a family chest whose epithet is the "Chosen Chest" (perhaps a chest which contained, in the Jewish custom, well-protected religious relics and was passed from generation to generation in the leadership of a family or tribe). He learns that the chest is lettered *Xi* (for Xanthus, the wife's uncle), *Mu,* and *Epsilon (ME)* for the present owner who is afraid to write his name and identify himself with the contents of the chest because of Christian persecution. Finally, note the geography of the poem as presented in the first paragraph. (One should consult a second century A.D. reconstructed map of the area.) The action of the parchment takes place near Ephesus, was probably written in or near Pergamum where parchment was used this early, and was related by a supposed Pamphylax the Antiochene, perhaps a pseudonym for someone from Antioch in nearby Pamphylia. Browning obviously had studied a map of second-century Asia Minor, and his ambiguities of location are probably intentional. Entire tribes and border designations were in a state of flux and fluidity.

In the next seven paragraphs of the poem Browning presents the first commentary by Pamphylax. The scene is set in the midmost grotto of a cave in a desert near Ephesus where John is dying on a camel-skin bed. Five people are present: Pamphylax, Xanthus, Valens, the Boy, and a Bactrian convert. All of the characters are probably Browning's creation, although there was a Valens who became a presbyter at Phillipi at the beginning of the second century. Most important, however, they represent ranges in age, geographical backgrounds, literacy, and points of view. For example, the focus of the action is the attempt to revive John. The Bactrian ("but a wild childish man, / And could not write nor speak, but only loved" 11. 649-50) did all that he could. At his own request he stood watch and "cried his cry / Like the lone desert-bird that wears the ruff, / As signal we were safe, from time to time," 11. 68-70. Pamphylax suggests wetting John's lips with wine; Valens tries some smelling-salts of perfume from a broken ball of nard; Xanthus says a prayer. But, the only method that works is the "inspired" Boy's who,

> . . . sprang up from his knees, and ran,
> Stung by the splendor of a sudden thought,
> And fetched the seventh plate of graven lead
> Out of the secret chamber, found a place,
> Pressing with finger on the deeper dints,

And spoke, as 'twere his mouth proclaiming first,
"I am the Resurrection and the Life."

(ll. 64-70)

Here certainly the structure of the poem itself hints at the power of the inspired written word on both the reader and the listener, for John "opened his eyes wide at once." Later in John's dramatic monologue this theme is repeatedly emphasized. Browning's achievement here as poet is that he does not need to state dogmatically this theme; rather, he can demonstrate through the Boy and through John.

Before commenting on John's dramatic monologue, a cursory remark about the interrupting bracketed glossa of Theotypas paraphrased by *ME* is in order. Perhaps Browning's structural purpose is two-fold here. He may be merely reconstructing an ancient manuscript. But he may also be demonstrating the development of biblical commentary and history which began in the second century with such men as Papias, Hippolytus of Rome, and Origen. Some early commentaries certainly began as marginalia, and the early commentaries are both the modern biblical historians' source of information and the basis of theological development.

John's dramatic monologue is, in itself, a complex study which deserves more careful explication and scholarship than it receives in this paper. Appreciation presupposes some research, and to begin with the reader should have a fresh knowledge of Renan's introduction to *The Life of Jesus* before closely examining the monologue, for Browning must be structuring this section on the knowledge of Renan's portrait of John.[5] For example:

Far removed from the simple, disinterested, impersonal tone of the synoptics, the Gospel of John shows incessantly the pre-occupation of the apologist—the mental reservation of the sectarian, the desire to prove a thesis, and to convince adversaries.

(p. 44)

This by no means implies that there are not in the discourses of John some admirable gleams, some traits which truly come from Jesus. But the mystic tone of these discourses does not correspond at all to the character of the eloquence of Jesus, such as we picture it according to the synoptics. A new spirit has breathed; Gnosticism has already commenced; the Galilean

era of the kingdom of God is finished; the hope of the near
advent of Christ is more distant; we enter on the barrenness of
metaphysics, into the darkness of abstract dogma.

(pp. 44-45)

The monologue seems to be addressing Renan's charges in many instances.
And Browning himself is responding and agreeing in part with Renan's
method. Imagine the reaction of the author of *The Ring and the Book* when
he read these lines by Renan on a theory of truth.

In attributing these new ideas to Jesus, he [John] only followed a very natural tendency. Our remembrances are transformed with our circumstances; the ideal of a person that we
have known changes as we change. Considering Jesus as the
incarnation of truth, John could not fail to attribute to him
that which he had come to consider as truth.

(p. 45)

Browning's John is a very carefully constructed John; he is faithful to his
own gospels, and he answers nineteenth-century Higher Critics. Sometimes he
is the "historical" John paraphrasing his own biblical verses. For example
(11. 158-59), Browning's John warns of the Antichrists. In his letter to the
church of Ephesus John of The Revelation writes, "I know your works, your
toil and your patient endurance, and how you cannot bear evil men but have
tested those who call themselves apostles but are not, and found them to be
false" (Rev. 2:2).

Sometimes he is Calvin's John who would have man use the optic glass
or spectacles to aid him in his myopia or hyperopia. And what he sees after
his vision is corrected is "plain historic fact" and that is the Life and Death of
the Christ. In life is the opportunity to learn love; if it is not learned, there is
eternal death (11. 220 ff.). And man's only hope to learn Love is through
his proper vision of and faith in the Life and Death of the Christ.

And sometimes he is Browning's John who finds the myth of Aeschylus exemplary. The myth referred to here (11. 284 ff.) is the Prometheus
myth of Aeschylus' *Prometheus Bound*. Elizabeth Barrett Browning translated the play from the Greek and published it in 1833, and Browning uses
the myth again later in the "With Bernard de Mandeville" (c. 1885) section of
Parleyings with Certain People of Importance. William O. Raymond suggests
that "The Myth of Prometheus" is used by Browning as "a symbol of Christ's

revelation of God to man" (p. 618). Browning's John foreshadows Buber's *I and Thou,* for the relationship of man to God is stressed as a personal relationship. Browning consistently analogizes the success in human love with God's love for man and man's relation with God. John says: "Such ever was love's way: to rise, it stoops" (1. 134). To begin to understand God's love, man must first comprehend and believe in human love.

Throughout his monologue John echoes his biblical self and answers the Higher Critics. He explains why he seems sectarian, why he is so preoccupied with proving a thesis, and why he must convince adversaries. He is old, the last eye-witness of Jesus, and he is living in the end of the first century, Christ's century, in which one might expect strength in the new faith. But he already sees doubts and adversaries, Cerinthus and the Ebionites, and he is concerned with how men of the future will be convinced when contemporaries who can cross-examine eyewitnesses are still skeptical.

John explains that the issue to be examined, the fact, the truth, the object under the optic lens now is far more complex than the fire that Prometheus brought to the world. The world could judge the value of Prometheus' gift— fire was obviously a benefit, a good truth. But how can one grasp love as a fact, examine the Spirit that carries the Power of Love over man's spirit to unblind him (11. 223-25) under an optic lens?

He tells why his gospel differs from the three synoptics and what his purpose was: "Whereon I stated much of the Lord's life / Forgotten or mis-delivered, and let it work" (11. 331-32). Then John speaks in Calvin's mode about the importance of using what is left (after the Fall) of God's gift of faith:

> I say, the acknowledgement of God in Christ
> Accepted by thy reason, solves for thee
> All questions in the earth and out of it,
> And has so far advanced thee to be wise.
> Wouldst thou unprove this to re-prove the proved?
> In life's mere minute, with power to use that proof,
> Leave knowledge and revert to how it sprung?
> Thou hast it; use it and forthwith, or die!
>
> (11. 474-81)

The theology of this passage can be glossed traditionally. Every man is given the seed of the power of Love which was activated through Christ. To deny the seed or to refuse to cultivate it means death. The growing-season for the seed is short and difficult; there is not time to dissect or trace the genus.

The rest of John's monologue is filled with equally well-informed theological apologies, and his defense is constructed with as much careful research and logical hypotheses as Renan's *The Life of Jesus.* Browning has already bettered the Higher Critics on their own ground, but he continues.

In Pamphylax's concluding remarks and explanation of his oral gift of the event to Phoebas he clarifies two of Browning's central themes. The five men present at John's monologue are mentioned as dispersing after the burial of John; all are accounted for one way or the other except one. The reader does not know what happens to the Boy or his point of view, inspiration. Pamphylax alone is left to communicate the event: Xanthus has been martyred, Valens has disappeared, the Bactrian could not speak or write. The Boy? Who would believe inspiration? Browning's point is well-taken. The event *must* be related for several reasons: to substantiate historically the death of John, to clarify his gospel and remove error from the natural unreliability of the oral tradition, and to explain the obliquity of his revelation. The modern reader knows that if the story of Pamphylax were extant the Higher Critics would solve the Johnnean controversy. Again, Browning's point is well-taken. The ancient documents available to nineteenth century biblical scholars often came by fortune and chance. To speculate about lost manuscripts is no basis for scholarly conclusions because the side of tradition can argue with the same weapons.

The concluding gloss of the poem summarizes Browning's central theme of the Power of Love through God in Christ. Cerinthus, as mentioned before, was a Gnostic heretic who denied the doctrine of the incarnation. Irenaeus, one of the earliest biblical commentators, records this legend concerning John and Cerinthus in this treatise *Against Heresies:*

> There are those who have heard him tell how when John the
> disciple of the Lord went to bathe at Ephesus, and saw
> Cerinthus inside, he rushed out of the bath without washing,
> but crying out, 'let us escape, lest the bath should fall while
> Cerinthus the enemy of the truth is in it'.[6]

So, it is Cerinthus who is lost, for by denying the divinity of Jesus he denies the Power of Love, Christ's gift. And by concerning himself with the truth of fact, he loses the divine Truth.

As in *The Ring and the Book* Browning is treating in "A Death in the Desert" the themes of love and truth from various complex points of view.

He meets the Higher Critics on their own ground certainly. He is obviously more than an amateur when he displays a sound knowledge of paleography, second-century geography, Reformation theology, the biblical texts themselves, the work of the Higher Critics, and the very sources used by these scholars. For example, in his letter to Isa Blagden right after reading Renan's *The Life of Jesus,* he criticizes Renan as a fellow biblical scholar who has traveled the same road of research: "His argument against the genuineness of Matthew—from the reference to what Papias says of the [logos] —is altogether too gross a blunder to be believed in a Scholar,—and is yet repeated half a dozen times throughout the book . . . " (p. 180).

In his own "A Death in the Desert" he presents the same sort of confusing ambiguity that biblical scholars face in building or rebuilding theologies from ancient manuscripts. The reader deals here with a partial manuscript, an unidentifiable number of removals from the original event (did Phoebas write the event down after Pamphylax told him, or did he tell someone else?), confusing marginal glosses, and a confusion of names. There is Xanthus, the present owner's uncle-in-law, Xanthus who was present at the death of John and who was later martyred in Rome, an Antiochene who is probably from Antioch in Pamphylia and not Antioch in Syria, and John the disciple of Christ who in his last hours of life is confused about his own identity because he is so withdrawn into his own depths.

But despite the confusion of one level of truth of fact, there can be little doubt in "A Death in the Desert" about the important truth which is a matter of life and death to man. John would have man see this truth through an optic lens of faith, for it is the only truth which would unblind man. Robert Browning would agree.

END NOTES

[1] *The Letters of Robert Browning and Elizabeth Barrett Browning,* ed. Elvan Kintner (Cambridge: Belknap Press of Harvard Univ. Press, 1969), *passim.*

[2] C. H. Herford's dictum on "A Death in the Desert" (*Robert Browning,* p. 160), as quoted in DeVane's *Handbook* (New York: F. S. Croft, 1935), p. 264.

[3] See pp. 152, 180, and 317 of *Dearest Isa* (Austin: Univ. of Texas Press, 1951), for example.

[4] For a complete discussion of the form and practice of writing early Christian manuscripts see Morton Scott Enslin, *Christian Beginnings* (New York: Harper, 1956), pp. 475-509.

[5] *The Life of Jesus* (New York: Random House, 1927).

[6] Cyril C. Richardson, ed. and trans., *Early Christian Fathers* (Philadelphia: Westminster Press, 1953).

An English Translation of the Ancient Greek Dedicatory Verses to Atalanta in Calydon

Apostolos and Lilika Marmaras

In March 1864, during the composition of *Atalanta in Calydon,* Swinburne visited Walter Savage Landor in Florence. It was the first time that Swinburne met his idol, and the impression of this visit stayed with the young poet forever. "Landor represented two things in his eyes: pagan rebellion and pagan art. *Atalanta* could be dedicated to him only."[1]

Swinburne visited Landor twice, and it was during the second meeting that he "had the long intimate conversation which he sought: his Greek verse met with approval, his dedication was accepted."[2] Swinburne would later record this meeting with Landor in a letter to Monckton Milnes, Lord Houghton, who had actually introduced him to the elder poet:

> . . . . [I] found him as alert, brilliant and altogether delicious
> as I suppose others may have found him twenty years since. I
> cannot thank you enough for procuring me this great pleasure
> and exquisite satisfaction—I am seriously more obliged for this
> than for anything that could have been done for me, . . . I
> should like to throw up all other things . . . and devote myself
> to playing valet to him for the rest of his days. I should black
> his boots if he wore any—moi. He has given me the great shock
> of adoration which one feels at thirteen toward great men . . .
> Not that I am disloyal to Tennyson, into whose church we
> were all in time born and baptised as far back as we can re-
> member at all; but he is not a Greek nor a heathen; and I
> imagine does not want to be; . . . [3]

Atalanta in Calydon, however, was published after Landor's death, on September 17, 1864, and Swinburne was left with the bitter disappointment that Landor would never read *Atalanta* and receive the tribute and satisfaction of the Ancient Greek dedicatory verses that Swinburne had composed especially for him. One can feel the genuine grief of the poet in the *new* verses that he finally had to compose at the publication of *Atalanta in Calydon* in 1865. The joyful lyric that Landor's eyes must have seen in Florence became an elegy. Swinburne expressed his grief and sincere affection beautifully in Greek. In his own dedication that precedes the elegy, Swinburne indicates the existence of an encomium which Landor must have seen and must have been very pleased with:

I NOW DEDICATE, WITH EQUAL AFFECTION, REVER-
ENCE, AND REGRET; A POEM INSCRIBED TO HIM
WHILE YET ALIVE IN WORDS WHICH ARE NOW RE-
TAINED BECAUSE THEY WERE LAID BEFORE HIM;
AND TO WHICH, RATHER THAN CANCEL THEM, I
HAVE ADDED SUCH OTHERS AS WERE EVOKED BY
THE NEWS OF HIS DEATH: THAT THOUGH LOSING
THE PLEASURE I MAY NOT LOSE THE HONOUR OF
INSCRIBING IN FRONT OF MY WORK THE HIGHEST
OF CONTEMPORARY NAMES.[4]

The three pages of Ancient Greek verse that precede the argument to the tragedy in almost all the standard editions of *Atalanta in Calydon* show Swinburne's mastery of the Ancient Greek language, and prove once more his poetic genius. Composing elegiacs in Ancient Greek had been a practice with Swinburne when he was at Eton. This practice proved useful in this case. The elegy dedicated to Landor shows the young poet's knowledge and experience in composing Ancient Greek verses.

In meter and language Swinburne's verses closely resemble Theocritus' dactylic hexameter and language, which were fashionable during the third and second centuries B. C. In context and tone, however, Swinburne's verses remind one of Moschus' (fl. c. 150 B.C.) *Lament for Bion,* and of Bion's (c. 100 B.C.) *Lament for Adonis.*[5]

Swinburne's elegy cannot be *closely* compared to either of the *Laments.* However, one cannot ignore the similarity of style and of tone of voice. Both works reflect the strong feelings and almost passionate affection that one finds in Swinburne's elegy to Landor. The *Lament for Bion,* written by a pupil of Bion, seems to be the more appropriate in this occasion even though it is clearly a pastoral lyric, for Bion's *Lament for Adonis* is specifically designed to be sung at Adonis's festival and is in effect an erotic lament from Aphrodite. However, Swinburne's elegy seems to resemble in language and tone Bion's lyric rather than the one ascribed to Moschus. Swinburne's tone is more restrained, of course, and he does not use the repetitive refrains of either poet. He does, however, use frequent repetition of phrases which become important to the theme of the elegy, and he too invokes the Nymphs and ancient deities in his lamentation of Landor's death. On the other hand, as in the *Lament for Bion*, he too refers to the world of the dead, and shows the same respect, admiration and deep sorrow that Bion's pupil feels at the loss of his teacher.

One can perhaps better appreciate this resemblance in a comparison of the styles of the two bucolic poets. Moschus *(Lament for Bion)*:

> ἄρχετε Σικελικαὶ τῶ πένθεος ἄρχετε Μοῖσαι.
> κεῖνος ὁ ταῖς ἀγέλαισιν ἐράσμιος οὐκέτι μέλπει,
> οὐκέτ᾽ ἐρημαίαισιν ὑπὸ δρυσὶν ἥμενος ᾄδει
> ἀλλὰ παρὰ Πλουτῆϊ μέλος Ληθαῖον ἀείδει.
> ὤρεα δ᾽ ἐστὶν ἄφωνα, καὶ αἱ βόες αἱ ποτὶ ταύροις
> πλαζόμεναι γοάοντι καὶ οὐκ ἐθέλοντι νέμεσθαι.
>
> . . . .
>
> τίς ποτὶ σᾷ σύριγγι μελίξεται ὦ τριπόθητε;
> τίς δ᾽ ἐπὶ σοῖς καλάμοις θήσει στόμα; τίς θρασὺς
>   οὕτως;
> εἰσέτι γὰρ πνείει τὰ σὰ χείλεα καὶ τὸ σὸν ἆσθμα,
> ἀχὰ δ᾽ ἐν δονάκεσσι τεᾶς ἔτι βόσκετ᾽ ἀοιδᾶς.[6]

Begin, Sicilian Muses, begin the dirge.

He whom the herds loved makes music no more: no more sits singing beneath solitary oaks, but chants in Pluteus's halls the song of Lethe. No voice is there on the hills; the cows that wander by the bulls lament and will not graze.

. . . .

Who will make music on thy pipe, O friend much missed? Who will set his mouth to thy flutes? Who be so bold? Thy lips, thy breath, live in them yet; those reeds still cherish the echo of thy minstrelsy.[7]

Bion *(Lament for Adonis)*:

> αἰάζω τὸν Ἄδωνιν, ἀπώλετο καλὸς Ἄδωνις.
>   μηκέτ᾽ ἐνὶ δρυμοῖσι τὸν ἀνέρα μύρεο Κύπρι.
> οὐκ ἀγαθὰ στιβάς ἐστιν Ἀδώνιδι φυλλὰς ἐρήμα·
> λέκτρον ἔχοι Κυθέρεια τὸ σὸν καὶ νεκρὸς Ἄδωνις.
> καὶ νέκυς ὢν καλός ἐστι, καλὸς νέκυς, οἷα καθεύδων.
> κάτθεό νιν μαλακοῖς ἐνὶ φάρεσιν οἷς ἐνίαυεν,

ᾧ μετὰ τεῦς [2] ἀνὰ νύκτα τὸν ἱερὸν ὕπνον ἐμόχθει
παγχρυσέῳ κλιντῆρι· ποθεῖ καὶ στυμνὸν Ἄδωνιν.
βάλλε δέ νιν στεφάνοισι καὶ ἄνθεσι· πάντα σὺν
    αὐτῷ,
ὡς τῆνος τέθνακε καὶ ἄνθεα πάντα θανόντων.
ῥαῖνε δέ νιν Συρίοισιν ἀλείφασι, ῥαῖνε μύροισιν·
ὀλλύσθω μύρα πάντα· τὸ σὸν μύρον ὤλετ' Ἄδωνις. [8]

No more in the oak-woods, Cypris, lament thy lord. It is
no fair couch for Adonis, the lonely bed of leaves! Thine own
bed, Cytherea, let him now possess,—the dead Adonis. Ah,
even in death he is beautiful, beautiful in death, as one that
hath fallen on sleep. Now lay him down to sleep in his own
soft coverlets, wherein with thee through the night he shared
the holy slumber in a couch all of gold, that yearns for Adonis,
though sad is he to look upon. Cast on him garlands and
blossoms: all things have perished in his death, yea all the
flowers are faded. Sprinkle him with ointments of Syria,
sprinkle him with unguents of myrrh. Nay, perish all per-
fumes, for Adonis, who was thy perfume, hath perished. [9]

A closer comparison, however, can be made with Swinburne's own English
poem, "In Memory of Walter Savage Landor," and his dedicatory elegy in
Atalanta in Calydon:

> By this white wandering waste of sea,
>   Far north, I hear
> One face shall never turn to me
>   As once this year:
>
> Shall never smile and turn and rest
>   On mine as there,
> Nor one most sacred hand be prest
>   Upon my hair.
>
> I came as one whose thoughts half linger,
>   Half run before;
> The youngest to the oldest singer
>   That England bore.
>
> . . . .

Not with disdain of days that were
    Look earthward now;
Let dreams revive the reverend hair,
    The imperial brow;

Come back in sleep, for in the life
    Where thou art not
We find none like thee. Time and strife
    And the world's lot

Move thee no more; but love at least
    And reverent heart
May move thee, royal and released,
    Soul, as thou art.[10]

Swinburne has been criticized at times for the expression of his "pathetic bereavement" at the loss of such great poets and idols of his, such as Landor and Hugo. We wonder whether the word "pathetic" is appropriate, for as one reads Swinburne's Ancient Greek verses and his poem in English, one cannot but deeply sense the sincerity of his feelings, and share with Swinburne the excitement and emotion he felt during his so frequently described visit to Landor, when the elder poet "with Olympian condescension laid his 'most sacred hand' upon the poet's hair."[11]

In the lofty and dignified manner of the dedicatory Ancient Greek elegy in *Atalanta in Calydon,* we find nothing that is pathetic or exaggerated. In Swinburne's dirge we find the sincere admiration of a young man for an older one, the respect of a young poet for the older bard, and most significant, the love of the student for the great teacher.

A. A Note on the Translation
In our translation of Swinburne's elegy, we decided to retain his verse line without being too literal. His elegy has been rendered into verse rather than prose so that the poet's tone, style and mood could be preserved.

B. A Translation of Swinburne's Ancient Greek Elegy into English
Title page
Those living should accomplish great things; for dead man becomes earth

and shadow; naught comes to naught.

EUR. *Fr. Mel.* 20 (537).

p. 262

You departed then from the North, far from men,
but sweet-breathing Nymphs welcomed you to the sea,
filling with honey your god-given mouth, lest Poseidon
should be disturbed by aught, hearing your melodious voice;
for you were born such a bard. And we are still lamenting
our loss in your death, always longing for you.
Then spoke on of the Pierides, turning to another:
Behold, he has come, the beloved of all mortals,
grasping fresh-budding garlands with his old hands
and covering with laurels his gray head,
singing sweet Sicilian songs and pleasant music
on the pipe; for he truly glorified the lyre.
Apollo found him often sitting in the glens,
crowned him with flowers, and enabled him to sing
the pleasures of memorable Pan and of awry Pitys Korythos,
the Hamadryad goddess kissed by a mortal.
Behold, the man who lulled Kymodameia in the palaces of the sea,
the goddess who restored the father to Agamemnon's son,
sending to sacred Delphi the god-stricken Orestes,
tormented hither and thither by loathsome goddesses.   20

p. 263

You departed then without friends without songs,
grasping flowers from gentle Persephone.
You died; you will be no more. Never again will I stand
in awe before you, my hands touching your divine hands.
Remembering you now, a sweetly-bitter reverence has come upon me,
such as I happen to have for such a person.
Never will I enjoy, elder, the dear glance of your beloved eyes;
never will I touch, dearest elder, your right hand.
What a friable dust, what a friable life. Which is
more ephemeral? Not dust but life.   10
Yet, you are still more pleasant to me than the living.

These verses I bring to your death,
and although few, are truly from the heart. Do not turn
away, let fall upon them your gentle glance.
Unable am I, beside my will, to offer you a worthy
burial; impossible it is for me; nor can I give you
splendid offerings of honey and milk. For if I am
ever to touch your hands, and if I am to see you again,
tears and offerings will tend your beloved head,
your sacred eyes and sacred body.   20
If only; for these would relieve much of my suffering.
Now far from your grave, I live in sorrow;
repelled, over your tomb I sing no lament;
far away, I suffer all-tearful passions.
But rejoice, for at your death, god you remain,
among the dead and the gods below.
Rejoice elder, dear father, rejoice; the best
of all singers, the best of the celebrated.
Rejoice, for you have the bliss and peace of the
dead, apart from hatred and love.   30
Your grave will last longer than monuments,
for your beloved memory is your monument.

p. 264

He whom the Graces lament, laments Aphrodite,
who rejoiced at the wreaths of the fair-dancing Muses,
for more than once old age wasted divine singers;
such splendour your monument reveals.
Indeed, you are beloved among the blessed dead, for if
the Nymphs were to bestow one with desired gifts, to you were
    offered the best.
Now, sound sleep and gentle eternity have advanced upon them,
buried together, their fate is one.   40
You sleep also, a beautiful, glorious sleep in the
hollow earth below, far away from your fatherland.
You sleep, far from the golden Tyrrhenian sea,
and you mother-earth still yearns for you.
But you remain afar rather than renouncing your beloved city.
Sleep; may you be blessed and enviable to us;

for men's time on earth is short, and fate the master,
giving mirth to some and grief to others,
who are often weeping, blinded by light or veiled
by darkness, and while waking are stung by *sleep*.   50
No more the dead fall asleep in the graves
either in darkness or in sunlight.
Nor do they have dreams and visions at night,
neither rejoicing nor mourning;
but they always hold one council and office,
immortal instead of mortal, beautiful instead of evil.

C. Swinburne's Elegy in Ancient Greek

Title page

Τοὺς ζῶντας εὖ δρᾶν· κατθανὼν δὲ πᾶς ἀνὴρ
Γῆ καὶ σκιά· τὸ μηδὲν εἰς οὐδὲν ῥέπει.

EUR. *Fr. Mel.* 20 (537)

p. 262

ᾤχεο δὴ βορέηθεν ἀπότροπος· ἀλλά σε Νύμφαι
   ἤγαγον ἀσπασίαν ἡδύπνοοι καθ᾽ ἅλα,
πληροῦσαι μέλιτος θεόθεν στόμα, μή τι Ποσειδῶν
   βλάψῃ, ἐν ὠσὶν ἔχων σὴν μελίγηρυν ὄπα.
τοῖος ἀοιδὸς ἔφυς· ἡμεῖς δ᾽ ἔτι κλαίομεν, οἳ σου
   δευόμεθ᾽ οἰχομένου, καί σε ποθοῦμεν ἀεί.
εἶπε δὲ Πιερίδων τις ἀναστρεφθεῖσα πρὸς ἄλλην·
   ἦλθεν, ἰδού, πάντων φίλτατος ἦλθε βροτῶν,
στέμματα δρεψάμενος νεοθηλέα χερσὶ γεραιαῖς,
   καὶ πολιὸν δάφναις ἀμφεκάλυψε κάρα,
ἡδύ τι Σικελικαῖς ἐπὶ πηκτίσιν, ἡδύ τι χόρδαις,
   ἀσύμενος· πολλὴν γὰρ μετέβαλλε λύραν,
πολλάκι δ᾽ ἐν βήσσαισι καθήμενον εὗρεν Ἀπόλλων,
   ἄνθεσι δ᾽ ἔστεψεν, τερπνὰ δ᾽ ἔδωκε λέγειν,
Πᾶνά τ᾽ ἀείμνηστόν τε Πίτυν Κόρυθόν τε δύσεδρον,
   ἥν τ᾽ ἐφίλησε θεὰν θνητὸς Ἀμαδρυάδα·
πόντου δ᾽ ἐν μεγάροισιν ἐκοίμισε Κυμοδάμειαν,
   τήν τ᾽ Ἀγαμεμνονίαν παῖδ᾽ ἀπέδωκε πατρὶ,
πρὸς δ᾽ ἱεροὺς Δελφοὺς θεόπληκτον ἔπεμψεν Ὀρέστην,
   τειρόμενον στυγεραῖς ἔνθα καὶ ἔνθα θεαῖς.

p. 263

ᾤχεο δὴ καὶ ἄνευθε φίλων καὶ ἄνευθεν ἀοιδῆς,
δρεψόμενος μαλακῆς ἄνθεα Περσεφόνης.
ᾤχεο· κοὐκ ἔτ' ἔσει, κοὐκ αὖ ποτέ σοι παρεδοῦμαι
ἀζόμενος, χειρῶν χερσὶ θιγὼν ὁσίαις·
νῦν δ' αὖ μνησάμενον γλυκύπικρος ὑπήλυθεν αἰδώς,
οἷα τυχὼν οἵου πρὸς σέθεν οἷος ἔχω·
οὔποτε σοῖς, γέρον, ὄμμα φίλοις φίλον ὄμμασι τέρψω,
σῆς, γέρον, ἁψάμενος, φίλτατε, δεξιτερᾶς.
ἢ ψαφαρὰ κόνις, ἢ ψαφαρὸς βίος ἐστι· τί τούτων
μεῖον ἐφημερίων ; οὐ κόνις ἀλλὰ βίος.
ἀλλά μοι ἡδύτερός γε πέλεις πολὺ τῶν ἔτ' ἐόντων,
ἔπλεο γάρ· σοὶ μὴν ταῦτα θανόντι φέρω,
παῦρα μὲν, ἀλλ' ἀπὸ κῆρος ἐτήτυμα· μηδ' ἀποτρεφθῇς,
πρὸς δὲ βαλὼν ἔτι νῦν ἥσυχον ὄμμα δέχου.
οὐ γὰρ ἔχω, μέγα δή τι θέλων, σέθεν ἄξια δοῦναι,
θαπτομένου περ ἀπών· οὐ γὰρ ἔνεστιν ἐμοὶ·
οὐδὲ μελικρήτου παρέχειν γάνος· εἰ γὰρ ἐνείη
καί σε χεροῖν ψαῦσαι καί σέ ποτ' αὖθις ἰδεῖν,
δάκρυσί τε σπονδαῖς τε κάρα φίλον ἀμφιπολεύειν
ὀφθαλμούς θ' ἱεροὺς σοὺς ἱερόν τε δέμας.
εἴθ' ὄφελον· μάλα γὰρ τάδ' ἂν ἀμπαύσειε μερίμνης·
νῦν δὲ πρόσωθεν ἄνευ σήματος οἶκτον ἄγω·
οὐδ' ἐπιτυμβίδιον θρηνῶ μέλος, ἀλλ' ἀπαμυνθείς,
ἀλλ' ἀπάνευθεν ἔχων ἀμφιδάκρυτα πάθη.
ἀλλὰ σὺ χαῖρε θανὼν, καὶ ἔχων γέρας ἴσθι πρὸς ἀνδρῶν
πρός τε θεῶν, ἐνέροις εἴ τις ἔπεστι θεός.
χαῖρε γέρον, φίλε χαῖρε πατὲρ, πολὺ φέρτατ' ἀοιδῶν
ὧν ἴδομεν, πολὺ δὴ φέρτατ' ἀεισομένων·
χαῖρε, καὶ ὄλβον ἔχοις, οἷόν γε θανόντες ἔχουσιν,
ἡσυχίαν ἔχθρας καὶ φιλότητος ἄτερ.
σήματος οἰχομένου σοι μνήματ' ἐς ὕστερον ἔσται,
σοί τε φίλη μνήμη μνήματος οἰχομένου·

p. 264

ὃν Χάριτες κλαίουσι θεαί, κλαίει δ' Ἀφροδίτη
καλλιχόροις Μουσῶν τερψαμένη στεφάνοις.
οὐ γὰρ ἅπαξ ἱερούς ποτε γῆρας ἔτριψεν ἀοιδούς·
τήνδε τὸ σὸν φαίνει μνῆμα τόδ' ἀγλαΐαν.
ἦ φίλος ἦς μακάρεσσι βροτός, σοὶ δ' εἴ τινι Νύμφαι
δῶρα ποθεινὰ νέμειν, ὕστατα δῶρ', ἔδοσαν.
τὰς νῦν χάλκεος ὕπνος ἔβη καὶ ἀνήνεμος αἰών,
καὶ συνθαπτομέναι μοῖραν ἔχουσι μίαν.
εὕδεις καὶ σὺ, καλὸν καὶ ἀγάκλυτον ἐν χθονὶ κοίλῃ
ὕπνον ἐφικόμενος, σῆς ἀπόνοσφι πάτρας,
τῆλε παρὰ ξανθοῦ Τυρσηνικὸν οἶδμα καθεύδεις
νάματος, ἡ δ' ἔτι σὴ μαῖά σε γαῖα ποθεῖ,

ἀλλ' ἀπέχεις, καὶ πρόσθε φιλόπτολις ὤν περ ἀπεῖπας·
   εὖδε· μάκαρ δ' ἡμῖν οὐδ' ἀμέγαρτος ἔσει.
βαιὸς ἐπιχθονίων γε χρόνος καὶ μοῖρα κρατήσει,
   τοὺς δέ ποτ' εὐφροσύνη τοὺς δέ ποτ' ἄλγος ἔχει·
πολλάκι δ' ἢ βλάπτει φάος ἢ σκότος ἀμφικαλύπτει
   μυρομένους, δάκνει δ' ὕπνος ἐγρηγορότας·
οὐδ' ἔθ' ὅτ' ἐν τύμβοισι κατέδραθεν ὄμμα θανόντων
   ἢ σκότος ἤ τι φάος δήξεται ἠελίου·
οὐδ' ὄναρ ἐννύχιον καὶ ἐνύπνιον οὐδ' ὕπαρ ἔσται
   ἤ ποτε τερπομένοις ἤ ποτ' ὀδυρομένοις·
ἀλλ' ἕνα πάντες ἀεὶ θᾶκον συνέχουσι καὶ ἕδραι·
   ἀντὶ βροτῆς ἄβροτον, κάλλιμον ἄντι κακῆς.

END NOTES

[1]Georges Lafourcade, *Swinburne: A Literary Biography* (New York. William Morrow, 1932), p. 119.

[2]Lafourcade, p. 119.

[3]*The Swinburne Letters,* ed. Cecil Y. Lang (New Haven: Yale Univ. Press; London: Oxford Univ. Press, 1959-62), I, 96-98.

[4]*The Complete Works of Algernon Charles Swinburne, Tragedies,* eds. Sir Edmund Gosse, C. B. and Thomas James Wise (London: William Heinemann; New York: Gabriel Wells, 1925), I, p. 261.

[5]We would like to thank Professor Terpsichori Tzavella-Evjen, Department of Classics, University of Colorado, for her suggestion of Theocritus and of Bion's work.

The *Lament for Bion* has been attributed to Moschus, but there is no sufficient evidence to this day. It was written by a pupil of Bion, and seems to have been suggested by Bion's *Lament for Adonis.*

[6]J. M. Edmonds, trans. *The Greek Bucolic Poets,* (Cambridge, Mass.: Harvard Univ. Press; London: William Heinemann, 1960), pp. 444-46, 11. 19-24, and p. 448, 11. 51-54.

[7]A. S. F. Gow, trans. *The Greek Bucolic Poets* (Cambridge: Cambridge Univ. Press, 1953), p. 134, and p. 135.

[8]Edmonds, pp. 390-92, 11. 67-78.

[9]A. Lang, trans. *Theocritus, Bion and Moschus* (London and New York: Macmillan, 1902), pp. 174-75.

[10]*The Complete Works of Algernon Charles Swinburne, Poetical Works,* eds. Sir Edmund Gosse, C. B. and Thomas James Wise (London: William Heinemann; New York: Gabriel Wells, 1925), I, 265-66.

[11]Samuel C. Chew, *Swinburne* (Hamden, Conn.: Archon, 1966), p. 56.

[12]Although 11. 31-32 are printed on p. 264 of the Gosse and Wise edition, we have transferred them to the passage of p. 263 for thematic purposes.

[13]Gosse and Wise, *Tragedies,* I, 262-64.

The Proserpine Figure in Swinburne's Poems and Ballads I

Douglas C. Fricke

If one had to pick a single year as the turning point in Swinburne criticism, it would be 1959, when Cecil Y. Lang sagely observed in his introduction to *The Swinburne Letters* (New Haven: Yale Univ. Press, 1959-62) that Swinburne had never been judged by his best poems. Lang's introduction encouraged Victorian scholars to reexamine a poet they had previously ignored or misread and, in a remarkable about-face, critical opinion of the last fifteen years has begun to take Swinburne seriously. Recent reevaluations suggest that in Swinburne's early poetry there lies beneath the schoolboy's delight in shock a more serious personality intent upon exploring and comprehending the nature and source of psychological and metaphysical troubles.[1]

The struggle of this personality to reach self-awareness becomes clear in a careful examination of the two main groupings of poems in *Poems and Ballads,* those poems illustrating the frustrations of love or failures of eroticism and those recording the oppressiveness of time and flux. Appropriately, significant poems of each group revolve, directly or indirectly, around a major deity, Venus or Proserpine. Venus in *Poems and Ballads* frequently appears, sometimes personally, sometimes as a presence or mood, in poems concerning the frustrations and inevitable failure of erotic love, and Proserpine often emerges with the "poppied sleep," or death, her antidote to the relentlessness of time and flux. The personality animating the volume often defines itself in relation to these goddesses, and in each encounter with them various states of mind are revealed, new discoveries made, new awarenesses reached.

In this essay I should like to examine the relationship of the animating personality of *Poems and Ballads* with Proserpine in the two poems bearing her name, "The Garden of Proserpine" and "Hymn to Proserpine." The first reveals the submission to Proserpine, the yearning for death and oblivion as a solution to the implacability of time and change. In the "Hymn to Proserpine," however, the response is markedly different. The personality behind the poem demonstrates a stoic courage and clarity of mind lacking in "The Garden of Proserpine." The point to be made is that although Proserpine remains a symbol of death and change, the response to her by the personality of *Poems and Ballads* is antithetical in these two major poems. Finally, I believe the degree of self-awareness attained in the "Hymn to Proserpine" illustrates not only a development beyond the death-wish of "The Garden of Proserpine," but also demonstrates a more positive and healthy attitude too often overlooked in *Poems and Ballads*.

There is certainly good reason why so many poems on the theme of time and flux appear in *Poems and Ballads*. Joseph Warren Beach notes that Swinburne was the first English poet to write all his major poetry after *The Origin of the Species* and concludes from this coincidence that Swinburne was an evolutionary poet. To me it is important because it stamps Swinburne as a child of his age. It was an age in which discoveries in geology reduced man's stature in time, knowledge of astronomy reduced man's stature in space, and exploration in biology simply reduced man's place. At the beginning of the nineteenth century before Swinburne was born the French astronomer Laplace made God more distant than the dimmest star. The controversy over Lyell's *Principles of Geology* raged at Swinburne's birth. *The Origin of the Species* was published in November, 1859, the same month Swinburne left Oxford. A year later, Oxford was the scene for the Huxley-Wilberforce debates on Darwin. In 1868, two years after the appearance of *Poems and Ballads*, Thomas Henry Huxley delivered his famous Edinburgh address, "The Physical Basis of Life." The point is that these scientific discoveries of his lifetime certainly must have affected Swinburne and he incorporated these concerns into his poetry.[2]

Critics, however, do not generally recognize a seriously philosophical Swinburne until *Songs Before Sunrise* (1871). But *Poems and Ballads* certainly reveals a personality oppressed by the implacability of time and change. The "triumph of time" is the overriding fear experienced in the volume and those who charge the volume with a philosophical emptiness or, at best, a simplistic art for art's sake, are simply wrong. Samuel Chew, one of these voices, claims that the positive motif of the poems is hedonism and allies *Poems and Ballads* with Pater's *The Renaissance*. It is true that the Heraclitean doctrine of flux on which Pater based his Cyrenaicism also affected Swinburne. But the answer to man's problems in *Poems and Ballads* is not merely to enjoy the fleeting moments of beauty in "this short day of frost and sun" but rather to confront the internal conflicts brought about by the very shortness of those days.

The speakers in *Poems and Ballads* react in varying ways to the discovery that the only certainty in their world is change. The refrain which begins and ends "Ilicet," with its mention of "The poppied sleep, the end of all," underlines a characteristic, though not final, response to the relentlessness of time and flux. The voice of languor and weariness sighs throughout the volume, expressing that sense of "depression and ennui" which Matthew Arnold claimed, in his opening lecture, probably attended by Swinburne, at Oxford in 1857, were "characteristics stamped on how many of the representative works of modern time."[3] The "poppied sleep," one answer to Heraclitean flux, is best illustrated in "The Garden of Proserpine."

Swinburne wrote in *Notes on Poems and Reviews* that "The Garden of Proserpine" expressed "that brief total pause of passion and of thought, when the spirit, without fear or hope of good things or evil, hungers and thirsts only after the perfect sleep." Critics have seized upon another comment in *Notes on Poems and Reviews*—that this poem, "The Triumph of Time," and "Dolores," as Swinburne claimed, "beyond the rest were autobiographical"—and have read the poem as an illustration of physical impotence resulting from physical excess. A closer reading, however, with attention to the relationship of form and meaning, punctures some of the inflated conclusions of such a biographical approach.

As Swinburne stated, "The Garden of Proserpine" reflects a longing for oblivion, a refuge from time. Meter enhances meaning; the functional monotony of the iambic trimeter lines imitates the thematic longing for peace in an eternal sleep. The stanzaic form ($ababcccb_3$) recreates in sound the languor of the speaker's being. The musical effect of the a and c lines, which always have feminine rhymes, produces a ceaseless, lulling and rolling movement, especially in the ccc lines. But the masculine rhymes of the b lines check the flow and add a necessary firmness to prevent the poem from dissolving into sugary music.

Iambic trimeter, the base meter, lends an evenness to the sound of the poem; there are always three stresses to a line, although the number of syllables may vary. Heavy alliteration, assonance, consonance, and internal rhyme also contribute to regularity and smoothness. Yet much of the meaning of the poem lies in Swinburne's manipulation of this metric regularity. In the iambic trimeter base, Swinburne substitutes in some 35 of 96 lines of the poem. These moments of counterpoint rhythm work against the slowly flowing monotony of the larger, external pattern of the verse and call attention to specific details and transitions of scene and thought. Spondaic and trochaic substitutions especially halt the verse and emphasize important images and states of mental activity.

Manipulation of images and setting also alerts the reader to transitions in the poem and points out areas of meaning. A central form-giving image of "The Garden of Proserpine" is its setting. As the first stanza immediately establishes, there are two specific locations in the poem; *here* is contrasted with *there*. *Here*, where the speaker stands, is the garden, the place of the irrevocable dead. *There* is the scene beyond the garden, the surrounding fields of growth and harvest bordering on a body of water, either a river, estuary, or sea. The stillness of the garden is contrasted with the activity of the men working in the fields, the wind blowing, and the ships drifting at sea. These two locations create a polarity, a place of life and a place of death, in the poem between which the speaker's mind fluctuates.

The effect of these contrasting locations is continued in the juxtaposition of images which gives a firm structural unity to the poem. The structure of "The Garden of Proserpine" is the contrast between fertility and sterility, appearing in the image clusters of life/death, activity/weariness, Demeter/Proserpine, light/darkness, mortality/immortality, permanence/change. These juxtapositions correspond, symbolically, to fluctuations of thought and mood and to the internal divisions the speaker experiences as he moves into the poem. The dominance of life-denying images near the end of the poem suggests that the speaker's thoughts have fixated on death and oblivion.

This movement is also illustrated by the cycle of seasons or growth operating in the poem, an appropriate image since the legend of Proserpine is associated with ancient explanations of the seasons. Images of both late summer and autumn harvest shape the first two stanzas. Harvest yields to Proserpine's wasteland, all barren save for the leaf from which she crushes "deadly wine," in the fourth stanza. The sixth stanza makes a brief reference to the last rose of summer; stanza eight alludes to spring, summer, and growth, with perhaps a hint of autumn and winter. Stanza nine is a bleak description of winter and a spring apparently ruined by late winter frost winds. Winter's desolation prevails at the end of the poem. In the last stanza, neither the leaves of winter nor spring flourish; the "eternal night" negates all seasons.

Thus in both seasonal imagery and in the image clusters of fertility and sterility, the poem moves more and more into sterility and death, from light to darkness. In stanzas one through six, the speaker, "weary of days and hours," fades from reality to a sleepy world where all things are adrift without direction. The barest hint of any activity in the first stanza ceases altogether in the third where, in the garden, no winds blow. In stanza four, one of the most heavily counterpointed, the speaker withdraws from the active world and moves, in thought now as well as in person, into the garden:

> No growth of moor or coppice,
> No heather-flower or vine,

> But bloomless buds of poppies,
>   Green grapes of Proserpine,
> Pale beds of blowing rushes
> Where no leaf blooms or blushes
> Save this whereout she crushes
>   For dead men deadly wine.
>
> (ll. 25-32)

The use of spondees in lines 28, 29, and 30 stresses the sterility of the garden. In the last line, a spondee, alliteration, and monosyllables imitate with a resounding finality the dark inevitability of the garden.

The initial trochee of stanza seven, which introduces Proserpine as the cold immortal who gathers all mortal things, signals a turn in the poem. From this point, images of sterility prevail. In stanza nine, for example, spondaic and trochaic substitutions, combined with elemental monosyllables, show what becomes of mortal things gathered by "cold immortal hands":

> There go the loves that wither,
>   The old loves with wearier wings;
> And all dead years draw thither,
>   And all disastrous things;
> Dead dreams of days forsaken,
>   Blind buds that snows have shaken,
> Wild leaves that winds have taken,
>   Red strays of ruined springs.
>
> (ll. 65-72)

As suggested by the plural nouns, Proserpine eventually scythes *all* life and growth in her barren harvest. This formative image of the grim reaper alters the tone of the poem. The sibilance in the stanza cannot disguise the unrelenting force of the rhythm which surges below the flowing monotony. The music of enervation subsides for a moment as mortal things begin to die.

Having figuratively moved down and into the garden, the speaker, in the last three stanzas of the poem, moves out of the darkness to contemplate the experience. He draws universal conclusions. In stanza ten, he accepts the fact that "Time stoops to no man's lure" and that although he may never be sure of joy and sorrow, he can be certain of change. Stanza eleven records the futility of hope or fear in face of the finality of death. Finally, in the last stanza, the speaker, enervated, surrenders himself, with all things—nature, sensations, seasons, days, light, sounds—to an end in "the sleep eternal / In an eternal night."

Close attention to the last stanzas of the poem, in which darkness engulfs both thought and image, reveals the relationship of form and meaning. I suggested earlier that the juxtaposition of the central image pattern of fertility and sterility establishes a dualism on which the movement of the poem operates. The eternal night which concludes the poem cancels all contrasts—light/dark, growing fields/barren harvest, life/death. All assume equal insignificance in the speaker's mind as he longs for release. And what should become clear by the end of the poem is that the speaker's mental movement towards this inevitable conclusion has been expressed in another form-giving image of the poem: "That even the weariest river / Winds somewhere safe to sea" (11. 87-88). The line "That even the weariest river" significantly contains nine syllables, more syllables than any other single line in the poem, and in its length and use of double anapests it suggests, as the meter of the poem has done throughout, a river slowly but steadily winding toward the sea. The last line of this stanza, "Winds somewhere safe to sea," imitates by the bluntness of its stresses a sense of finality. What is happening in these lines is the conversion of the speaker's animating feeling into the image of a river winding to the sea, to peace and sleep in the negation of discord.

Maud Bodkin, writing about Arnold's "Sohrab and Rustum" in *Archetypal Patterns in Poetry* (1934; rptd. London: Oxford Univ. Press, 1965), p. 66, discusses how the death-wish is often symbolically fulfilled in the image of the sea. The neurotic views death not as the end of life, but as "a quiescent resolution of affective excitement." Like the neurotic, Professor Bodkin writes, "the poet or his reader, dreaming on the river that breaks at last into the free ocean, sees in this image his own life and death, not at all in their social and legal implications, but in accordance with a deep organic need for release from conflict and tension."

This image which Professor Bodkin singles out operates throughout "The Garden of Proserpine." In the first stanza, the speaker watches a "sleepy world of streams." In the ninth stanza, further reference is made to this river, or perhaps estuary, in line 29: "Pale beds of blowing rushes." The image suggests a sea or river marsh often found in the mouths of rivers flowing out to sea. The speaker mentions in the second stanza that he, like the river, is "weary," and in the third stanza he pictures the image of ships lazily adrift at sea. When the image of the weary river winding to oblivion in the sea appears in stanza eleven, it becomes clear that Swinburne has used this recurring motif to illustrate, analogously, that the discord and weariness of the speaker's own mind have found refuge in oblivion. The "Then" which begins the last stanza indicates this mental turn, and the initial "Nors" which accumulate and echo in that stanza reinforce the finality of the mind's journey. In the fifth stanza, the speaker saw morn come out of darkness, but in the last stanza there is

> Only the sleep eternal
> In an eternal night.

(11. 95-96)

The force with which Swinburne stresses the idea of eternal night does not make this poem an illustration of the "dark night of the soul." The darkness is not despair but release, not anxiety but security. The eternal night which cancels the juxtaposed images of the poem also negates the anxiety and strife in the speaker's consciousness. Professor Bodkin writes that "Within the poetic vision, however, this death-craving is not a mere crude, repressed impulse; it is, as Vivante says, an impulse actively realizing itself anew in consciousness, attaining a new character in synthesis with other tendencies" (p. 66). Clearly there is no such renewal of consciousness or synthesis in "The Garden of Proserpine."

Although there is a degree of honest evaluation in the poem, "The Garden of Proserpine" does not approach the honesty or austere stoicism with which the speakers confront and resolve the horrors of their age or personality in other major poems in the volume. "The Garden of Proserpine" represents a characteristic, though not necessarily dominant, mood of *Poems and Ballads,* but as I have suggested earlier, there is a more positive feeling which runs counter to this yearning for death or oblivion. And, as if to underline this conflict, Swinburne chose another Proserpine poem, "Hymn to Proserpine," to illustrate a very different response to that goddess of death and change. Whereas "The Garden of Proserpine" leaves the speaker in darkness, self-discovery is at the heart of "Hymn to Proserpine." Proserpine, of course, plays a major role in the poem, and so does that other commanding goddess, Venus. To swell the host of deity, the Christian God and the Virgin Mary also make an appearance. In fact, as in "Laus Veneris," the God/Venus conflict helps give structure to the "Hymn to Proserpine." In this poem, however, the concern of the speaker is not specifically the mental struggle between God and Venus, as it is in "Laus Veneris," but between the way of life those deities represent.

The stimulus for this dramatic monologue is probably Constantine's Edict of Milan (313), the proclamation in Rome of the Christian faith,[4] and the sentiments expressed in this monologue were so decidedly anti-Christian that some of Swinburne's closest friends strongly urged him to omit this poem from *Poems and Ballads*. Swinburne wrote to Lady Trevelyan on December 10, 1865 that "Hymn to Proserpine" (which was a favorite of Lady Trevelyan's) was one of the poems "I have been advised to omit as likely to hurt the feeling of a religious public" (Lang, I, 141). "Hymn to Proserpine," however, when viewed within the framework of the dramatic monologue, is neither anti-Christian nor pro-pagan. Proserpine, here goddess of both death and change, finally emerges as a more powerful deity than Christ or Venus. The affirmation of Proserpine at the end of the poem confirms the speaker's recognition that, as the pagan gods have been replaced by the Christian, so, in turn, must the Christian gods give way before endless change and flux which determine all life, especially, as the Roman discovers, his own. If there is a deity worshipped in the poem, it is the overwhelming force of life itself.

The movement of the poem is really the expanding awareness of the speaker's mind as he examines both sides of the pagan/Christian conflict which distresses him. The speaker's series of direct addresses gives shape to the external structure of the poem. In lines 1-12 he addresses Prosperine; lines 13-22, the pagan gods, lines 23-88, Christ, the Galilean; lines 89-90, the pagan gods again; and, in lines 91-110, as in the beginning of the poem, Proserpine. The Roman's direct addresses to Proserpine at the beginning and end of the poem create a definite ordered movement. He has progressed down into the poem and back out of it but, in the middle sections of the poem where he confronts the pagan and Christian gods, he arrives at a new understanding and self-awareness. Consequently, his return to Proserpine at the end of the poem is characterized by an expanded consciousness and wisdom.

These clear divisions in the poem (more characteristic of Swinburne's poetry than his critics will acknowledge) do establish, of course, an external structure, but the activity and development of the speaker's mind, the animating feeling expressed within the larger structure, also generate the poem. Not at all static, the speaker's mind develops as he moves through the various direct addresses and explores the conflicts which provoke those direct addresses. Changes in imagery, tone, and diction within the series of direct addresses reflect the speaker's active and changing mind and growing awarenesses. The conflict which besets him, and which he tries to resolve, is essentially between the spirit of life (pagan gods) and the spirit of death (the death-in-life of Christianity; the death as sleep of Proserpine). Once again, this conflict appears as the fertility/sterility image cluster which gives structure to so many of the lyrics of *Poems and Ballads,* to perhaps even the volume itself. Here the conflict specifically juxtaposes pagan and Christian. The life and joy images associated with the pagan gods,

> The laurel, the palms and the paean, the breasts
>   of the nymphs in the brake;
> Breasts more soft than a dove's, that tremble
>   with tenderer breath;
> And all the wings of the Loves, and all the joy
>   before death;
> All the feet of the hours that sound as a single
>   lyre,
> Dropped and deep in the flowers, with strings
>   that flicker like fire.
>
> (ll. 24-28)

can never be rejuvenated by ascetic Christianity which the speaker visualizes as "the leavings of racks and rods," and "ghastly glories of saints, dead limbs of gibbeted Gods!" The juxtaposition is condensed in a comparison of the beautiful and flower bedecked Venus with the life-denying sorrow of the Virgin in the speaker's direct address to Christ, the "pale Galilean":

> Not as thine, not as thine was our mother, a
>   blossom of flowering seas,
> Clothed round with the world's desire as with
>   raiment, and fair as the foam,
> And fleeter than kindled fire, and a goddess,
>   and mother of Rome.
> For thine came pale and a maiden, and sister to
>   sorrow; but ours,
> Her deep hair heavily laden with odour and colour
>   of flowers,
> White rose of the rose-white water, a silver
>   splendour, a flame,
> Bent down unto us that besought her, and earth
>   grew sweet with her name.
> For thine came weeping, a slave among slaves,

and rejected; but she
Came flushed from the full-flushed wave, and
    imperial, her foot on the sea.
And the wonderful waters knew her, the winds
    and the viewless ways,
And the roses grew rosier, and bluer the
    sea-blue stream of the bays.

                                        (11. 78-88)

   The confrontation with this conflict is only one means which illustrates
the dynamism of the speaker's mind. In the course of his monologue, he
comes upon choices which he must make, a choice between the pagan gods,
who make life like life, but are gone, and the Christian gods, who make life
like death. There enters into the struggle between these two choices a third
alternative, Proserpine, who makes death like sleep. The speaker's changing
states of mind, his inability to decide which is the right decision, contribute
to the animating feeling of distressed activity struggling toward resolution.
And in the course of contemplating these three choices, the Roman speaker
arrives at a series of discoveries which lead him to a final awareness. Early in
the poem, the Roman bitterly recognizes that the pagan gods are gone, replaced by Christian:

O Gods dethroned and deceased, cast forth,
    wiped out in a day!
From your wrath is the world released,
    redeemed from your chains, men say.
New Gods are crowned in the city. . . .

                                        (11. 13-15)

But a further discovery mitigates this frustration and despair; because of inevitable change, the Christian gods too must go:

In the darkness of time, in the deeps of the
    years, in the changes of things,
Ye shall sleep as a slain man sleeps, and the
    world shall forget you for kings.
Though the feet of thine high priests tread
    where thy lords and our forefathers trod,
Though these that were Gods are dead, and thou

> being dead art a God,
> Though before thee the throned Cytherean be
>   fallen, and hidden her head,
> Yet thy kingdom shall pass, Galilean, thy dead
>   shall go down to thee dead.

(ll. 69-74)

This awareness leads, ultimately, to the speaker's third and most important discovery that he too must submit to change and die. In his final address to Proserpine, he expresses this self-discovery.

> Thou art more than the Gods who number the days
>   of our temporal breath;
> For these give labour and slumber; but thou,
>   Proserpine, death.
> Therefore now at thy feet I abide for a season
>   in silence. I know
> I shall die as my fathers died, and sleep as
>   they sleep; even so.

(ll. 103-06)

The caesura after "sleep" and the brevity of "even so" in line 106 help convey this very effective understated power of discovery and acceptance.

Ignorant of these things in his first address to Proserpine, in which he talked vaguely about the sleep she offered, the speaker, in the course of the poem, comes to *know* ("I know," he says at the end of the poem, "that I shall die as my fathers died") and accept the hard facts of time and mortality. The euphemistic "sleep" of his first address to Proserpine becomes, in the end, what it really is—death. The paramount discovery is that no things will last, not gods (nor worship of them), not men, and that the only permanent thing is change. Although the poem leans toward these darker tendencies, the ending is not pessimistic. "Hymn to Proserpine" expresses the triumph of the clarity and integrity of a man's mind, a mind able to resolve conflicts and face the facts of existence without dispair or the cowardice of suicide. As the last two lines indicate,

> So long I endure, no longer; and laugh not
>   again, neither weep.
> For there is no God found stronger than death;
>   and death is a sleep.

(ll. 109-10)

the speaker will endure while he lives. "The Garden of Proserpine" longs for death; "Hymn to Proserpine" stoically endures until death comes.[5]

The speaker's animating feeling—the dynamism of his mind illustrated as he moves through changes and indecisions, resolves conflicts, and, finally, through a series of discoveries, perceives a pattern for living in the chaos of time and flux—is very carefully converted into a form-giving image. The dynamism of the central metaphor of the poem, the "wave of the world," imitates the dynamism of the speaker's mind as he struggles toward discovery. A symbol of confusion, change, and flux, the wave also represents the darker, pessimistic tendencies in the speaker's mind at this point in the poem:

> All delicate days and pleasant, all spirits
>   and sorrows are cast
> Far out with the foam of the present that
>   sweeps to the surf of the past:
> Where beyond the extreme sea-wall, and between
>   the remote sea-gates,
> Waste water washes, and tall ships founder,
>   and deep death waits:
> Where, mighty with deepening sides, clad
>   about with the seas as with wings,
> And impelled of invisible tides, and fulfilled
>   of unspeakable things,
> White-eyed and poisonous-finned, shark-toothed
>   and serpentine-curled,
> Rolls, under the whitening wind of the future,
>   the wave of the world.
> The depths stand naked in sunder behind it,
>   the storms flee away;
> In the hollow before it the thunder is taken
>   and snared as a prey;
> In its sides is the north-wind bound; and its
>   salt is of all men's tears;
> With light of ruin, and sound of changes, and
>   pulse of years;
> With travail of day after day, and with trouble
>   of hour upon hour;
> And bitter as blood is the spray; and the crests
>   are as fangs that devour:

> And its vapour and storm of its steam as the
>   sighing of spirits to be;
> And its noise as the noise in a dream; and its
>   depths as the roots of the sea:
> And the height of its heads as the height of the
>   utmost stars of the air:
> And the ends of the earth at the might thereof
>   tremble, and time is made bare.
>
> (ll. 47-64)

The speaker voices this metaphor at the exact mid-point of his monologue. Occurring at this point, the metaphor, like the wave it describes, enables him to look behind and ahead, to view past and present, even future. When he looks backward in the poem, to the pagan gods, the speaker sees only their demise. But as he comes to realize, partly in this description of the wave and certainly by the end of the poem, all change is not destructive. Change, symbolized by the wave, will eventually destroy life-denying Christianity: "Ye are gods, and behold ye shall die, and the waves be upon you at last." And although the imagery which describes this wave of flux and change is largely destructive, life-affirming images survive. The wave is "poisonous-finned, shark-toothed, serpentine-curled," its "crests are as fangs that devour," but, opposed to these are such life images describing the wave as "pulse of years," "the sighing of spirits to be," and "the roots of the sea." The wave, then, as an agent of change, is not all destructive; there is a duality in the central metaphor. The "sighing of spirits to be" and "the whitening wind of the future" announce the possibility of a new world and new life emerging out of old forms. The future is not necessarily maligned. The sea is destructive, chaotic, but it is the chaos out of which all life comes, the source of life and creativity. The speaker intimates in the description of the wave that new life will arise out of destruction and chaos; he realizes at the end of the poem that although he must die, life will go on.[6]

This recognition by no means tilts the balance of the poem toward optimism but does qualify the pessimism. The speaker's two triumphs in the poem are really minimal, even anti-triumphs. He can take some consolation in the fact that "his" goddess, Proserpine, wins out in the end, but Proserpine is not as good as Venus. And, secondly, although he is willing to realize that life must go on, that life is not his. The final mood of the poem is neither optimism nor pessimism but stoicism. The speaker realizes and accepts that, although he must die, not all change is destructive and that there are order and creativity in chaos, a pattern in flux and confusion. The dual aspects of the wave reveal the strength and clarity of the speaker's discovery, his ability to reconcile the opposing forces in his life.

This reconciliation of opposites and perception of order in chaos is reinforced by the particular verse form of "Hymn to Proserpine." Swinburne again, as in "Anactoria," borrows the couplet principle but manipulates it to his own desired effect. Swinburne rejects the epigrammatic quality inherent in most rhymed couplets, softens it with frequent run-on lines and long cadences, but retains the sense of restraint. The long hexameter lines, for example, accumulate cadences and imitate musically the poem's central metaphor, the rushing of the wave. But interlaced or crossed rhymes, that break the long hexameter couplet into four alternating rhyming shorter lines, balance the cascading rush and flow. The particular effect of the interlaced rhyme is to create, rhythmically, a unity and pattern beneath the sweeping rush of the hexameter lines. Thus there is a pattern which runs clear through the rushing verse just as the speaker perceives there is a pattern in chaos, the effect of law and life beneath destruction and chaos.[7]

Especially in the lines describing the wave does meter imitate meaning. Clangorous and explosive consonants, like d, b, capture the destructive dynamism of the wave. The speaker's thoughts seem to dwell on destructive change, but the appearance of life-affirming images, the use of trochaic and spondaic substitutions that give weight without noticeably slowing the verse, and the repetition of w and s sounds which creates resonance and sonority all emphasize the dual aspect of the wave and, by analogy, the growing synthesis of opposing thought and emotion in the speaker's mind. The speaker's final synthesis, his perception of oneness in the diversity and flux of life, transforms a poem from what was mistakenly interpreted as anti-Christian bitterness to a poem of discovery and stoicism.

These antithetical responses toward Proserpine by the personality of *Poems and Ballads* reveal not an inconsistency but rather evidence of a psychologically agonizing struggle within that personality. Given the uncomfortable knowledge that the only certainty in life is death and change, how does one confront Proserpine, emblem of those forces? "Hymn to Proserpine" and "The Garden of Proserpine" reflect the extremes of positive and negative response between which the personality of *Poems and Ballads* vacillates, and the tensions and conflicts inherent in these poems suggests the larger pattern of self-conflict and struggle which gives *Poems and Ballads* its formal unity and intense, dynamic quality.

END NOTES

[1]Lang's monumental edition of *The Swinburne Letters* touched off the critical re-assessment of Swinburne and has created a movement which in the 1970's has grown to revival proportions. Book-length publications in the last five years include biographical studies by Mollie Panter-Downes, *At the Pines* (London: Hamilton, 1971) and Philip Henderson, *Swinburne: Portrait of a Poet* (New York: MacMillan, 1974); a critical study by Jerome J. McGann, *Swinburne: An Experiment in Criticism* (Chicago: Univ. of Chicago Press, 1972); a survey of important past criticism edited by Clyde K. Hyder, *Swinburne: The Critical Heritage* (London: Routledge and Kegan Paul, 1970); and important chapters on Swinburne in Morse Peckham's *Victorian Revolutionaries* (New York: George Braziller, 1970) and Lionel Stevenson's *The Pre-Raphaelite Poets* (Chapel Hill: Univ. of North Carolina Press, 1972). Peckham has also edited *Poems and Ballads and Atalanta in Calydon* (Indianapolis and New York: Bobbs Merrill, 1970), and a special issue of *Victorian Poetry* (vol. 9, 1971), edited by Cecil Lang, was devoted to Swinburne.

[2]"Hertha," the keynote poem of *Songs Before Sunrise* (1871), is certainly evidence that Swinburne was brooding over the scientific explorations of his age. But I think that the total impact of *Poems and Ballads*, his first volume, could only be the result of a man very much aware of these scientific and intellectual currents. And certainly the august circle of intellectuals and artists with whom Swinburne associated in the years during which he wrote *Poems and Ballads* discussed these events.

[3]Matthew Arnold, "On the Modern Element in Literature," in *Matthew Arnold*, ed. John Bryson (Cambridge, Mass: Harvard Univ. Press, 1954), p. 279. In this particular section of his inaugural address as Professor of Poetry at Oxford, Arnold refers specifically to Lucretius who, he claims, "is overstrained, gloom-weighted, morbid; and he who is morbid is no adequate interpreter of his age" (p. 281). According to Edmund Gosse, in *The Life of Algernon Charles Swinburne* (London: MacMillan, 1917), although Swinburne admired Arnold's lyric poetry, he was lukewarm about the lectures, perhaps because of the influence of his friend John Nichol (pp. 52-53).

[4]In a note to "Hymn to Proserpine" in his edition of *Poems and Ballads*, Morse Peckham suggests that the subtitle "Proclamation in Rome of the Christian Faith" may also refer to the edict of toleration of emperor Galerius, in 311, or to the official establishment of Christianity as the religion of the Roman Empire by Theodosius the Great (379-85).

[5]The fact that Swinburne in a footnote alerts the reader that line 108 is a quote from Epictetus, the Greek Stoic philosopher, may also be a hint pointing toward the emerging stoic personality of the speaker at the end of the poem.

[6]The section describing the wave (11. 47-64) in "Hymn to Proserpine" corresponds somewhat to the Yggdrasil (tree of life) section of "Hertha" (11. 96-135). The description of the wave and the tree of life both manifest a great volcanic energy able to synthesize elements of life and death. Although "Hymn to Proserpine" lacks the clear expression of the humanistic, pantheistic evolutionism of "Hertha," it does share common thoughts with that keynote poem of *Songs Before Sunrise* and demonstrates, with other poems of the 1866 volume, that the gap between *Poems and Ballads* and *Songs Before Sunrise* is not so great as might be believed.

[7]Even the appearance of "Hymn to Proserpine" on the page is organic. When the poem is printed correctly, so that each hexameter line is unbroken, the rhyme patterns, otherwise terribly confused, and the unusual sweep and width of appearance imitating subject, are clearly brought out.

Henry James and the Bluestockings: Satire and Morality in The Bostonians

Sallie J. Hall

In these days when feminist activism has become an accepted fact of academic life; when courses are springing up dealing with "neglected woman writers" or "the image of woman in literature"; when symposia are held on the subject at professional conventions; when Courtly Love, the Virgin Cult, D. H. Lawrence, and Norman Mailer are alike excoriated by militant feminists, it strikes me as curious that little mention is ever made of Henry James. One can speculate on possible reasons for critical silence on the question of where James stood in the battle of the sexes. Let us postulate that on the one hand, bewildered males, caught off-balance by the unexpected vehemence of the feminists' attacks, do not feel that they can enlist James on "their" side. Some of James's male critics traditionally have entertained doubts about his sexual proclivities, partially because of his life-long celibacy (we remember the tedious debates about the nature of the famous "obscure hurt"); partially because they see in his works a seeming lack of Hemingwayesque "machismo." The Jamesian hero, the cliché goes, is the man who is always deciding *not* to marry the woman. And then they may look at the gallery of formidable females which populates the Jamesian fictive world, ranging from the defiant Daisy Miller and the strong-minded young Isabel Archer (who had a "vague feeling that people were right when they treated her as if she were rather superior") to the over-bearing dowagers such as Mrs. Newsome and Mrs. Lowder. They may look at these women and feel "threatened." Of course, they generally acknowledge that James had insights into feminine psychology unusual among male writers; nevertheless, they seem to feel vaguely uneasy with the number, variety, and unconventionality of the women in James's fiction. So they retreat to the comfortable security of a conviction that, after all, if James's women do not conform to traditional masculine notions of what a woman should be and do, that fact is simply the predictable result of what they see as James's own thwarted and attenuated masculinity.

Continuing our hypothesis, radical feminists, also viewing him selectively, similarly might find grounds for uneasiness, albeit different ones. They might note the aridity of the fates with which James seems to "punish" some of his heroines: Catherine Sloper, Nanda Brookenham, Daisy Miller, for instance, or Isabel at the end of *The Portrait,* or Kate Croy after Densher has refused to marry her on the dowry of Milly Theale's money. The image of the "silken noose" at the conclusion of *The Golden Bowl*—"his wife's immaterial tether . . . held ever so lightly" around Charlotte Verver's neck by her husband—may register forcibly, evoking outrage. Or, they may feel annoyed at the (by now) tired theory that the governess of *The Turn of the Screw* is a classic case of neurotic sex repression. And particularly, they may react with the most violent indignation of all to James's most explicitly satirical novel, in which the subject is specifically the feminist movement of the mid-and-late nineteenth century, known popularly and pejoratively as the Bluestocking Movement. Any lingering doubt, they might say, as to where James stands in the battle of the sexes, is settled finally and forever by the damning evidence of *The Bostonians.*[1] James is yet another male chauvinist, admittedly a little more polite than Mailer but chauvinist nonetheless.

It is true, as Alfred Habegger has noted, that *The Bostonians* has been exposed to its share of critical attention and, as he further suggests, that most recent criticism has "found the novel to be of value largely because of its cultural significance—its criticism of American sexuality."[2] But it is also true that most of those who have devoted their considerable critical acumen to analyses of the novel have been men; therefore, I take exception to Habegger's further claim that "the vein opened by [Lionel] Trilling and [Irving] Howe has been exhausted." I believe that one of the more fortunate results of the current women's movement has been the re-examination of certain works of literature in the light of new perspectives. I further believe *The Bostonians* is among those works which demands such a re-examination.

Therefore, as a Jamesian who also happens to be a woman, I take that task upon myself. My purpose here is not to proselytize for either of the extreme stances posited above, but rather to suggest that neither is complete or accurate. I suggest rather that among the reasons for the ambivalence (and resulting silence) of reaction to James in the context of the modern women's movement, and the difficulty of determining his sexual "partisanship" are precisely the facts that he saw no need for such partisanship, that he saw women as human beings as men are human beings, and, further, that his was a syncretic vision, transcending limited traditional cultural stereotypes of sex roles and definitions in favor of the recognition of a common humanity, a recognition that assumes the fact, so often overlooked, that all human beings

are compounds in various degrees and proportions of qualities and characteristics that have only been culturally designated as "masculine" or "feminine."
One's biological sex is but an index, and sometimes an indefinite one, to the
proportions of "masculine" or "feminine" traits within any particular individual. In fact, his fiction, taken as a whole, registers a cumulative protest
against just such cultural stereotyping, especially when it involves the failure
of a person's—male or female—full realization of his or her intrinsic right to
dignity as a human being. His fiction reveals a broad comprehensive concern
with the ordinary, everyday problems of simply being human, and since he
saw those problems primarily in relational terms, the relationship between the
sexes is one of his continuing concerns. Christina Light, in the early novel
Roderick Hudson, seems to speak for her creator when she says:

> "One doesn't want a lover one pities, and one doesn't want—
> of all things in the world—a husband who's a picturesque
> curiosity. . . . I should like Mr. Hudson as something else.
> The world's idea of possible relations, either for man or wom-
> an, is so poor—there would be so many nice free ones. I wish
> he were even my brother, so that he could never talk to me of
> marriage. Then I could adore him. . . ."[3]

But "the world's idea of possible relations, either for man or woman" was
(and in many ways still is) poor, so, pragmatically, James seemed to set out
for himself the task of suggesting through his fiction what one might do in
the face of that fact. The first step is to come to terms with one's self, including one's sexual being, and to achieve the kind of self-realization that James
posited as an ideal for the civilized (in the Jamesian sense) man or woman.[4]
The second step is to establish such relations with other people, both male
and female, as the society in which one lives will accept or tolerate, and to
derive whatever fullness of satisfaction such a relationship can give. Involved
in this struggle is a resolution of the tensions within oneself that Naomi
Lebowitz has called the "masculine ego" and the "feminine sensibility."[5]
The pervasive ironies so frequently noted as an integral part of the Jamesian
vision often result from a failure to achieve such a resolution.

But, returning to our imagined debate between the sexual extremists:
"Granted," each side might say, "all of this might be fine as generalization,
but there still remains *The Bostonians.*" And the male partisans would
triumphantly point to Ransom's "victory" over Olive, and the feminists
would insist even more rigorously that the novel "proves" James's male

chauvinism. Clearly it is time to proceed with an examination of *The Boston-ians* with our hypothetical debate in mind.

The first point to be recognized and, I think, insisted upon, is that *The Bostonians* is satire, not merely in the first book, as nearly everyone has acknowledged, but throughout. There is abundant use within the novel of such traditional devices of satire as comic exaggeration, ridicule, wit, and satiric reduction. I shall point out examples of these as I proceed, but the most important element, I believe, that identifies the novel as satire (as op-posed to being a novel with satirical elements—a significant difference) is its positing of a relationship between art (the novel) and morality (the satiric norm). Aubrey Williams has said:

> In any satiric work art stands in close and peculiar relationship
> with morality from the beginning. Such works appear to spring
> from a blend of the artistic faculties and of the moral attitude,
> either real or assumed, within the satirist. The satirist, either in
> terms of biographical reality or in terms of a fictive person-
> ality, takes a moral position from which he lashes out at what
> appear to be, in the light of his or her assumed standards, the
> vices and follies of mankind. *In one way or another the ques-
> tion of morality is raised by the author himself* (italics mine).[6]

Williams' comments come close to what I see as the central problem plaguing critics of *The Bostonians.* His comments occur in the context of his argument that criticism of *The Dunciad,* for at least a century and a half, had been obscured by the critical assumption that Pope the satirist was the same being as Pope the man, and that therefore the aesthetic merits of the poem *qua* poem had been obfuscated by what his critics saw as the vitriolic immorality and vindictiveness of the man. Today we have perhaps reached a degree of critical sophistication that we can chuckle condescendingly at the notion that an immoral man cannot produce a great work of art, but that attitude was not current in James's time; indeed, Leslie Stephens (one of James's greatest friends) was one of the most outspoken critics of *The Dunciad* on those very grounds. But I suggest that James was keenly aware of the fine line of connection between art and morality and that, further, he was suffi-ciently versed in the devices and conventions of traditional satire to know that in order for satire to be effective, the adoption of a satiric *persona*— whether biographically consistent with the author himself or not—is a neces-sity for a satirical work.

Williams' stance, as he acknowledges, is based essentially upon Maynard Mack's classic essay on the subject, "The Muse of Satire," in which Mack identifies three possible classifications of *personae* which the satirist may assume. First, there is the *"vir bonus:* the man of plain living, high thinking, and lasting friendships." Second is the *ingénu:* "the simple heart . . . the vehicle of ironies about matters he professes not to understand, and is amazed by his own involvement in the literary arts"; and, finally, the "hero: the fellow [who] has somehow got Goliath's head in his hand (and also, the hero's accents in his voice)."[7]

I believe that, for his satirical purposes in *The Bostonians,* James the author adopted the voice of the *vir bonus,* who in virtually every particular comes very close to James's biographical reality. Certainly, anyone who has perused Leon Edel's exhaustive biography comes to realize that, whatever his human faults may have been, James was a man of high intentions, fond friendships, genuine good humor, and kindliness. Perhaps an even more telling argument is that in this novel, alone among his major works, there is no "centre of consciousness" consistently maintained; even in those portions where he seems to be presenting information or impressions through the eyes or sensibilities of one or the other of the characters, he has not abandoned his own authorial role of satiric *persona.* If he had intended Ransom as the hero, or Verena as the heroine (both claims have been made), he would not have made them so frequently objects of satire. A claim has even been made for Olive as a "tragic heroine on the model of Antigone," but again such an interpretation cannot stand up in the face of the fact that she too, perhaps most of all, is the target of the satirical thrust. Only the moral standards posited by reverse implication through the voice of the satiric *persona* (i.e., the authorial voice) are consistent throughout the work.

Even the setting and the minor characters are included in the satiric treatment, as a means of providing what Oscar Cargill calls the "environment of ideas" which is such an important part of the total satiric effect.[8] For instance, the view from Olive's comfortable parlor reveals "casual patches of ice and snow; the desolate suburban horizons, peeled and made bald by the rigor of the season; the general hard, cold void of the prospect . . . straight, sordid tubes of factories" (p. 178). Because most of the action takes place in New England, James provided himself with the opportunity to recreate the ambience of what Van Wyck Brooks called New England's "Indian Summer," which James saw as the unfortunate aftermath of the great mid-century surge of humanitarian reform that the region had fostered. The dessication of that once-vigorous spirit is incarnated in the figure of Miss Birdseye, who, while not totally exempted from the satiric treatment, is accorded a degree of tender if ironic indulgence. It is perhaps significant in this regard that her death, symbolizing the final extinction of the true humanitarian spirit (grown old and impotent), immediately precedes the novel's powerful climax. Miss Birdseye further functions as a foil to the charlatanism of the present age of pseudo-reform, most vividly embodied in Selah Tarrant, the greedy, exploitative mesmerist who feeds, vulture-like, on a feast of gullible females. James further associates, through imagery and scenic rendering, the growth of industrialism with the decline of genuine humanitarianism. The pictures of Boston and New York, of which the passage quoted above is but one of many examples, as they passed into the age of industrialization are masterful, as James captures and satirizes the very sights, sounds, and smells of the musty, dimly lit meeting rooms of the reformers, the vulgar lecture-hall flickering with gaslights and bustling with self-important women, the traffic-choked streets, the defiled vistas, the gaudy ostentation of Mrs. Burrage's music room with its potted palms and marble busts. It is a picture far removed from the atmosphere of picturesque antiquity in which his evocations of many European cities are customarily enveloped. The defining difference is that which James saw and despised as a pervasive and distinctly American vulgarity.

But it is the three central characters as they function within this setting who are the main focus of the satire in *The Bostonians*. The already noted omission of an explicit "centre of consciousness" in the usual Jamesian sense, besides telling us that the authorial voice is the spokesman for the satiric norm, also suggests that in this novel we are dealing with differing forms of the limited consciousness, or, to be more specific, with the kind of character whom (as he confesses in the preface to *The Princess Casamassima*) he had never been able to see as a truly "interesting" character, as a "leading interest" (his terms). The *vir bonus* stands in direct, if at times implicit, contrast to both the hero and the *ingénu* as satiric *personae*. But this fact has not always been recognized: Abigail Hamblen has said, for instance, that "it is difficult to escape the feeling that [Verena] is James's . . . ideal of perfect femininity."[9] In the face of this and similar statements by others, let us consider Verena.

Many readers have been charmed by James's red-haired oratress, and it is true that there is something at least superficially engaging about Verena Tarrant. Her striking appearance, her disarming ingenuousness, her desire to please others—any and all—make comprehensible, if not unarguable, Charles R. Anderson's comment that she is "the embodiment of the feminine principle."[10] But such a conclusion is brought severely into question when one considers the types of girls to whom James elsewhere in his works chose to accord his most sympathetic treatments: Verena is far from being an Isabel Archer, for instance, or even a Daisy Miller, to use again these examples from this period of his career. She is not even a *"femme fatale,"* as William Mc-Murray has claimed, in the sense that Christina Light (or, as she appears later in the canon, the Princess Casamassima) is; Verena lacks the cleverness, sophistication, and genuine beauty required for that role.[11] In short, she possesses none of that capacity for intelligent discrimination and courageous independence that characterizes James's major heroines; even Kate Croy and Charlotte Stant Verver, the so-called "bad heroines" of the late novels, are given a higher degree of authorial sympathetic understanding and psychological probing than is either Verena or Olive Chancellor. But it is not really necessary to go outside the novel, even to James's own other works, to support my claim that Verena, far from being the heroine or *ingénu,* is an object of satire.

Of course it was necessary to James's scheme for the novel that, as the character upon whom the conflict was to be centered, she be sufficiently credible for the role. But even her charm is qualified: her beauty appears as beauty largely because of the satiric contrast afforded by the dinginess and sordidness of her background, and because of the obliquities of vision on the parts of those whom it affects. The authorial voice makes frequent references to the cheap vulgarity of her appearance. It is difficult to imagine that the man whose surrogate-character in *The Ambassadors* could wonder whether the charming Madame de Vionnet, a genuine *femme du monde,* wears under her long black sleeves perhaps more bracelets than a lady might wear would present as an "ideal of femininity" a girl whose "idea of enjoyment . . . is an abundance of feather on her hat"; who, "with her bright, unique clothes . . . might have been a ropedancer or a fortuneteller." Verena's ingenuousness and desire to please, delightful as they might momentarily appear in a young *naif,* go deeper than her naiveté; they reveal her essential malleability. She is a plastic being whose mold has not been cast, true, but there is lacking in her basic endowments both the capacity for fine aesthetic discrimination and the potential for meaningful moral development, desiderata James consistently posited elsewhere for his major characters. Verena's mold will never be cast; she will never achieve form, only an imposed posture. She will always assume the form determined by whatever stronger influence is brought to bear upon her. McMurray has said that she has "an absolutely open and selfless consciousness," but he qualifies his statement, rightly I think, by continuing, "if she gives herself effortlessly, it is because she is 'anemic' of any self to give." We remember Verena's pale complexion, suggesting both physical anemia and this anemia of selfhood. Like Browning's Duchess, she has a heart too soon made glad, too easily impressed: "she liked whate'er/She looked upon, and her looks went everywhere." This plasticity is the quality in Verena that causes Olive her moments of greatest anxiety, as the scene of the Tarrants' tea-party (a scene of uncontestably overt satire that borders on broad parody) makes abundantly clear. A literary source for Verena has been suggested in Dinah Morris of Eliot's *Adam Bede,* but despite the evidence Robert L. Selig marshals in support of his thesis, Verena displays not even the sense of sincere conviction in her proselytizing for women's rights that gives depth and substance to Eliot's lady-preacher.[12] Verena's "gift of elo-quence" is brought severely into question by the air of charlatanry surround-ing it, by the uses to which it is put, by the intellectual spuriousness of those whom it affects, by its ostensibly spontaneous but in reality carefully re-hearsed "sincerity," and (worst of all) by the few examples of it to which we are privy. Whatever commitment she may have to the feminists' cause is a pale refraction of the atmosphere of "causes" in which she has been reared and, more importantly, of Olive's unyielding pressure. Mrs. Luna, for once, is right in her ungenerous conviction that "Verena cared as much for the rights of women as she did for the Panama Canal. . . . She will give Olive the greatest cut she has ever had in her life. She will run off with some lion-tamer; she will marry a circus man" (which, while exaggerated, is not a totally inaccurate picture of Basil Ransom, especially when we recall the "leonine" aspect of Ransom's appearance). In short, Verena is a fool—"one that will do/To start a scene or two/An easy tool/Deferential, glad to be of use"—a pretty fool ("though she had red hair"), but a fool nonetheless. The fact that the cousins, Olive Chancellor and Basil Ransom, contend so bitterly over this relative nonentity is one measure of their own limitations.

Verena, then, cannot be the "heroine," especially in the sense of Mack's definition of the satiric *persona* of *ingénu.* Ingénue she is, but only in a pejor-ative sense, as an object of satire. She is, further, the object for the posses-sion of which the novel's basic conflict takes place, and now I should empha-size the words *object* and *possession,* for they suggest most nearly the es-sential satirical purpose of the novel: pointing out the folly, indeed, immoral-ity of dehumanization, the treating of another human being, however shallow or foolish, as a thing to be appropriated, possessed, and used.

Verena's father, Selah Tarrant, is of course the first culprit in this regard, but from the moment Olive lays eyes upon the girl, early in the novel, it is obvious that she will soon take Verena over. In direct contrast to Verena's extreme malleability, Olive is a case of extreme inflexibility. Hamblen has said of her, "she is a single-minded intense character . . . whose hatred of men is pathological." It is hard to escape the feeling that she represents, in a concentrated dose, all that James disliked about his native country, which might explain why he chose to make her the major target of his satire. Olive has all of the morbidity of the brooding, introspective sensibility that is one strain of the Puritan heritage as James saw it: "she took things hard. . . . She was a woman without laughter." She has the rigidity, intolerance, and desire to control and manipulate others that is part of that strain, and she has the sense of moral self-righteousness that seems inevitably to follow when one is convinced that he (or she) is in sole possession of The Truth. "She has a fastidious, exclusive, uncompromising nature." That nature is imaged forth vividly—and satirically—as one reads that her smile "might have been likened to a thin ray of moonlight resting on the walls of a prison," and that "when she turned [her eyes] upon you, you thought vaguely of the glitter of green ice."

But Olive, for all her cold moral rigidity, has an aesthetic sense; though, again like her Puritan forebears, she harbors a distrust for beauty as morally suspect. She registers distaste at the dinginess and ugliness of Miss Birdseye's lodgings but tries to convince herself that these things are unimportant:

> The bareness of her long, loose, empty parlor . . . told that she had never had any needs but moral needs, and that all her history had been that of her sympathies. . . . [Olive] mortally disliked it, and . . . in a career in which she was constantly exposing herself to offense and laceration, her most poignant suffering came from the injury of her taste. She had tried to kill that nerve, to persuade herself that taste was only frivolity in the disguise of knowledge; but her susceptibility was constantly blooming afresh and making her wonder whether an absence of nice arrangements were a necessary part of the enthusiasm of humanity (pp. 29-30).

The juxtaposition of "nice arrangements" with the concept of an "enthusiasm of humanity" is a perfect example of what Joseph Bentley has described as "semantic gravitation," a device resulting in satiric reduction that occurs when a higher moral or social value is juxtaposed with a lower, or more trivial, one. The effect inevitably is that the higher is reduced to the level of the lower.[13] And when we remember that Olive's own parlor suffers no such privation of "nice arrangements," we see even more clearly the spuriousness of her claim to "an enthusiasm of humanity." She regards the experience of "Europe" (in the special Jamesian sense as a means of opening oneself to new experiences and ideas) in similar terms. Mrs. Luna comments that although Olive had been to Europe, "she stayed only an hour or two. She hates it; she would like to abolish it." Even Mrs. Luna's obviously comic exaggeration does not mitigate the bite, or the truth, of the satirical comment. Olive's attitude toward Europe is akin to that implied in the little satirical sketch of the Reverend Mr. Babcock, another product of the Puritan culture, in *The American*, and anticipates the more fully developed Waymarsh and Sarah Pocock of *The Ambassadors*. All of these characters are struck from the same Puritan mold. Olive is not, like Catherine Sloper in *Washington Square*, merely indifferent to Europe; she "hates it," because it touches that sensibility deep within her that her perverted moral sense tells her must be crushed. Yet, like most such efforts, her attempt to "kill that nerve" is unsuccessful, and the nerve surfaces as her unhealthy attraction to Verena, no small part of which is attributable to her sense of the girl's beauty. It is essential that Verena be flamboyant (thus the images of the "ropedancer" and the "for-tune-teller"). She must be totally different from that which Olive might have regarded as "tasteful," for taste, perversely, is what Olive seeks to sublimate. Verena must have the "common" touch. She would not have served nearly so successfully as an illustration of this particular aspect of Olive's neurosis had she been plain or even just ordinarily pretty.

But, as Babcock and Waymarsh illustrate, these negative aspects of James's view of the refracted Puritan character are not confined to women. Olive's is an extreme case because in her these qualities are combined with an innate sexual insecurity. In her view that insecurity takes the form of her "compre-hensive contention . . . that the peculiar wretchedness which had been the very essence of the feminine lot was a monstrous artificial imposition, crying aloud for redress . . . [and] men must take *their* turn, men must pay!" (p. 186). But we see that beneath the rhetoric lies her fear of the implications of her sex, a fear that manifests itself as a pathological hatred of men:

> . . . Miss Chancellor was a signal old maid. That was her qual-
> ity, her destiny; nothing could be more distinctly written.
> There are women who are unmarried by accident, and others
> who are unmarried by option; but Olive Chancellor was un-
> married by every implication of her being. She was a spinster
> as Shelley was a lyric poet, or as the month of August is
> sultry (p. 18).

Whatever the cause or concatenation of causes—hereditary, environmental, biological, or psychological—and despite the fact that this particular quotation occurs as an impression of Ransom's, the point of Olive's insecurity as a sexual being, and specifically a female, is emphatically iterated and reiterated throughout the novel. In this respect she serves, along with other female characters, to illustrate a pervasive sexual distortion, the "decline in the sentiment of sex" as James called it in his Notebooks, that theme that Habegger claims has been overemphasized. I side, however, with Howe when he suggests that a crucial element of the novel is its depiction of "the disarrangements of society . . . embodied in the often deformed and grotesque sexual lives of the characters, particularly the women." Howe continues, quoting liberally from the novel:

> Mrs. Luna's "hair was in clusters of curls, like bunches of grapes; her tight bodice seemed to crack with vivacity." Verena Tarrant, predictably, has a "flat young chest," and Miss Birdseye "no more outline than a bundle of hay." Dr. Prance is "spare, dry, hard, . . . If she had been a boy she would have borne some relation to a girl, whereas Dr. Prance appeared to have none whatever." Olive Chancellor's appearance is deliberately left vague, except for the clue given our sense of catastrophe when we learn, upon her first meeting with Ransom, of "the vague compassion which [her] figure excited in his mind."[14]

No defense of these descriptions as explicit satire would seem to be required. They employ, in fact, a standard satirical technique, one of which Pope was particularly fond. I refer to the device of ridiculing individual examples of deviations from the satiric norm for the purpose of suggesting the pervasiveness of such deviations. In "An Epistle to Dr. Arbuthnot," for example, the famous "Sporus" passage satirizes not only "Lord Fanny" (Lord Hervey) as an individual, but all the foppish Court sycophants whom the satiric *persona* saw Lord Fanny as representing. So here: Olive's personal problems are generalized and extended to other participants in the crusade for women's rights, and then are re-particularized in her own perverted zeal. James runs no risks that the cause might appear in his satiric rendering as a viable or admirable campaign; however much he elsewhere demonstrated his admiration for the courage and independence of modern young American women, he makes it clear in his satire that the form assumed by the organized movement of his time and place was both ineffective and meretricious. One of the novel's great moments, illustrating my point, occurs with the often-admired description of Mrs. Farrinder, a "national leader" who is the featured speaker of the evening at Miss Birdseye's:

> She was a copious, handsome woman, in whom angularity had been corrected by the air of success; she had a rustling dress (it was evident what *she* thought about taste). . . . There was a lithographic smoothness about her, and a mixture of the American matron and the public character. There was something public in her eye, which was large, cold, and quiet; it had acquired a sort of exposed reticence from the habit of looking down from a lecture desk, over a sea of heads, while its distinguished owner was eulogized by a leading citizen. Mrs. Farrinder, at almost any time, had the air of being introduced by a few remarks. . . . She was held to have a very fine manner, and to embody the domestic virtues and the graces of the drawing room; to be a shining proof, in short, that the forum, for ladies, is not necessarily hostile to the fireside. She had a husband, and his name was Amariah (pp. 30-31).

While these excerpts can give only an indication of the satiric force which accumulates through the passage in its entirety, they sufficiently illustrate the point that the authorial voice, in the *persona* of the *vir bonus,* is in full control. The grandiose formality of the prose reflects Mrs. Farrinder's own conscious sense of inflated self-importance; the use of the clichés of the lecture platform is heavily ironic; the analogy of the lithograph (as well as her expressed desire to make the Sunday Supplement) underscores her deliberate pose as a swayer of public sentiment; and the superlative flatness of the final sentence laconically expresses the total insignificance of the male in Mrs. Farrinder's—and by simple extension, the movement's—scheme of things. It is almost mock-heroic in the Fielding manner; it reminds me of nothing so much as the *tour de force* of the description of Beau Didapper in *Joseph Andrews.* This scene at the novel's beginning is balanced by equally satirical ones at the mid-point (the occasion of Verena's first New York performance at the home of Mrs. Burrage), and at the end (the climactic scene at the Music Hall). Whatever other faults might be found with the structure of *The Bostonians,* the satirical thrust is an undeniable unifying thread.

   All of which simply serves to underscore Olive's distorted values in allying herself with such a movement for, unlike the opportunistic Mrs. Farrinder, she is sincere (to the limits of her self-understanding, at least), and, unlike Miss Birdseye, she possesses a superior intelligence, one indication of which is the depth and breadth of her researches into the subject of her monomania. The fact that her motivation stems primarily from her personal aberrations is seen in the ineffectuality of her attempts at active involvement in the movement. When she asks Mrs. Farrinder what she may do to help the cause, that lady, shrewdly surmising Olive's relative affluence, suggests that she "contribute," by which she obviously means money. This is clearly not what Olive envisions. Elsewhere the point is made that Olive had tried on several occasions to befriend "poor, downtrodden shopgirls," but had become discouraged when it seemed that they "were all odiously mixed up with Charlie"; it is further noted, significantly, and, again, in the authorial voice, that the girls "seemed afraid of her" for some reason that Olive cannot comprehend. So while she quivers intensely for "the long martyrdom of woman" and feels it "as a deep, unforgettable wrong . . . as one feels a stain that is on one's honor," her actual participation in the movement is more desire than fact.

Her meeting Verena seems to offer the opportunity she has been awaiting. Olive's motives—public and private—in trying to appropriate the girl are really two sides of the same coin. She tells herself that she wants to help Verena to become an instrument in the "holy cause," with Olive supplying the financial backing and spiritual determination necessary to effect a significant surge forward in the campaign for justice. The public motive, then, has its exploitative side, in Olive's using Verena's "gift" to rectify her own deficiencies in public speaking. But the private motive is more important and more exploitative, for secretly Olive admits even to herself that "she found here what she had been looking for so long—a friend of her own sex with whom she might have a union of soul." The form of Olive's neurosis has been generally recognized, as it should be, for there seems no doubt that James was perfectly aware of how accurately he was drawing in Olive the very type of the latent lesbian. From the moment when Olive "came to her slowly, took her in her arms, and held her long—giving her a silent kiss" (p. 309), Olive is terribly doomed. She desires a solemn vow of fidelity "for life"; she habitually speaks of their relationship as "our union"; she admits she is "jealous, that she didn't wish to think of the girl's belonging to anyone but herself"; she literally buys Verena from her parents; she writhes in an agony of apprehensive terror as Verena innocently flirts with the Harvard men; and she conceives a mortal hatred for Ransom that is terrible in its ferocity when she divines his interest in Verena. Every passage describing or even referring to the relationship between the two girls is rife with such implications, so that the point is made inescapable that Olive's passion for Verena and her espousal of the "sacred cause" are equally emblematic of her deep-seated sexual neurosis. And, lest the reader be tempted to suffer empathetically with Olive, the voice of the satiric *persona* reveals it all in the pitiless glare of his devastating, albeit subtle, satire.

The detachment of the consistently satirical treatment, implying a lack of general human sympathy, should not be construed, however, as minimizing Olive's suffering. She does indeed suffer, but suffering, as well as justice and love, can be blind. James would not have agreed with some modernists that suffering *per se* is tragic; it becomes tragic only when accompanied by moral insight. It is this point which denies to Olive the role of tragic heroine.[15] We remember May Bartram's comment to John Marcher: "You were to suffer your fate; that was not necessarily to know it," a point effectively dramatized in that scene of tragic intensity at the end of his story when Marcher experiences, too late, his moment of insight, when his beast finally springs. But up to that moment, his character as the morally blind solipsist had been unshaken. So with Olive Chancellor, except that Olive never does see; therefore, never reaches tragic stature. She never sees the underlying cause of her passion for Verena and the movement, and she never sees the root of the perversion of sensibility which manifests itself as the "secret, the most sacred hope of her nature was that she might some day . . . be a martyr and die for something" (p. 13). She seeks out tasks, duties, responsibilities, and the more unpleasant they are, the better they serve her masochistic desire for self-flagellation. "She expected to suffer intensely; . . . the prospect of suffering was always, spiritually speaking, so much cash in her pocket." The financial metaphor (besides casting aspersions on the so-called "Protestant Ethic," another unfortunate heritage of the early Puritans) is yet another example of semantic gravitation resulting in satiric reduction. After her satisfactorily distressing interview with the opportunistic and vulgar journalist, Matthias Pardon, we read that Olive "seemed to see the glow of dawning success; the battle had begun, and something of the ecstasy of the martyr." In sum, Olive's quasi-religious desire for self-sacrifice is the *reductio ad absurdum* of genuine selflessness; it is perverted ego gratification masquerading as moral self-righteousness. It further illustrates that blindness into her own nature already adumbrated and, even more serious, the perversion of her moral sense into what can only be regarded as a parody of true morality. She may be sick, and we may feel compassion for her on that account, but that fact would not have mitigated James's view that in her motives and actions she is essentially immoral.

Olive finds the martyrdom she ostensibly seeks, but not in the form she had envisioned, and, ironically, at the end she is fighting desperately for life. When Ransom by sheer brute force wrenches Verena from Olive's frenetic clutches while the restless crowd in the Music Hall roars its impatience, with Olive left to face that crowd alone to drown in the vulgarity she hated, one feels that the stake would have been infinitely preferable to her. She believes that she is prepared and even desirous of giving up her physical life, but she cannot endure the loss of Verena. Without Verena as her strut and support, she has no sense of self; she needs the girl to supply her own desperate lack of conscious human identity. But this kind of appropriation of another human being for one's own selfish ends is blatant immorality in the Jamesian moral universe, and it defines Olive as the victim, however inadvertent, of a perverted martyr-complex. Olive violates Verena's spiritual integrity, intrinsic to her as a human being, by attempting to appropriate, control, and manipulate her; her desire for martyrdom is the index of her inability to recognize and realize her own. She is the *sine qua non* of the essential Jamesian sin of failing to integrate feeling and living into an organic, unified, moral and aesthetic whole.

So far, my discussion might seem to support the male side of the hypothetical debate with which we began, and seem even to suggest that Ransom, Olive's opponent and mortal enemy, does indeed embody the novel's positive values and represent the satiric norm, as some have claimed. But such is by no means the case. It is true that Ransom is subjected to less satirical treatment than is his cousin, but this is strictly a matter of degree. James casts his ultimate vote for the normal heterosexual relationship, but he makes it clear that it is anything but a happy alternative that Verena faces.

There are many reasons why Ransom cannot qualify as the hero or the spokesman for the satiric norm. I stand with Oscar Cargill and Irving Howe against Philip Rahv, Trilling, and Anderson, who tend (in Cargill's words) "to inflate him." Howe, in particular, seems to me to dispose effectively of most the arguments in favor of Ransom in his essay already quoted, which he concludes by saying, "what James thought of Ransom's pretensions, what he made of the whole affair, how thoroughly he maintained the critical and ironic tone throughout the book, is suggested in this hint [the novel's last lines] that Ransom and Verena, married at last, would live unhappily ever after." But none of the critics has addressed himself specifically to the most thoroughgoing defense yet published of Ransom as hero, Anderson's "James's

Portrait of a Southerner."[16] Since Anderson raises some points that I believe require answers, I shall attempt to supply them.

His thesis is baldly stated: "Ransom became properly the hero, for what began as a satire of the Bostonians ended by being the triumph of a Mississippian." It is true, as Clare R. Goldfarb has recently pointed out, that there are regional implications in the conflict between Olive and Basil, echoing certain circumstances, in come cases ironically, of the late conflict between North and South.[17] Just as Olive represents in a certain sense the reform-minded North of the 1850's and the Burrages represent the post-war Northern *nouveaux-riches,* so does Ransom embody certain of the characteristics of the ante-bellum Southern myth. James reversed the direction of the war by having his Southerner "invade" the North and (again, as Goldfarb has punningly said), ironically winning the "Battle of Chancellorsville." Further, he wins not only that battle, but the war. At this point, however, the irony becomes painfully pointed, for he wins that war by the exercise of brute force analogous, say, to Sherman's march through Georgia, perhaps the single campaign in that bloody struggle which to this day arouses resentful indignation on the part of Southerners. A further qualification inherent in Ransom's "victory" is that, again like the ultimate military victory of the Union forces, the end of the fighting guaranteed no definitive resolution of the sources of conflict. One need only look at recent history to realize that.

Anderson further cites as positive virtues the facts that Ransom espouses the "righteous causes of chivalry and conservatism," and that he is the "champion of love and marriage," yet he admits that Verena is "loved possessively by both Ransom and Olive." Anderson is damning with faint praise here, for any knowledgeable reader of James knows that possessive love—even when directed from male to female, a traditional attitude modern feminists highly resent—is to be condemned. Anderson does admit some of Ransom's absurdities and inadequacies, pointing out his evident unfamiliarity with the "material panoply," by which one assumes he means the notions of taste, beauty, and gracious living commonly associated with the Margaret Mitchell version of the ante-bellum South, and even saying, "how could Ransom's cavalier pride, his aristocratic conservatism, his cult of chivalry, be anything but tinsel and pretension?" Yet he draws the conclusion that Ransom's fault are attributable to "James's lack of familiarity with the South and Southerners."

It seems clear that Anderson is trying to reconcile what he recognizes as contradictory qualities in Ransom by placing the blame on James's ignorance of the "Southern character." Admittedly, James may have been drawing upon certain stereotypes of the unreconstructed Southerner in his portrait of Ransom, but I suggest that his aim was larger than any desire to depict the "Southern character" (or, for that matter, the Northern) in any narrow, local-colorist sense. I maintain, rather, that Ransom's obvious absurdities and con-tradictions, his inflated sense of self-importance, his outmoded convictions, are evidence, again, of the satirical purpose of describing the "disarrange-ments of society." For instance, the author says, describing Ransom's ap-pearance, "these things, the eyes especially, with their smouldering fire, might have indicated that he was to be a great American statesman; or, on the other hand, they might simply have proved that he came from Carolina or Ala-bama." "Here thou, Great Anna! whom three Realms obey,/Dost sometimes Counsel take—and sometimes Tea": the satiric device of zeugma is as ap-parent and effective in *The Bostonians* as in "The Rape of the Lock."

But the final, and I hope clinching, argument remains to be made: the dif-ferences between Ransom and Olive are more apparent than real. Anderson comes close to this realization in his point about the possessiveness of the "love" (I qualify the word as I think James intended) each entertains for Verena. The very terms of the conflict define the basic immorality of each contender, for they have identical aims. Each "loves" Verena in a wholly egocentric way. Each sees her solely as the bolster for his or her own partic-ular insufficiency of self and conviction of superiority: Ransom as an advocate of male supremacy and Olive as an espouser of women's rights. Both of them are inflexible in their respective convictions; Ransom says at one point, for instance, "God forbid, Madam! I consider women have no business to be reasonable." Both cling to *a priori* judgments regarding right and wrong, on both the personal and the social levels; both are selfish in their respective attempts to appropriate, control, and manipulate Verena. Herein lies the force of the novel's devastating ending: after wresting Verena from Olive's grasp and forcing their way through the guards onto the street, Verena says, " 'Ah, now I am glad!' . . . But though she was glad, he presently dis-covered that, beneath her hood, she was in tears. It is to be feared that with the union, so far from brilliant, into which she was about to enter, these were not the last she was destined to shed" (p. 464). In short, all of those qualities and characteristics which I have identified as evidence of Olive's immorality—with the exception of the motive and form of the martyr com-plex—are shared, albeit in different forms and emanating from different motives, by Ransom. Both are absolutists, attempting to impose stasis upon the dynamic substance of life. Thus both deny the full range of life-potential to themselves and, what is worse, to Verena. Both are immoral, for Kant was not the first, nor will he be the last, moralist to contend that the essence of morality is to "so act as to treat humanity, whether in thine own person or in that of any other, in every case as an end withal, never as a means only."

And this point, I suggest, is the heart of *The Bostonians;* indeed, of all of James. On this occasion, he chose to depict the figure in his carpet by means of satire. Perhaps, paradoxically, his use of the forms and devices of satirical tradition was too successful, or perhaps just overly subtle, since it seems to have led to some serious misreadings of the novel. I hope that I have successfully demonstrated not only that James was a skillful satirist who knew the tradition well, but that, further, he conformed to the tradition by confronting—and answering—the matter of the relationship between satirical art and morality.

I began this essay by raising the question of the relevance of James to the modern mood, particularly some of the issues that have surfaced as a result of the current movement for Women's Liberation. I hope, at the very least, that I have succeeded in suggesting that *The Bostonians* deserves careful study by partisans of both feminine extremists and "male chauvinists." I believe that James, in a strangely prophetic way, may have succeeded in suggesting a necessary balance between the sexual extremes. In his overt satirization of the grotesquerie which in recent times has characterized much of what is commonly thought of as the "bra-burning" branch of modern "women's libbers," he has pointed out that such means, to reasonable persons of whichever sex, arouse at best amusement and at worst contempt. But in his positing of a standard, a satiric norm, he has also made an important point, in fact, *the* important point that society, and American society in particular (since it was American society that he chose here to satirize) needs to take a long, hard look at its traditional assumptions regarding the nature and function of women. As I said at the outset, James saw women as human beings, which is neither to denigrate nor to derogate their roles as women, but in fact to enhance those roles, to suggest a fuller definition and realization of just what it could mean to be a woman—and, for that matter, to be a man. Maybe, just maybe, that is what it is all about.

END NOTES

[1](New York: Random House, Modern Library ed., 1956). Orig. publ. 1886. Further references to *The Bostonians* are to this edition and will be noted in the text within parentheses.

[2]"The Disunity of *The Bostonians*,"*NCF*, 4 (1969), 193-209.

[3](New York Edition: Scribner and Co.), I, 53.

[4]Dorothea Krook, in *The Ordeal of Consciousness in Henry James* (Cambridge, England: Cambridge Univ. Press, 1962), pp. 17-19, has provided a lucid definition of the special sense in which James uses the word "civilized": "In the moral world that James has created . . . perfect lucidity, perfect composure, and perfect good humor . . . are the transcendent virtues of man as man, by which the greatness and dignity of the human spirit are affirmed in the very midst of suffering in itself degrading and demoralising. . . . This is the vision of human perfection that lights the way of the Jamesian vessels of consciousness with a radiance consistently splendid."

[5]*The Imagination of Loving: Henry James's Legacy to the Novel* (Detroit: Wayne State Univ. Press, 1965), pp. 58-66 and *passim.*

[6]*The Dunciad: A Study of Its Meaning* (Hamden, Ct.: Archon Books, 1968), p. 4.

[7]*Yale Review*, 41 (1951), 80-92.

[8]*The Novels of Henry James* (New York: MacMillan, 1961), p. 137. The passage in which the phrase occurs reads in part: "The most neglected point about *The Bostonians* is the pains which James took to establish the environment that produced Olive Chancellor and made the contest for Verena possible. . . . If we apply Zola's test of the adequacy of an environment (that which 'determines' and 'completes' the man), *The Bostonians* is as satisfactory as any French naturalistic novel. . . . In his first major effort in their direction James demonstrated that he had read the French naturalists to his advantage. His *environment of ideas* is as substantial as Zola's environment of things."

[9]"Henry James and the Freedom Fighters of the Seventies," *GaR*, 20 (1966), 35-44.

[10]"James's Portrait of a Southerner," *AL*, 27 (1955), 309-31.

[11]"Pragmatic Realism in *The Bostonians*,"*NCF*, 16 (1962), 339-44.

[12]"The Red Haired Lady Orator: Parallel Passages in *The Bostonians* and *Adam Bede*,"*NCF*, 16 (1961), 164-69.

[13]"Semantic Gravitation, An Essay on Satiric Reduction," *MLQ*, 30 (1969), 3-19.

[14]Introd., *The Bostonians*, p. xix.

[15]See Oscar Cargill and Daniel Lerner, "Henry James at the Grecian Urn," *PMLA*, 66 (1951), 318-25.

[16]See note 10 above.

[17]"Names in *The Bostonians*,"*IEY*, 13 (1968), 18-23.

Ring Around A Christmas Garland

Marshall Ledger

Christmas 1912 must have been cheerier than usual, if only because of the publication of Max Beerbohm's *A Christmas Garland.* Seventeen of Beerbohm's contemporaries were amusingly parodied in this work; no one, I suppose, found difficulty in reading past the asterisks in J*m*s, K*pl*ng, W*lls, H*rdy, B*nn*tt, G*lsw*rthy, C*nr*d, M**re, M*r*d*th (among novelists); Ch*st*rt*n, H*rr*s, G*sse, B*ll*c, H*wl*tt, B*ns*n, and Str**t (among belletrists); and Sh*w.

The book had had a long gestation. In 1896, Beerbohm conceived a collection of parodies grouped around the central event of Christmas; perhaps he was thinking of an extended lesson in point of view. His working title, "Seasonable Tributes Levied by Max Beerbohm," was itself part of the lesson—one pays tribute and one exacts tribute from others. Although Beerbohm dropped this title, he never relinquished the implications of levying tribute. He makes the original writers pay for what is in fact their artistic treasures, their styles; and their collective payments constitute Beerbohm's artistic wealth.

In 1896 "A Christmas Garland, woven by Max Beerbohm" appeared in the *Chap-Book* (Chicago); it contained parodies of Wells, Meredith (the only ones re-parodied in 1912), Alice Meynell, Beerbohm himself, and a few others. In December, 1906, he published parodies of James, Kipling, Wells, Shaw, Chesterton, Hewlett, and Moore in the *Saturday Review* (London); Meredith, "improved" from the 1896 version, appeared again in the *Review.* In 1912, these, some revised, appeared with nine new ones to form the final "garland."

A collection of parodies was not a new idea. In 1736, Isaac Hawkins Browne wrote *A Pipe of Tobacco,* praises put into the mouths of major authors of the day on what they put into their mouths; in 1784 a few cynical and disregarded poets gathered *Probationary Odes for the Laureateship;* in 1797-98 Canning, Ellis, and Frere parodied the politics of radical poets in the *Anti-jacobin,* and in 1812, James and Horace Smith wrote *Rejected Addresses,* supposed speeches celebrating the opening of the rebuilt Drury Lane

Theatre. Collections of parodies such as Thackeray's *Novels by Eminent Hands* (1845) and Swinburne's *Heptalogia* (1880) appeared throughout the nineteenth cent y.

What distinguishes Beerbohm's collection from these others is a unique unifying agent: the use of the parodies to define the parodist's position as artist. All parodies can be read as being critical, fault-finding, or appreciative of their originals. All parodies bring up the question of dominance or control and suggest that the parodist is finding his place by taking this particular tack on the original. But only Beerbohm thought of himself as an artist who finds his identity exclusively through parodying others.

Beerbohm himself suggests this meaning in a prefatory "Note" to the book. He says that as a youth he parodied—"played the sedulous ape"—to find models for his own style, sometimes to discover what to avoid. This explanation is pat enough, common to many writers. But he caps his statements with revealing and typical wit: "The book itself may be taken as a sign that I think my own style is, at length, more or less formed."[1] And of course there is nothing here that is not also someone else's. The laurel wreath, figured in the garland, belongs on Beerbohm's head. He is the hero, represented by no narrow set of literary devices describable as "Maxian" or less elegantly "Beerbohmian," but represented by the Jamesian and Shavian and Conradian devices all serialed together; nowhere pinned down and fixed by his own style, everywhere suggested by whosoever style he chooses to present.

No parodist of skill parodies gratuitously, any more than a serious writer chooses his themes, characters, issues, arguments, by whim. But the parodist is at a disadvantage because no one takes him seriously. Readers appreciate a dextrous parody, they like to apprehend the illusion of the original writer, and they are willing to allow it critical significance. But they go only so far as to discern whether the parodist loves or hates his original, and, as a corollary, the critical stance implied by the parody. All they want is a rough-hewn sense of style, as in word choice, imagery, and characters; and they want this brought into the purview of a laugh.

For the space of this essay, let us treat parody as we would treat a work whose seriousness was beyond question. Let us assume that whatever in a work is separable from other elements and "can be thought of as distinct"[2] is potentially grist for a parodist. So he will work not only with word choice, but also with larger elements like structure, situations, patterns. Let us look at the content of the parody as a serious choice of the parodist, not one forced on him by an author he has randomly chosen to parody. For a parodist, content is another element of style. Finally, since when a parodist chooses someone to parody, he commits himself to the original's entire bag of tricks, let us assume that each and every trick is one willingly taken on, not simply a requisite part of the original's paraphernalia, like the contents of a suit-case bought unopened at a post-office auction.

These requests are not outrageous. We grant them constantly, as far as they apply, to other kinds of literature. Here, they will permit me to make a case for the unity of *A Christmas Garland* as more than a string of parodies. My case is this: Beerbohm works himself up from the subservient position of parodist into the position of master over the original, overtaking the artist on his own grounds and, beyond the point of burlesque or ridicule, supplanting him; this is Beerbohm's way of laying claim to the title of artist. His parodies of James, Conrad, Kipling, and Shaw are the best examples, and concern the writers most familiar to us today.

II

The Jamesian parody, "The Mote in the Middle Distance," is the most famous and most often reprinted. It is the story of Keith Tantalus's moral awakening. He and his sister Eva wake up Christmas morning to find their stuffed stockings dangling at the foot of the bed. Keith wants to plunge right into them, but sensing something wrong with that act, tries to feel out Eva's attitude. She is a master of restraint—so much so that her sheer presence, rather than direct warning, wins Keith back from his unseemly impetuousness. They never do peek.

The parody includes what we usually term "style" and then extends out to subtler aspects which we also ought to call "style": "broken sentences, roundabout simplicities, syntactical quibbles, colloquialisms made genteel by inverted commas, italics for delicate intonation, stunning double negatives, accumulated homely adjectives, abruptly placed, vague adverbs, banal metaphors worried and reworried, the narrator's unsettling glances into the future and his intimacy with 'our friend' Keith, the exasperating, magnified scruples, and, at last, the vibrant moral renunciation."[3] To which let us add, terminology from painters, physical gestures and positions which seem like dynamic stills, the change wrought in the title through the development of the narrative; indefinite statements ("Oh, as to that!") and the assumption that the interpretation following such attenuation is correct; speculation about the other person, which seemingly could be put to rest by a direct question or two; indefiniteness of motive ("Perhaps it was to test this theory, or perhaps merely to gain time . . . "), raising doubts about how successfully one can penetrate the mind of another (Keith of Eva's mind, the narrator of Keith's); and the unknown line between fantasy and a good reading of another's intentions.

This list only begins to describe the parody's relation to the original. Distressingly it may not even approach the way Beerbohm actually apprehended James. Beerbohm pencilled on the rear cover of his copy of James's *The Finer Grain* what seems to be a few notes to himself:

> Never wrote verses—
> suppressed poet came
> out in letters—
> rhetoric
> alexandrines[4]

The last word suggests that Beerbohm perceived in terms of rhythm, which he proceeded to parse in the vocabulary of his sound classical education. In "The Mote," alexandrines abound:

> "They so very indubitably *are,* you know!"   (p. 5)

> It was with a certain sense of his rashness in
> the matter, therefore, that he now, with an air of
> feverishly "holding the line," said "Oh, as to that!"
>   (p. 6)
> [The narrator won't ask if they peeked because of his impression]
> —my sometimes all but throned and anointed certainty—
> that the answer, if vouchsafed, would be in the negative.
>   (p. 10)

Rhythm is doubtless a much deeper aspect of technique, one much less susceptible to cancellation or revision, than most of the preceding list, although all the items on the list tend, in James, to build to the rhythm Beerbohm heard.

Given all these elements, it is difficult to say exactly where burlesque or ridicule sets in. John Felstiner thinks of the parody as a "fetish for anyone who either loves or disparages James,"[5] expressing the delicate balance the parody maintains. The parody is so complete that it is difficult to ascertain Beerbohm's critical reaction to James; we see merely that his artistic reaction is reception in the highest degree. And no doubt we ought to take that felt balance as a way of looking at the parody. We might see Keith and Eva as a reduction of Merton Densher and Kate Croy in *The Wings of the Dove* (as Felstiner suggests), we can also see the toys in the stockings as a reduction of the beasts in Jamesian jungles. But reduction is not always belittlement; it can be a way of getting a handle on something. Beerbohm praised James' characters for their "passion of conscience, a sort of lyrical conscience, conscience raised to the pitch of ecstasy, both in great matters and in small."[6] If we think in these terms of technical accomplishment, rather than weight, we begin to think as Beerbohm did, with a mind tuned to psychology and art rather than to criticism.

To get at this parody, then, we must leave off measuring the critical stance, and treat it as a work with its own integrity. We don't look at it apart from the original—even though it does have a self-enclosed and complete story—but we ask what is in the parody that intrigued Beerbohm. To do this, we must examine the narrative as more than merely a peg on which Beerbohm hung Jamesian devices.

To Keith, Eva is "magnificent." He thinks this because she is apparently able to read his every thought, anticipate his moves. But at the start of the story, the word is only air; as her "magnificence" works a change in Keith's personality, it becomes a real quality, one which we are convinced Keith believes in, if not actually a part of Eva.

The magnificence is based on "remoteness," distance. Keith has never been close to his sister, doesn't know how she thinks or what she is capable of. So after his first thought, upon awakening, to look into his stocking, he suspects that Eva has already peeked. He is immediately checked—she is asleep. Then he is corrected—she is awake and, even being so, did not peek. Not only is she magnificent for that, but she adds to it by noting the presence of the stockings without chiding him for being tempted to violate them:

> She really was—he had often told her that she really was— magnificent; and her magnificence was never more obvious than in the pause that elapsed before she all of a sudden re- marked "They so very indubitably *are,* you know!" (p. 5)

The stockings are real. Eva, however, is a bit unreal to Keith, who launches an elaborate telephone metaphor to comprehend the distance between him and his sister, "the most telephonic of her sex." The metaphor is hilarious, simply because the slightest attempt to treat it literally becomes instantly absurd. As Keith draws out the metaphor, he leans, naturally enough, on telephone jargon, and we are asked to apply that jargon to human relations. We have already quoted Keith's biding for time—"holding the line"—and when he fears that she will not speak, he fears she has "rung off."

The telephone is not simply a burlesque of a Jamesian metaphor. It is immensely appropriate to the situation between the children. Though they speak to one another, they lack genuine closeness. " 'Oh, you certainly haven't, my dear, the trick of propinquity!' was a thrust she had once parried by saying that, in that case, *he* hadn't"—and indeed, over the telephone, the distance from Keith to Eva is equal to the distance back again. At least, Keith sees it this way.

But Eva is already reading his mind—he discovers this during the remainder of the parody. He becomes worried that she will discover his near-betrayal of looking into his stocking, and then the worse betrayal of silently accusing her of being capable of peeking. Her rarified statements and allusions, "Well, one does, anyhow, leave a margin for the pretext, you know!" leads him to test her. And when he swings his stocking, and she sits stock still without recrimination—another sign of restraint—he apotheosizes her magnificence. For the stockings hold "a very plenary fulfillment of desire"—and to look into that would be to destroy the loving mystery of it. " 'One doesn't,' she added, 'violate the shrine—pick the pearl from the shell.' " He understands: " 'One doesn't even peer.' " As an epilogue the narrator also understands; he refuses to ask Keith and Eva, in later days, if they ever had "in fact, 'peered.' "

The theme is renunciation; Eva knows it and teaches it to Keith, the narrator shares in it. In learning it, Keith closes the distance between Eva and him, and her magnificence is made palpable. Even the toys they wanted reflect the narrative development. Eva wanted a doll (self) of "ample proportions" (her magnificence) and "practicable eyelids" (she sees). Keith wanted a sword and helmet, elements of aggression, as if force were a proper action when necessary; but he outgrows these gifts even before he gets a chance to play with them. The "mote" turns from being an interruption, a "herd of elephants," to the inviolable shrine which implies the reality it houses. It becomes the best way to "see" that reality.

What attracts Beerbohm to this story is more than its Jamesian origin. It is Beerbohm's own story of his relation to James. Eva and Keith are eidolons for James and Beerbohm. The awareness Keith grows into is analogous to the understanding a parodist has for his original. Although Eva may guess what is in the stockings, she restricts herself to the sure knowledge that they must not be pried into. What is *in* the stockings represents the real nature of the children's desires and hopes and fatuities, but one doesn't get at them by ravage. The material thing, a reflection of the personality that wants it, must be approached gingerly, as one would deal with oneself, not grabbed. If one doesn't pick the pearl from the shell, it is not simply to play up to a mystery for mystery's sake, but to avoid missing the diaphonous personality by manhandling it. This is Jamesian. Analogously Beerbohm can get "at" James by showing that he understands the intricacies of the Jamesian mode of thought without flattening those intricacies by his own critical terms or by imposing his own interpretations. So he thinks in terms of "motes," which conceal, but to the perceiving eye reveal by suggestion, innuendo, implication, all the ways of Jamesian indirection. At the threshold of his realization, Keith says of the mote in the middle distance, "Did you ever, my dear, know me to see anything else? I tell you it blocks out everything. It's a cathedral, it's a herd of elephants, it's the whole habitable globe. Oh, it's, believe me, of an obsessiveness!' " In Jamesian style, these words are *about* the Jamesian style, figured in the stockings. Keith swiftly comes to know that they sufficiently imply everything. In the course of his own reading and understanding, Beerbohm found himself in this relation to James.

The details in "The Mote" bear out the relation between original and parodist. The telephone is a device which lends aural closeness, but demands that the whole personality be inferred through voice alone. This is good enough for a parodist. When Keith falls into a momentary fit of disaffection and accuses Eva of his own failing, the lack of "propinquity," she (James) is perfectly right in turning his own phrase back on him. Keith calls propinquity a "trick," as we might label the tricks (not trickery) of a clever illusionist. Ultimately, propinquity becomes identification—Keith's with Eva's ways, Beerbohm's with James'.

At this final stage, Keith's idolatry is called "the bigotry of the convert." Jamesian, it suits Beerbohm as well. Beerbohm is won over to James, and then outdoes him at his own endeavors.

The narrative subject, then, which seemed exclusively Jamesian to start, is fully Beerbohm's. The parody succeeds not simply because Beerbohm has mastered James, but because what was there to master matters deeply to Beerbohm. Taking material seemingly forced upon him by the fundamental choice of parodying James, the parodist keeps it as tightly organized and unified as a work by James. We cannot appreciate the coherence in a mere list of parodied devices, which alone are bones lacking unifying tissue.

Our general desire to know things is constantly countermanded by James, whose characters frequently turn their backs on direct knowledge. They send back unopened letters announcing inheritances, they do not state what others assume is on the tip of the tongue, they die with their secrets. James' point is that sheer knowledge is secondary to the way personalities have an impact on one another; he loves exploring how one sensitive mind grows aware of another. The serious parodist raises the same question. To imitate another's style is kid's play. What, however, are the implications of so thoroughly getting into another's mind as to be able to anticipate, even, what another mind might write?

James felt that this parody had successfully penetrated the deep recesses of his own mind. He told someone who asked him a question to consult Beerbohm: " 'Ask that young man,' he said. 'He is in full possession of my innermost thoughts.' "[7] Upon the publication of *A Christmas Garland,* James said, "No one, now, can write without incurring the reproach of some-what ineffectively imitating—*you!*"[8] James realizes an excellent parody and more—a realignment of the relation of original and parodist. Beerbohm goes far beyond amusement and ridicule; there is much more at stake than exposure of vices, of something to be learned and avoided in forming one's own style. The parodist not only devours the original, but even anticipates any possible new style. Beerbohm's parodies make the author so self-conscious that all he can do is play up to himself. And so, according to James, Beerbohm has put an end to writing. Beerbohm's talents point to literary suicide (as Zuleika Dobson's search for love results in the suicides of all of Oxford's undergraduates). This certainly is an extreme form of renunciation.

Beerbohm's mastery through words—over the telephone, so to speak—is corroborated by an anecdote he tells of meeting James in the street. James asked him to be his guide to a new London exhibition. Beerbohm was on his way to his club to read James' new story "The Velvet Glove," and turned him down. Mulling over his decision while reading the story, Beerbohm concluded that he preferred to infer the master than be with him.[9] Beerbohm was living out the experience of Fanny Hurter in "The Death of the Lion," James's story of the renunciation of a woman who came to see her favorite writer and who convinces herself that the greatest tribute is not to bother him.

Both Beerbohm's writing and his life seem to confirm that James was long writing what Beerbohm found apt to mythologize about James and himself. Letting life follow art. Beerbohm turned James's art into an expression of his own artistic life. James is always larger, more important, the "master." But, as a sketch Beerbohm did in 1911 suggests which shows James lecturing to a receptive Beerbohm, Beerbohm's one quality is the ability to look James in the eye on an even keel, to have his receiving eye on exactly the same plane.

III

Like "The Mote in the Middle Distance," Beerbohm's parody of Conrad, "The Feast," is an excellent parody pertinent to Beerbohm's own interests. The narrative tells how Williams, a clerk for commerce stationed in Africa, has been led by his servant Mahamo to a place where he will exchange trinkets for valuable ivory. The time is Christmas Day, and Williams' thoughts drift back to his fellow Englishmen celebrating the Christmas feast. Mahamo says that today is a feast-day for his own people, and Williams discovers that he has been brought to the feast—as the entree.

The parody is built on both little and large items associated with Conrad: postpositive adjectives, pairings, abstractions that lend themselves to philosophic statement (rivalling the concrete aspect of the narrative), foreshadowing, "exoticism," vegetation given the vigor of conscious beings, mystifying atmosphere, failure to read the landscape, misleading patterns in sensory things, ironies—of statement, of title, of situation, of job, the centrality of illusion, the "partnership" between black man and white, men seemingly getting along without feeling for one another, one's identification with one's office (at the sacrifice of the human and personal), the mocking of "human solidarity," the exploited outdoing the exploiter at his own game, the disaster befalling a lack of "imagination," and finally the fantasies represented by social institutions and "aims" in life, which prevent us—or protect us—from attending to the dark side of existence, the unknown and unintelligible.

Opinion about "The Feast" has varied. One of Beerbohm's reviewers, Richard Curle, felt the parody poor because it missed Conrad's "romantic intensity." Influential Conrad critics Guerard and Mudrick agree that the parody flails the weaknesses of early Conrad, most flagrant in "The Lagoon"; from this perspective the parody illustrates the obvious. Most recently, Addison C. Bross has enlarged the list of works Beerbohm likely drew upon and concludes that the wide reference indicates Beerbohm's appreciation for Conrad; Bross shows Beerbohm steeped in Conrad but does not account for the excellence of the parody. Conrad's own comment is curbed, although he is thinking of something else, his reputation as a writer. In the "Author's Note" to *Tales of Unrest,* he points to "The Lagoon" as having been

> most agreeably guyed by Mr. Max Beerbohm in a volume of parodies entitled *A Christmas Garland,* where I found myself in very good company. I was immensely gratified. I began to believe in my public existence.[10]

If we are going to give Beerbohm due credit for his parody, however, we must see what is in the parody that reaches beyond an interest in Conrad's literary techniques or his need for publicity.

Williams is an unknowing victim of the real world. He is human: he dreams of home, itches when bitten by mosquitoes, and resents the fate which he sees at last will be his. He has what he thinks is a responsible job of collecting ivory from natives, but in that office he has relinquished some human traits. He takes his own imperialistic work for granted, including his mastery over Mahamo. In Conrad, it is personally disastrous to be unaware of the implications of your work. Accordingly, although Williams doesn't intend to cheat the natives or sell Mahamo out, he ignores what it means for him to do what he is doing. He has rationalized his life—not in the sense of making the best of a bad situation, but in the basic sense of thinking thoughts and performing actions which conveniently protect him from questioning the status quo.

On this point, Beerbohm deeply understands Conrad; it happens to be a point of overlap with James. Beerbohm loves the rationalizations that one makes of one's situation. In James this typically human behavior is called "attenuation"; in Conrad, "illusion." The illusions Conrad writes of are those constructions of reality which prevent a person from ever shaming himself in front of his full consciousness (not to mention others). In the parody, Williams never lets go. Even in the moment of dawning that he shall not feast, but be feasted upon, he resorts to his structure of the world:

> As he turned in his flight he saw the goods so neatly arrang-
> ed at his orders, and there flashed through him, even in the
> thick of the spears, the thought that he would be a grave loss
> to his employers. This—for Mr. Williams was, not less than the
> goods, of a kind easily replaced—was an illusion. It was the last
> of Mr. Williams' illusions.   (p. 130)

Even as this theme is Conrad's, so is it Beerbohm's. As a parodist and especially as a dandy, Beerbohm cautiously held himself in, playing up to ideas and styles that were already established in art.

Williams' mental shelter is paralleled by a series of physical ones: a mosquito net, a hut, the roofs of trees, the blue sky. All are ineffectual. The mosquito net was "itself illusory like everything else, only more so." This should have been an illusion Williams himself perceived! But even here he suppresses himself for his office; first he checks the goods, and only after seeing that they are safe does he relieve his agony by scratching. The other illusions are rendered as Conradian ironies. Williams stands in the "mouth" of the hut. Under the roofs of the trees takes place that "warfare implacable and daily" among all the insects of the jungle, even on this holy morning "newly roused to the task of killing and being killed." And the trees are silhouetted against the sky "like shapes cut out of black paper by a maniac who pushes them with his thumb this way and that, irritably, on a concave surface of blue steel"—a simile whose elements foreshadow the spear that finally imposes on Williams, "a young sapling tremulous, with a root of steel."

Ultimately there are no shelters, physical or mental. Williams is a man out in the open, exposed. In living up to his job, he closes out a sense of the world as it really is; he is "not imaginative." He lives in a dream-world as unreal as his nostalgic fantasy of lying in his bedroom in Marylebone, "late dozing, with great contentment." He is not so much punished for his faults as he is forced to succumb to the way of the predatory world.

"The Feast" does lack Conrad's moral seriousness. The eating of Williams is expected more as a psychological event than as a moral one. If Williams is a careless master, he is not brutish; if Mahamo is wily, he is not secretive and mysterious. There are no philosophic implications—no metaphysical skepticism, no parodic comment on Conradian pessimism; the cannibalism is not seen, as it is in "Heart of Darkness," as "unspeakable rites." In such words as "inexplicable" and "inilluminable," the parody has what Leavis has called in Conrad the "adjectival insistence upon inexpressible and incomprehensible mystery,"[11] but Beerbohm does not care about that mystery as Conrad does (or as Conrad, in purple passages, convinces himself he does).

Beerbohm chooses to ignore this rich aspect of Conrad because it does not suit his definition of self that is being made through Conrad. Only Conrad's sense of human relation is relevant, not the nature of man's mind and the fearful question of what man's mind is. The parody raises the question of who is in charge, a deep question to both Conrad and Beerbohm: the story is about how the servant is really the master. Talking about illusions and presenting them dominate the narrative because they are persistent Conrad motifs, and Beerbohm's major ones as well. For master or Williams, read Conrad; for servant or Mahamo, read Beerbohm.

The details of the parody point to this conclusion at the same moment that they perfectly recall Conrad. On the floor of the jungle, writes C*nr*d, "by force of habit, the lush herbage went through the farce of growth—that farce old and screaming, whose trite end is 'decomposition.' " Growth in Conrad might be called a farce because it is seen as the perennial destruction of created things, life being always in a stage of passing away. The eternal repetition, especially caught in its dying phase, is undoubtedly a "trite end." Growth ought to be composition or progression (just as we speak of Conrad's own growth from his early works to his later ones[12]). Uniting these opposites of growth and repetition or death is the parodist. To him, growth is suspect because his business is to reveal the original at a point of stopped growth. In going over the original's devices, presenting them for our recognition and enjoyment, the parodist stills the original, making a farce of growth and a virtue of arrested development. He catches the original at the height of his compositional powers; anything afterward is implied to be only a decline (*vide* James's suggestion that writers cannot write after their own styles are consciously forced upon them, unless they are resigned to imitate themselves or even Beerbohm). The parodist, then, puts an end to the writer's style by replicating it humorously. The slow and gradual assimilation of nature contrasts to the motif of devouring, which is exactly the process perpetrated by Beerbohm upon Conrad. By "decomposing" Conrad, both in the sense of taking him apart, device by device, for study and parody, and in the sense of leaving him now to rot, Beerbohm is making his own composition. Beerbohm's process parallels the "growth" Mahamo and his friends shall shortly enjoy, which is not through the trite end of decomposition, but through the meaningful ritualistic ceremony of a "feast."[13]

More briefly, let us take another sentence: stars reflect off Mahamo's body and in his eyes, "creating an illusion of themselves who are illusions" (p. 125). This recalls the final sentence of "The Lagoon":

> He stood lonely in the searching sunshine; and he looked
> beyond the great light of a cloudless day into the darkness of
> a world of illusions.[14]

The reflections off Mahamo's body are indeed illusory stars. The stars in the heavens, however, are a different kind of illusion. Although they are real bodies, they are not in that place in the heavens where, from the source of the light, we expect them to be. The stream of light has been traveling so far and so long that the body of the star has already moved on, and we are "seeing" its light from where it used to be. (It might even have already exploded, and no longer exist.) Beerbohm is conveying a real phenomenon, not ridiculing or exaggerating something from Conrad. It reinforces the main theme: Mahamo, about to betray his master, is, like the star, not where he used to be (and not where Williams thinks he is). And it describes Beerbohm, for where is *his* body? We can see it only in the style of Conrad, in the reflected glass of parody, and then perceive it only in its past. Like light from a distant star, it has no present self; yet in borrowing its "present," it seems to take on greater lustre than the lender's.

In two different writers, James and Conrad, Beerbohm found ways to insinuate his own place as artist; yet his parodies lose nothing for this extra interest. In fact, I would reverse the priorities: his own interests are not "extra" but entwined with the parodies. They doubtlessly conditioned the kinds of styles he could parody most fully. For instance, despite his excellent hold on Conrad, Beerbohm limits himself to the style we see exemplified chiefly in "The Lagoon," which preceded the parody by eight years. By the time the parody was written, Conrad had moved on to other subjects and other styles. Throughout his life, Beerbohm didn't have much to say about Conrad—an essay in 1905, caricatures in 1904 and 1921 are most of it—so it is significant that he chose to parody something Conrad had already personally superceded. He did not grow with Conrad because he had already made with him his imaginative identification. With James, Beerbohm found identification with material James was writing in the 1890's, but had to wait, as it were, for James to develop the famous dense style of his last phase. (Perhaps James didn't make it into the 1896 "garland" because he, rather than his parodist, was not sufficiently "mature.") As we read the parodies, we don't feel any lack of fulness, but we can readily suppose that, in defining himself through parody as an artist-scholar, Beerbohm selected with as careful an eye towards his own needs as towards adherence to his original authors. Interestingly, even if the original's style were not current, Beerbohm demanded that the writer himself be so. He restricted his parodies to contemporaries, and disliked publishing a parody after the original author died (he did so in the *Garland* only in Meredith's case). Since he saw the "personality" of the author and the author's works as one entity, the end of the man's life spelled the end of the work's vitality. He might not cease reading the author, but he could no longer catch the spark of creative identification.

IV

By searching through all of the parodies in *A Christmas Garland*, we will find the same overall principle: Beerbohm transcending the ordinary requirement of parody that it give pleasure, demonstrating a mastery that makes the original dwindle by comparison, and making that mastery a significant part of the content. Fifteen parodies remain, but I shall comment on only two, those of Kipling and Shaw, both of whom touched Beerbohm oddly.

K*pl*ng's "P.C., X, 36" stands second in *A Christmas Garland,* following the James parody; a contrast seems intended. The narrative tells of a police-man named Judlip, bored and philosophical on Christmas Eve, until he sees Santa Claus suspiciously hovering on the roof-tops; he springs into action, arresting him. Santa is fully compliant as Judlip marches him off to the police station, physically brutalizing him every step of the way. We hear the story through a nameless narrator who acts as Judlip's factotum; he plays up to Judlip in exchange for being allowed to ignore the curfew, he buys him drinks, reinforces his self-righteousness, and helps out in beating up Santa.

The viciousness in this story is paralleled by a viciousness in the parodic flavor. No one has missed it. Kipling, although never once answering this or other attacks by Beerbohm, seems to have felt stunned, and avoided passing Beerbohm on the street. Kipling's critics don't dwell on it. Beerbohm's admirer Felstiner calls one sentence the "cruelest" Beerbohm ever wrote: " 'Frog's-march him!' I shrieked, dancing. 'For the love of heaven, frog's-march him!' " Beerbohm himself grew to wonder about his own ferocity, especially as it multiplied in the many caricatures he made of Kipling: "I couldn't stop. You know, I couldn't stop. As his publication increased, so did my derogation. He didn't stop; I *couldn't* stop. I meant to. I wanted to. But I couldn't."[15]

The customary explanation for Beerbohm's break from usual decorum is hatred towards Kipling's imperialism. This fits many of the caricatures (in-cluding a famous one from *The Poets' Corner,* depicting a diminutive Kipling, tooting a horn, hanging on to the arm of the giantess Britannia, who doesn't relish the accompaniment). But political comment was not Beerbohm's line, and despite attempts to color him as a liberal, he was uninterested in politics, especially in his writings. With political opinions only haphazardly dropped throughout his prose, he would hardly take Kipling to task so frequently un-less he saw in Kipling, as in James and Conrad, a sign of himself.

Imperialism in general, or the performance of a single peace-officer, is a cousin to the theme of dominance we have seen earlier. If the social or political question is who shall be master and who servant, then the K*pl*ng subject represents another angle on the parodist's relation to his original. Judlip enforces his mastery by use of a truncheon and clever neck-twists and an assortment of body-chops, all upon a consistently docile victim. He over-kills. The restraining hand of law knows no restraint in executing its duty; it in fact negates the principles of its own existence, making anarchy and force the rule. Judlip unknowingly gives himself away:

"Life ain't a bean-feast. It's a 'arsh reality. An' them as makes
it a bean-feast 'as got to be 'arshly dealt with accordin'. That's
wot the Force is put 'ere for from Above. Not as 'ow we ain't
fallible. We makes our mistakes. An' when we makes 'em we
sticks to 'em. For the honour o' the Force. Which same is
the jool Britannia wears on 'er bosom as a charm against
hanarchy."   (p. 16)

Beerbohm saw Kipling as similarly persistent—as an artist inclined to over-
assertion, exaggeration, and exhibitionism. In a review of the dramatized
version of Kipling's *The Light That Failed*, he ironically states that "Rudyard Kipling" is surely a female's pseudonym, for the manly veneer which
Kipling insistently urges is so excessive that it implies its very opposite.
Kipling's way is Judlip's. The eyebrow-raising violence obliterates any decent
purpose in law or art. Kipling, like Judlip, lives up to a distorted idea of his
role, rather than dealing with reality in a manner consistent with that role. As
a result, the artist ruins the psychology of his characters: "They are men seen
from the outside, or rather, not seen at all, but feverishly imagined." They are
the fantasies of Kipling's impatience, his failure to adhere to reality for the
sake of the literary illusion. They are malformations produced by the "abrupt
jargon of alternate meiosis and hyperbole which is Mr. Kipling's literary
style."[16]

Beerbohm's complaint does not seem to be in anger against Kipling for
spending his imagination on jingoism, although he felt that good jingoism
precluded good fiction. He may also have sensed Kipling's internal contradiction in celebrating soldiers and merchants as men of action superior to men of
ideas or writers, but this should not have riled him—especially since Judlip
acts like Kipling. Perhaps Kipling's artistic direction was dangerously close to
Beerbohm. We would never suspect it now, since Kipling's excesses are a polar
opposite to Beerbohm's restraint, but the two writers were once linked together as bright stars on the literary horizon.[17]

Judlip himself gives us a clue to Beerbohm's anger. In a few statements of
self-pity, he helps explain why he finds his own identity in smashing Santa's
cervical vertebrae:

" 'Wot am I?' he said, as we paced along. 'A bloomin' cypher.
Wot's the sarjint? 'E's got the Inspector over 'im. Over above
the Inspector there's the Sooprintendent. Over above 'im's the
old red-tape-masticatin' Yard. Over above that there's the

'Ome Sec. Wot's e? A cypher, like me. Why?' Judlip looked up
at the stars. 'Over above 'im's We Dunno Wot.' "   (pp. 15-16)

Understandably he yearns to be more than "X, 36"; the attention cf the
groveling narrator does not suffice, even though Judlip is "over 'im." Judlip
gets a solid sense of himself only when his foot is in Santa's stomach. For the
individuals in this Kiplingesque world, the needs are the same as for those in
the Jamesian and Conradian worlds—to find an identity. Here, however,
there is utter helplessness except through stridency and violence and excess,
unBeerbohmish to the hilt. But there was a snare in parodying these ugly
qualities. In order to articulate the savagery he perceived, Beerbohm became a
version of that same Judlip.

Shaw seems an unlikely contrast to Kipling, but Beerbohm implies a link.
The ego he finds repugnantly surfacing in Kipling's prose and poetry he finds
praiseworthy in Shaw's plays. In describing the Shavian ego, he describes an
artistic personality directly opposite his own, yet one in which he can
rejoice—rather than find his fury rising in the opposite represented by Kipling. Shaw, according to Beerbohm, sees the world as populated by versions
of "his own unrecognised self" and peoples his plays with the same. Beerbohm remains unimpressed by Shaw's theories and totally unconvinced by
Shaw's attempts to convert his audiences. Furthermore, he thinks that ego
and the didactic are truncheons in art: "they kill illusion." Despite these
problems, Shaw survives for Beerbohm, and mightily. Shaw can "caricature
his own thesis" and do it so laughingly that he nullifies the seriousness. The
result is not ideas, not ego, but a "personality," the artist revealed through
the works, the quality Beerbohm preserved in James by refusing to spend the
afternoon with him. Shaw, wrote Beerbohm, has "the most distinct personality in current literature."[18]

Beerbohm's parody of Shaw, "A Straight Talk," is a Shavian Preface to
"Snt. George: A Christmas Play," celebrating the fact that Sh*w has plagiariz-
ed his material: "Flatly, I stole this play." Sh*w begs off, saying he was too
lazy to invent his own play, but in taking someone else's, has "crammed in"
an idea, "the stiffening of civistic conscience." He claims in doing so to have
raised a good play into a "masterpiece." He goes on to explain the allegory
he had in mind, with himself in the heroic role of Snt. George.

Beerbohm was always aware of Shaw's use of "sources." He certainly
read the preface to *Man and Superman* in which Shaw says that he would
acknowledge the "authors whom I have pillaged in the following pages if I
could recollect them all" and the preface to *Three Plays for Puritans,* in

which Shaw claims that his Caesar (in *Caesar and Cleopatra*) is "an improvement on Shakespear's."[19] On November 24, 1906, just before the parody appeared for the first time, Beerbohm reviewed "A Doctor's Dilemma" as "Mr. Shaw's Roderick Hudson." More bitingly, he caricatured Shaw in 1914 in the process of pawning his second-hand clothes. The title and caption make the point of "A Straight Talk":

LIFE-FORCE, WOMAN-SET-FREE, SUPERMAN, ETC.
George Brandes ('Chand d' Idees): "What'll you take for the lot?"
George Bernard Shaw: "Immortality."
George Brandes: "Come, I've handled these goods before! Coat, Mr. Schopenhauer's; waistcoat, Mr. Ibsen's; Mr. Nietzsche's trousers—"
George Bernard Shaw: "Ah, but look at the patches!"[20]

"A Straight Talk" represents Shaw on the defensive as Beerbohm might see himself if his parodic mask were to crack. But his mask doesn't crack or even wrinkle because Beerbohm has nothing to assert other than the sheer presence of the mask. His game of stylistic beggar-thy-neighbor is the core of the point he makes, not a sign of artistic poverty or critical cleverness.

Since the nature of parody is derivative, we may wonder at Beerbohm making Shaw's borrowings a subject for mockery. He might criticize another's lack of originality, but he could not have missed the parallel to his own procedures, certainly not regarding Shaw, with whom in 1901 he had likened writing careers.[21] Beerbohm freighting a parody with the burden of his own artistic identification is akin to Shaw's own combinations of thoughts and jests. In his reviews of Shaw's plays, Beerbohm insisted that Shaw's brilliance lay in the simultaneous presentation of seriousness and fun. We have been praising Beerbohm for the same combination—the mocking being the jest, his identity as artist being his earnestness. He lauds Shaw for a quality he himself displays: "conspicuous fairness." In Broadbent of "John Bull's Other Island," Beerbohm wrote, Shaw delicately unites the insights of observation and the darts of satire; he keeps in perspective "all Broadbent's good points, and lays stress on everything that is not absurd in him. . . . We are quite sure that justice is being done."[22] This is the impression we are to get from the parodies (even that of Kipling): a thorough replication of style, "conspicuous" so that the skill of the parodist-artist may be detected and praised.

Beerbohm parodies Shaw in prose rather than drama because he felt prose

was a more honest form for Shaw; in prose there is no pretense of ventrilo-
quism. And prose even offered an advantage: sitting comfortably in his
chair, a reader could proceed at his own pace, backtrack to corrolate
thoughts, meditate in peace. Beerbohm often thought of Shaw's plays as
pieces more aptly read than staged; when *Man and Superman* first appeared,
Beerbohm looked on it as Platonic in form and called it "Mr. Shaw's New
Dialogues."[23] So Beerbohm knew the value of prose held in one's hand
and knew how to manipulate it. Since we can look back over the pages of
A Christmas Garland and contemplate, we can be sure we are meant to. And
what we find is the unity of the whole—not that it builds to a particular
climax, but that it has a recurring motif: the parodist's affinity with the role
of artist, wherever an "artist" might be found and deftly shaped.

Beerbohm's writing fools us. Accustomed as we are to digging for meaning,
we find the meaning on the surface; yet humor has its own protective coat, in
the myth that says if you explain humor, you destroy it. So Beerbohm seems
to resist exploration. But material is there to observe and interpret, even
though it dangles, like Eva's and Keith's stockings, at once tantalizing and unapproachable. Conrad expressed something like it when he reversed the relation of the story and its meaning:

> The yarns of seamen have a direct simplicity, the whole mean-
> ing of which lies within the shell of a cracked nut. But Marlow
> was not typical (if his propensity to spin yarns be excepted),
> and to him the meaning of an episode was not inside like a
> kernel but outside, enveloping the tale which brought it out
> as a glow brings out a haze, in the likeness of one of these
> misty halos that sometimes are made visible by the spectral
> illumination of moonshine.[24]

This statement, itself a tough nut to crack, provides an image for the parodist
as we have seen exemplified by Beerbohm: the parodist envelops his original
who brings him out as a glow brings out a haze.

Parody is an effective medium because it is intimation, something more
than verbalized, something less than fully spelled out. It resembles the elastic
rhythms of an Art Nouveau flower-stem. In encircling an object the stem becomes a frame which controls what and how we see. Its function is to lend
the object a new content and a new life; at the same time, it itself takes on
life. At first ornamental, the stem comes to have its own significance (the
object begins to serve *it*). Analogously Beerbohm's parodies, at first perhaps

merely pleasure-seeking, come to dominate the originals and take on lives of their own. They cannot be separated from their originals, nor would Beerbohm wish them independence. Like the stems they come to have a significance surpassing their function, but only when they are in full harmony with the objects which call them into being.

END NOTES

[1]*A Christmas Garland* (London: William Heinemann, 1912), p. vi. Hereafter cited in the text.

[2]Kenneth Burke, *A Grammar of Motives* (Berkeley: Univ. of California, 1969), p. 503.

[3]John Felstiner, *The Lies of Art: Max Beerbohm's Parody and Caricature* (New York: Knopf, 1972), pp. 142-43.

[4]Daniel N. Roselli, "Max Beerbohm's Unpublished Parody of Henry James," *RES,* n.s. 22 (1971), p. 62.

[5]*The Lies of Art,* p. 142.

[6]Review of "The High Bid" in *Around Theatres* (New York: Simon and Schuster, 1954), p. 544.

[7]S. N. Behrman, *Portrait of Max: An Intimate Memoir of Sir Max Beerbohm* (New York: Random House, 1960), p. 231.

[8]Evan Charteris, *The Life and Letters of Sir Edmund Gosse* (New York and London: Harper, 1931), p. 347.

[9]"An Incident" in *Mainly on the Air* (New York: Knopf, 1958), pp. 131-33.

[10]Richard Curle, "Max Beerbohm's Parodies," *Rhythm,* 1 (March, 1913), pp. xxix-xxx; Albert J. Guerard, *Conrad the Novelist* (Cambridge, Mass.: Harvard Univ. Press, 1958), p. 65; Marvin Mudrick, "Introduction," *Conrad: A Collection of Critical Essays* (Englewood Cliffs, New Jersey: Prentice Hall, 1966), p. 5; Addison C. Bross, "Beerbohm's 'The Feast' and Conrad's Early Fiction," *NCF,* 26 (1971), 329-36; Joseph Conrad, "Author's Note" to *Tales of Unrest* (Garden City, New York: Doubleday, Page, 1923), p. viii.

[11]F. R. Leavis, *The Great Tradition* (New York: New York Univ. Press, 5th printing, 1973), p. 177.

[12]E.g., Guerard's chapter "The Discovery of a Fictional World" in *Conrad the Novelist,* pp. 60-99.

[13]In a revised ending to "The Mote in the Middle Distance," now in the O'Connell Collection, Princeton University Library, Beerbohm has Eva Tantalus laud her and Keith's renunciation as "the garland at the feast." Thus he unites literary cannibalizing and praise of restraint, his own chief qualities.

[14]*Tales of Unrest* (London: T. Fisher Unwin, 1898), p. 297.

[15]Vasant A. Shahane, *Rudyard Kipling: Activist and Artist* (Carbondale and Edwardsville, Illinois: Southern Illinois Univ. Press, 1973), p. 80; C. E. Carrington, *The Life of Rudyard Kipling* (Garden City, New York: Doubleday, 1955), p. 264; Bonamy Dobree, "Rudyard Kipling" (*Monthly Criterion,* 1927) rpt. in *Kipling: The Critical Heritage,* ed. Roger Lancelyn Green (New York: Barnes and Noble, 1971), pp. 342, 347; Felstiner, p. 159; Behrman, p. 70.

[16]"Kipling's Entire" in *Around Theatres,* pp. 245, 248.

[17]Dixon Scott on Rudyard Kipling: "The youngster was bracketed with Beardsley, was bracketed with 'Max.' " From "Rudyard Kipling" (*Bookman,* 1912), rpt. in *Kipling: The Critical Heritage,* p. 310.

[18]*Around Theatres,* pp. 172, 175, 272.

[19]"Epistle Dedicatory to Arthur Bingham Walkley" prefacing *Man and Superman* in Bernard Shaw, *Complete Plays with Prefaces* (New York: Dodd, Mead, 1962), III, 506; and "Preface to Three Plays for Puritans," *Ibid.,* III, lv.

[20]In *A Survey* (London: William Heinemann, 1921).

[21]"Mr. Shaw's Crescent" in *Around Theatres,* pp. 118-19.

[22]"Mr. Shaw at his Best," *Ibid.,* p. 357.

[23]*Ibid.,* p. 268.

[24]"Heart of Darkness" in *Youth: A Narrative and Two Other Stories,* ed. Morton Dauwen Zabel (New York: Doubleday, 1959), p. 70.

Roger Vitrac and the Drama of Surrealism

Annette S. Levitt

The literature of Surrealism offers many obstacles to the formalist critic: conceived in revolt against traditional modes and values, it is philosophically opposed to mimetic or symbolic representation, to logic and coherence in presentation. Its primary goal is the representation of the dream state itself or, as André Breton, high priest of the movement, proclaims, the "resolution of these two states, dream and reality, which are seemingly so contradictory, into a kind of absolute reality, a *surreality*. . . . "[1]

These aims, both negative and positive, do not particularly create problems in the analysis of poetry, in which subjectivity often transcends literal representation and brevity may well obviate the issue of coherence. But drama is another matter, for at its center are the various manifestations of mimesis, whether seen in the naturalistic accuracy of a set, the psychological credibility of characterization, or the mere physical possibility of a sequence of events. With isolated exceptions, the drama that preceded Dada and Surrealism maintained these traditional requisites. But the drama of Surrealism, at once the most challenging and the most frustrating genre of the movement, flaunts the limits of reality, uses language alternately to mesmerize and to shock, and, in the words of Guillaume Apollinaire,

> Often connecting in unseen ways as in life
> Sounds gestures colors cries tumults
> Music dancing acrobatics poetry painting
> Choruses actions and multiple sets
>
> . . . actions
> Which add to the central drama and augment it
> Changes of tone from pathos to burlesque
> And the reasonable use of the improbable
> And actors who may be collective or not
> Not necessarily taken from mankind
> But from the universe

For the theatre must not be "realistic"

It is right for the dramatist to use
All the illusions he has at his disposal
. . .
It is right for him to make crowds speak and inanimate things
If he wishes
And for him to pay no more heed to time
Than to space[2]

These characteristics of Surrealist drama are hardly conducive to reasoned analysis, and the temptation for the critic is to write impressionistically—or not at all. Indeed, there has been relatively little criticism of Surrealist literature since its birth fifty years ago,[3] still less specifically on its drama, and, avers John Weightman in *The Concept of the Avant-Garde,* "even expository books about Surrealism tend to be written in a non-rationalistic way."[4] Weightman, too often wrongheaded in his brief chapter on Surrealism, clearly overstates and generalizes the issue. But even J. H. Matthews, probably the best known and most prolific scholar of Surrealism, feels compelled to translate into critical theory the anti-intellectual bias of the Dadaists and Surrealists:

> if we try to evaluate the plays . . . on their literary merits, we
> are in danger of losing sight of what is essential . . . [and]
> diverting [this material] from its true purpose. For, in surreal-
> ism, no less than in Dada, the conflict between form and
> technique, on the one hand, and expression of latent content
> and a nonliterary anti-artistic spirit, on the other, is resolved
> invariably to the detriment of formal and technical require-
> ments, and in disregard of aesthetic standards.[5]

Matthews may well be correct in terms of the Dada "manifestations," which eschew all goals but the desire to shock, as well as all links with humanity; the drama of Dada exists only for its destruction as a form. But Surrealism developed in response to Dada as well as to the appalling times in which both movements flourished, and it sought to revolutionize rather than to destroy. Just as Breton attacks the naturalistic novel, and not the novel form *per se* (his own novel, *Nadja,* was published in 1928), Surrealist drama revolts against the naturalism of Ibsen, the farce of Feydeau, the well-made play of

Scribe. It maintains certain forms, abandons others, but does so, I believe, consciously and with a certain degree of aesthetic control. To quote Antonin Artaud, foremost theoretician of Surrealist drama,

> No one ever thought of considering Surrealism as the sort of activity achieving release solely through the agency of automatic writing. Surrealism is perfectly reconcilable with a certain clarity of mind. Higher logic is a part of this clarity, leading us to choose a certain number of elements put forward by the subconscious which systematic logic would set aside. In such operations it follows new paths, higher than those of ordinary understanding, tending to destroy such understanding.[6]

We recognize in Artaud's statement a subtle linking of conscious and unconscious, the former organizing the creative leaps made by the latter; the process which he describes parallels Breton's resolution of dream and reality, and the result, too, this higher understanding, is akin to the surreality which Breton seeks to achieve.

At its best, Surrealist drama does achieve this surreality for its reader or viewer. It is thus appropriate that Artaud's comment occurs in a review of *Les Mystères de l'Amour (The Mysteries of Love),* a play by Roger Vitrac, his partner in the Théâtre Alfred Jarry and the writer described by Martin Esslin as "the ablest dramatist to emerge from Surrealism. . . ."[7] Esslin adds that *Mysteries* "is probably the most sustained effort to write a truly Surrealist play,"[8] and Michael Benedikt, in his introduction to the fine anthology, *Modern French Theatre,* calls it "the culmination of the Surrealist drama. . . ."[9]

Vitrac's play well merits these encomia, for it succeeds in fulfilling the goals of both Surrealism and dramatic form. Moreover, the tightness of its structure, the intricate patterning of its imagery, make it not merely accessible to literary analysis, but richly revealing of Surrealist values, in life and in art.

II

André Breton's aim, "the future resolution . . . of dream and reality . . . into a kind of absolute reality, a *surreality,"* is the focus of all Surrealist acts, the goal of all its art. Breton considers "the waking state . . . a phenomenon of interference,"[10] breaking into our continuous and organized dream life.[11] When we dream, we move without hesitation through places and events ranging from the most mundane to the most fantastic. As Breton describes it,

> The mind of the man who dreams is fully satisfied by what happens to him. The agonizing question of possibility is no longer pertinent. Kill, fly faster, love to your heart's content. . . . Let yourself be carried along, events will not tolerate your interference.[12]

Of *The Mysteries of Love* Antonin Artaud proclaims,[13] *"Pour la première fois un reve réel fut réalisé sur le théatre."* (For the first time a real dream was enacted in the theatre.) It is precisely the dream's enmeshing of the commonplace and the supernatural, Breton's resolution of dream and reality, at which Vitrac excels. He makes literal upon the stage a sur-real world; he "makes concrete" (as Anna Balakian says of Surrealist language) "the ineffable dream."[14] And he does so not with "indifference to the medium of the play" (Matthew's view of "Dada and Surrealist writing for the stage")[15] but, indeed, by means of the play's very structure.

Mysteries provides a frame of reality interpolated by two distinctly oneiric segments. The opening scenes of each of its three acts develop the prosaic plot: a young couple, Leah and Patrick, moves in them from courtship through marriage, unhappiness, separation and finally reconciliation. Interspersed between these scenes are the apparent dream sequences: in the first (Act I, scene 2), neatly lodged between courtship and marriage, Leah takes part in a banquet, hosted by Lloyd George, which is preceded and interrupted by his dismemberment of several bodies; in the second (Act II, scene 2), immediately following the couple's separation, she is presented with a child, dogs, and a husband (Mussolini) by her strangely unfamiliar mother, and she moves disjointedly through varied and disturbing experiences without pause. The dreams would appear to be Leah's, expressing her unspoken desires and fears.[16] She is the protagonist in each; Patrick in each plays the lesser role, a silent voyeur in the first (the role of Lloyd George, according to the cast of characters, is "taken by Dovic," Leah's former lover—we might call him Dovic's surrogate), and in the second a surrogate himself (Mussolini, the cast list says, is a "role taken by Patrick").[17]

Vitrac pointedly does not label these scenes as dreams (as he does similar scenes in his earlier play, *Free Entry*).[18] Moreover, to confuse reality with fantasy still further and to convey a sense of continuity which denies "rationally simplified correspondences between dream and reality,"[19] the play's scene divisions are numbered consecutively from one to five, thus ignoring the formal division into three acts—the divisions between dream and reality.

Vitrac uses set design to provide additional contradiction between reality and dream. The "reality" scenes are offered with minimal set directions, while the dream scenes appear in the context of extremely detailed and realistic, believable settings. In scene two the action is grotesque and disjointed, defying logic and credibility: Lloyd George serves a banquet of "lobsters, chickens, dressed roasts, sherbets, pyramids of fruit" to Leah, to her mother "in mourning" and to the late Mr. Morin. "The lamp lights of itself" (241). After reminding Leah of her complicity in his actions and mocking Patrick's inadvertent arson ("The assassination victims themselves fail in their attempt," he declares [242]), Lloyd George agrees with the loquacious Mr. Morin that Leah is crazy. When the men leave, Leah and her mother "go toward the bed where two arms are being raised which resemble two dead branches, but whereon are flowering two enormous, very white hands." Despite her mother's warning that "She has leprosy," Leah kneels, saying, "She has my slanted eyes. My blond hair. My gleaming mouth. You must agree that you don't die of love. END OF THE SECOND TABLEAU AND OF THE FIRST ACT" (243).

In striking contrast to these totally unreal occurrences, Vitrac provides a set for this scene with detail appropriate to the most naturalistic of dramas:

> The stage represents, on the left, the Quai des Grands-Augustins in Paris. To the right, a bedroom. In the center stands a small cabin with a porthole overlooking the Seine. In the background, in the space which should be occupied by the Palais de Justice, stands an advertising sign bearing this inscription in large blue letters: Le Petit Parisien. On the parapet, booksellers' stalls affecting the shape of coffins. Above, red tugboat stacks. The bedroom has closed windows, formed like narrow arches, the tops of which are lost in obscurity; they are adorned with very white muslin curtains. In front of the fireplace and a couple of yards from the entrance to the room stands a stove of the "salamander" variety. But it is from the fireplace that, from time to time, blue flames emerge. The bed is entirely covered by the sheets. A table. Chairs. A pedestal lamp with a green shade on the table. A glass-fronted side-

> board is filled with dishes. In a corner, some old newspapers. A
> package of medicated cotton wool stands in front of the stove.
> (239)

Not merely naturalistic, this is the kind of precise detail that we see in our dreams.

A similar contradiction between oneiric situation and realistic setting occurs in scene four. The situation is not at all macabre, merely a mélange of unlikely occurrences in the most natural of places. The scenes shift quickly from a railway station to the train itself, from the seashore to a hotel lobby, a yard-goods shop, and the main square of a provincial town. Vitrac's directions include various props to simulate these locales, and a projector to light each appropriate part of the stage. All is very carefully arranged, all very incongruous with the frantic tone of Mussolini, who fears the sea and kicks the dog, and that of Leah herself, who runs "like a madwoman" from place to place.

In contrast to Leah's dreams, the scenes of the couple's waking life occur in the simplest of sets. Scenes three and five take place in the hotel in which Leah and Patrick live. In scene three, "The stage represents a hotel room. A bed. A table. Chairs. A wardrobe, and so on" (243). Vitrac leaves the details to our imagination. Similarly, in scene five, all that we are told of the set is that it "represents a hotel lobby at midnight" (257). In scene one, there is still less attempt at naturalistic detail; indeed, most of the scene takes place not on the stage at all, but in a box overhanging the stage, with the house-lights on during much of the action. Only in the last moments, when Vitrac suddenly interposes a brief symbolist drama, seemingly unconnected with the main plot, does the action shift onto the stage itself, where it remains for the rest of the play.

The use of the loge and the interpolated play are aspects of Vitrac's attacks on conventional dramaturgy, attempts to fulfill the need expressed by Artaud "to re-establish a subconscious link between actor and spectator."[20] Unlike Pirandellian games, which appeal to the intellect, the goal here is a visceral reaction: one is shocked when the author of the symbolist drama, after being declared a suicide, appears, dripping blood and laughing. Similarly, shots into the audience and speeches addressed to the audience are meant to unnerve the complacent spectator.[21] When The Author (not Mr. Mouchet, the suicide, but another with the same title) appears in the third and fifth scenes, to discuss the outcome of the play, it would seem that we are back in Pirandello's territory. But the final resolution is not at all what he planned, and we are ultimately left, not in a state of philosophical perplexity but, rather, in a state of shock equal to Patrick's, when he discovers that Leah has in fact killed a spectator.

III

Not all of the surreal effects in the play come from the violence, strangeness, or illogic of its action, nor even from the juxtaposition of these events with the more mundane aspects of life. Vitrac lays open the psyches of his two lovers so that, in the words of Artaud, "factual logic is excluded and . . . every feeling is instantly turned into action. . . . every state of mind is registered with direct imagery. . . . "[22] It is language, finally, with which the Surrealists perform their magic, language which produces, to quote Balakian, "unremembered, previously nonexistent realities—but realities just the same, in the full, concrete, dimensional sense of the word."[23]

It is language at which Vitrac excels, in all of its Surrealist uses: language contradicted by action—Patrick says, "I'm going to take a stroll," and sits down to look at the audience (231); language used to convey hallucinatory images—"a hat gliding along six feet above the sidewalk" (235); the illogical progression of language—Patrick, the child says, "would have been restored to you a eunuch, Leah. And my father would today have that bayonet-like voice which is the sign of imminent genius" (262). The Surrealist potential of language is best seen in dialogue, according to Breton: "Here, two thoughts confront each other . . . My attention . . . treats the opposing thought as an enemy; in ordinary conversation, it 'takes it up' almost always on the words, the figures of speech, it employs; it puts me in a position to turn it to good advantage in my reply by distorting them."[24] Dialogue as Vitrac uses it is thus not necessarily a means of communication, as when Leah says, "It already smells like brains," and Patrick replies, "Some good advice. Throw some sound and sweep under the armchairs. This mud is an infection" (234).

Isolated phrases, however, can convey little of the effect that Vitrac achieves, and the key to the effectiveness of his language is similar to the basis of his structural achievement; it is, in fact, the element basic to Surrealist imagery—the juxtaposition of unlike entities. As Pierre Reverdy describes it,

> "The image is a pure creation of the mind.
> "It cannot be born from a comparison but from a juxta-
>   position of two more or less distant realities.
> "The more the relationship between the two juxtaposed

> realities is distant and true, the stronger the image will
> be—the greater its emotional power and poetic reality.
> . . ."25

Vitrac not only makes this theory the basis of his imagery but uses it as a metaphor for the construction of his drama, another parallel to Breton's resolution of reality and dream. Thus against the chaos and confusion of Surrealist language he juxtaposes patterns of imagery full of meaning and significance, patterns which convey his central themes, the renewal of the love relationship and the need for creativity.

Love and the free imagination, however trite they may now seem, are values basic to Surrealist life and art. Vitrac revitalizes these potential clichés by presenting them with their accepted emphases and at the same time with his own subtle parody. He renews these themes as, in his epigraph from Jarry, *"Les femmes qui nous aiment renouvent le vrai Sabbat."* (The women who love us renew the true Sabbath—even in its most unquestioned aspects, that is, love is revitalizing.) It is appropriate that Vitrac quotes Jarry, for Jarry is, of course, the progenitor of Surrealist drama, and the senseless violence that we recall from the Ubu plays manifests itself here very clearly. His is the voice of irrationality. But Vitrac also evokes Apollinaire, whose theories of Surrealist drama ultimately make great sense: in his preface—*"En tout cas, Guillaume Apollinaire disait qu'il faut tout publier."*26 (Anyway, Apollinaire said that you must publish everything—as if to discount this play); in the several appearances of The Author, whose discourses on theatre seem to parody Apollinaire's Director in *The Breasts of Tiresias;* and in a speech of Leah's which directly parodies Thérèse-Tiresias. *The Breasts of Tiresias* is another play about love—about the need for more love—and Vitrac conveys a similar message with much greater complexity and depth.

The Mysteries of Love, while it evolves from Jarry, also partakes of Apollinaire; its movement seems chaotic perhaps, but it is developed with care. Vitrac takes, for example, the tritest of conventions—the sun which shines on the lover—and revitalizes it, causing it to serve as a basic pattern of his imagery, a structural device which unifies the play. In sentimental drama the sun shines, the sky is blue when life and love go well; in *Mysteries* the imagery of sunlight provides a paradigm for the events of the romance, occurring, appropriately, in the prologue and in scenes one, three, and five but not in the intervening oneiric scenes. In the prologue, Patrick draws in the mud the hair for a female portrait painted on a house wall. His love is as yet unreturned, and the "weather is cloudy. It has been raining" (229). Not unexpectedly, after Leah confesses her love and they receive congratulations, Patrick declares, "What beautiful sunshine! What beautiful sunlight" (233)! In the same scene, after he has fought and sent away Leah's former lover, Patrick shrugs off Leah's headache with the comment, "Never mind. Look, what sunshine" (237). In each case, he has been victorious in one of the rituals of romance. It is not until Leah goes off to have their baby that Patrick again sees the sunlight (250). But when he leaves Leah, after killing the baby, at the end of scene three, there is no sun: "PATRICK: Enough, Leah. You will light the torches and prepare my travelling gear. I have things to do in the neighborhood. LEAH: Goodnight, Patrick" (252).

Leah alludes to light only once—just before Patrick's return: "The light keeps shining. It keeps shining by itself" (259). But after he returns, and before they resolve their difficulties, "the sky is like lead," and there is thunder in the heavens (260). The sun reappears only at the end of the play, within the lyrical dialogue in which Patrick and Leah consider the values of their lives; here, "Forgiveness" is "like the sun" (267). But much must happen to Leah and Patrick before they can make this mature and sensitive analogy.

The play's final speeches reveal maturity in both Leah and Patrick, a fulness and acceptance that is in striking contrast to the callowness we encounter in the first scene. There Patrick complains of his "plaster"—his "hollow Space"—hurting, and asks Leah to "pump up the red," his heart's blood, to fill his emptiness. But she does not understand. She has "confessed" her love for Patrick, but only after initially refusing to do so, and commenting even then that she is unsure of what she has confessed. His declaration of love is so excessive that it makes hers seem almost flat:

> Do you see Leah, I'm happy. I don't need anything else. I'm stifling. It's the oysters. Do you hear? (Shouting.) It's the oysters. But what is the lemon doing? Ah, Leah, will you hide that leg, that knee! Will you hide that thigh! (Screaming.) Oh! Oh! Oh! Oh! I will shout it out. I will shout it out from the rooftops, from the stars, from above the stars! (Taking the audience into his confidence.) Leah loves me, Leah loves me, Leah loves me. She confessed it. She loves me. (To Leah.) It's your turn now. Shout it out, Leah. Go on my little Leah, my Lele, my Leah-Leah. Shout it out, now, shout it, my Leahleahleah.

And Leah responds, also addressing the audience:

> I love Patrick. Oh! I love his guts. Oh! I love the clown. I
> love the clown. From every viewpoint, from every seam, from
> every form. (233)

They are both, they tell the audience, "Madly" mad—Vitrac's wry variation
on the romantic cliché, "madly in love." Leah has told her mother of Patrick's love, and when asked if she loves him, responds glibly, "Why, naturally" (231). But Patrick's courting, despite his enthusiasm, has been all along a
mockery of romantic ritual: "Then do accept these few flowers. (He slaps
her.)" (230). He tells her to shut up, calls her a "little bird-brain," and insists that she reminds him of "a slashing knife. A wound" (235). Dovic,
Leah's former lover, appears and proclaims his undying love to Leah, inter-
polating his declarations with slaps, pinches, and kicks. He then fights with
Patrick over the woman they presumably love. In the tradition of romantic
comedy, Patrick ousts his rival. But then Patrick's former mistress appears,
and when Leah asks, "Who's this tart?" he responds, "She's the virgin, Leah;
she's the virgin. Are you happy" (238)? Unlikely un-resolution seems to be
de rigueur, for clearly he assumes a positive response. And clearly in this
parody of a conventional romance, Leah's role requires her to accept all and
comprehend little.

By the play's final scene, however, Leah and Patrick have endured and
learned much. Patrick has functioned as involuntary voyeur when Leah
joins with Lloyd George; their marriage is filled with battles, dreams shared
but not comprehended, and a baby, unwanted by Patrick, which dies through
his carelessness. Patrick abandons Leah, who is burdened with domestic
responsibilities and who is presented, at the start of the fifth and last scene,
as "mad," "hysterical," and "wrecking everything" in their room at the
hotel. But she has good reason, as she explains in a lyrical passage which
conveys the destruction of all her romantic dreams:

> I did not come here, sir, to occupy a number, not even Num-
> ber 53. You say I smashed the wardrobe: Patrick had promised
> to take me to the pole. Did he do it? You say I made a sham-
> bles of the bathroom? Patrick had promised me some stars
> which he had made himself. You press on a coiled spring:
> you're supposed to see the sea, the trees, and the clouds. What
> did I see? You say I strangled the goldfish in their tank? I
> sold all I could of Saint Patrick's body. The rest had gone on a
> trip. Has the rest come back? (258)

Patrick then miraculously appears, affirming Leah's (and Vitrac's) faith in "the power of words" (259). She declares to the police—and to herself—

> The night gets along without us. It passes all by itself. But I,
> I say, I am going to say, that I carry him . . . and he passes . . .
> as though molded by my throat and sprung from my mouth:
> "Patrick."

Enter Patrick. The Policemen flee in terror. (260)

The power of words is at the heart of the Surrealist mystique, and we experience throughout the play their power to disturb, to shock, to create the sudden revelation which Vitrac describes in his preface: *"Mais les mystères drapés d'éclairs ne se révelent pas. Ils éclatent aux yeux fermés."*[27] (But the mysteries draped in lightnings cannot be disclosed. They burst forth to closed eyes.) Eluard's aim for poetry, *"donner à voir,"*[28] is to give sight; *éclater,* however, connotes both information and explosion, and is thus closer to Breton's goal, the sudden destruction of the boundary between conscious and unconscious, real and unreal. Vitrac's play repeatedly breaks down these barriers, both by means of dramatic action and by the impact of language itself. Some of the most lyrical language occurs in the final scene, in which disparate images converge and suddenly reveal a pattern within seeming chaos. To read or to see *Mysteries* we must first become like dreamers ourselves; but analysis follows, and is rewarded, for Vitrac provides an intricate design of imagery that conveys valuable insights into love and creativity among the Surrealists. As it began, the play ends with a dialogue on love; the tone, however, is strikingly different from that at the start. The lovers now recognize the limitations of conventional romance, and for the first time they perceive the deeper spiritual values of mature love:

> PATRICK: Ah, Leah, there's still love!
> LEAH: Love worn down to the bare rope, and the rope to
>   hang yourself. Love: the secret work of wear. There's
>   just you, Patrick.
> PATRICK: Me, let's talk about it! Me, a little cork of marrow
>   bobbing on a string. There's you, Leah.
> LEAH: Ah, Patrick: the beautiful architecture of wrath! I
>   would be quite willing to live on roses: they have a flowery
>   odor. I need coal and bedsheets. There is pain, Patrick.

PATRICK: Pain? A burning drop of oil engendering a body. The curving of the earth is the pain of the world, as the tongue is the pain of thought, as the isthmus of the neck is the pain of the body and, when it is sliced through, the most painful criminals are severed from life. Pain? The great genesis. But there is kindness, Leah.

LEAH: Kindness? No, Patrick. Kindness, a gift at the end of a rubber band, the flabby malady of death. Fat cheeks and overburdened knees. Don't try to touch me with that. The trained-dog factory. But there is forgiveness, Patrick.

PATRICK: Forgiveness, like the sun. Forgiveness, like returning. Forgiveness, like a boomerang. Forgiveness, like births. Forgiveness, like seasons. Forgiveness, without any ill-feelings.

LEAH: There is death.

PATRICK: Yes, death. But death like forgiveness. Like snow on the mountain. Forgiveness, like fire you slice with a knife. Forgiveness, like the water houses are made of. Forgiveness, like the murderer other crimes are made of. Forgiveness, like the secret the storms are made of. Forgiveness, like the horse fortunes are made of. Forgiveness, like the old man the clouds are made of. Forgiveness, like me, whom I am making a criminal of. Forgiveness, like you whom I am making a deadly acid of. The heart is red already. Flow. Leah. Hands on the copper of shadows. The heart is red already as far as the end of the theatre where someone is about to die. (266-67)

Vitrac's poetry is both in and of the theatre, both heard and experienced; it recalls the best of Surrealist poetry. As Anna Balakian describes that poetry, the "unexpected linking of words became the foundation of a new metaphor, which, instead of being based on analogy, is derived from divergence and contradiction. . . . The surrealist associates what we normally dissociate and the word 'like' is inappropriate because the connections are nonsequential or psychic rather than rational."[29] The Surrealists do use the word "like," however, to stress the very incongruity of juxtaposed images, and Vitrac follows the mode—begun by Lautréamont and used so effectively by Péret— in which a line begins *beau comme:* "Beautiful like a hole in a windowpane / beautiful like the unexpected encounter of a cataract and a bottle. . . ."[30]

Vitrac modifies the *beau comme* formula, offering abstractions (pain, kindness, forgiveness, death) and their equivalents, moving from layered metaphor ("The curving of the earth is the pain of the world, as the tongue is the pain of thought") to simple simile ("Forgiveness, like fire you slice with a knife"), shifting from abstraction to concrete detail with no more apparent logic than that in the sequence of the images themselves: "Forgiveness, like the sun. Forgiveness, like returning. Forgiveness, like a boomerang." There is, however, a psychic connection between "returning" and a "boomerang," and a certain psychic, if not totally rational, logic does persist throughout the play, beneath the surface level of dissociation. In this, the play's final dialogue, we see a recapitulation and assimilation of the various themes and images set forth earlier in the play.

The play's central image is the human body and its relation to the great "mysteries" of human love. The imagery of the body pervades the play, although it may seem difficult to connect the hacked up bodies of scene two with Patrick's references to Leah's leg, knee, and thigh, in scene one. There is, however, a thematic connection which ties even that strange and obscure scene into the greater coherence of the play as a whole: the state of the body and the state of love are one. The sexual overtones of Patrick's lines recur, primarily in the courtship scene. For example, Patrick, referring apparently to women in general, declares to Leah, "Oh! Sirens! You all have it, you're all fishheaded" (235). We normally think of sirens and mermaids as seductive, but "fishheaded" reverses their customary physiology and conveys as well certain gross connotations of dismemberment and garbage heaps. The human body is thus denigrated, as it is in Patrick's reaction to Leah's proposed nakedness. "Be a little discreet," she says, "if you force me to it, I'll be stark naked." And he responds: "How useless it all is. Only clothing interests me. An empty dress or suit or shirt walking about. All these constructions of chalk, wax, wood, bone and flesh should be incinerated" (235). Bodies are merely "constructions" when they are empty of spirit, of love, as Patrick seems to realize when he declares that his "plaster hurts."

LEAH: Your plaster?
PATRICK: My hollow space.
LEAH: So?
PATRICK: Oh! So you can take your place at the pump.
LEAH: Why, Patrick?
PATRICK: Why, to pump up the red, my dear child.
LEAH: Bladders and lanterns, my love?

PATRICK: Isn't that always the way with bearded women!
The intelligence of the extremities. (236)

"The intelligence of the extremities" is clearly lesser than that of the heart
or brain. Leah's insensitivity prevents her from recognizing Patrick's needs,
from "pumping up the red," from filling his "hollow space." This failure of
passion and imagination, of mutual fulfillment, and the resulting distortions
of perspective both in their world at large and more particularly in that
human microcosm, the body, appear with still greater intensity in scene
three, in the married life of Leah and Patrick. Leah offers herself to Patrick
as "the world," but he rejects her: "Pardon, Leah. The world, if you please"
(245). Reclining on the bed, she invites him to join her, but again he rejects
her, declaring that she protects the land of Tahiti, "Tahiti the shoe of spring."
"LEAH: Tahiti? My hips. You boor!" Patrick's rejection appears less a reaction to Leah than a manifestation of his own skewed world and body:

> I'm not doing anything any more. I am the machine that is to
> turn in a vacuum. That's the brain, you say? It's poisoned by
> work.[31] It's at the stage of tetanus. A nice animal, that one.
> Only yesterday I could still eat. Today, Leah, it's all over. The
> brain is in the belly. We let that outcast do anything. The
> heart? You can look for it in the bed. The stomach? It licks
> my feet beneath the table. The liver makes faces in the mir-
> rors. The spleen is in the drawer next to the corkscrew, and
> my lungs are having fun making holes in your canaries. My
> poor brain, that divine dough, bends under any yoke. (246)

The organs are disembodied, the human body is reduced to a plaything for
the mayhem of Lloyd George and to scraps for the butcher, who refuses
them:

> Well, now, Miss Leah, I'll not be coming to your place any
> more. Not worth the bother. Just some bones where even a
> whore wouldn't find a pittance! You can keep your garbage
> for the soldiers. You could give me the skin with the hair and
> nails on it now, and I still wouldn't give you another penny.
> (247)

Heart, as well as brain, has lost its power, and the erstwhile lovers reiterate their feelings of emptiness, as Leah proclaims, "You're hard, Patrick. You're heartless" (249). Both literal and metaphorical meanings of her comment are reinforced by Patrick's reply:

> Well, I get along as I can—that's no one's lookout but my own. My behavior is my own. What was it someone once said? Love: the need to come out of oneself, someone once said. And that is why I ask you this: Are you through looking for what has been left me? Are you through looking at my skeleton? You're certainly quite an X-ray.

He goes on to recite "The Skeleton and the Spinning Top (a fable)":

> A skeleton six feet tall
> Happened to run out of plaster
> The worms no longer cared for it it had become so brittle
> and lovely
> And the rest what did you do with it
> When sitting down at the table
> We made animals out of it
> And the reason is this speed supplied
> By the momentum of my darling's heart
> That top
> (The heart or the darling?
> —Both) (249)

Clearly marriage has not filled his emptiness, and his love has all the depth and tenderness of a spinning top. Indeed, he seems to have been physically diminished, as the plaster which previously pained him has disappeared, and "the rest"—the disembodied organs, presumably—has been reduced from human to animal levels.

While the heart is compared to a child's toy, which moves without feeling, the brain is both ridiculed and glorified—ridiculed for its rational capacities, glorified for its imaginative potential. The Surrealists scorned reasons as much as they revered imagination, and thus when Patrick asks, "would you dare suppose that I don't have my reason?" Leah mockingly responds, "Far from it. Reason is balance, isn't it? You climb ladders well enough" (248). In contrast, the brain, "that divine dough" which is "poisoned by work," is also capable of extraordinary visions, of worlds remote from the hotel room,

the quai, and the other realistic settings in which we encounter Leah and
Patrick.

The visions are Patrick's, and they are distinct from Leah's dreams. They
occur first in the courtship scene and thereafter during the marriage. The
first, filled with pastoral imagery, offers an apotheosis of romantic tragedy:
youth cut down abruptly in the brilliance of its potential. The scenario might
be Patrick's foreshadowing of his own thwarted life; in outline, it also
parallels the events of the play within the play, which takes place in scene
one. This brief symbolist drama, in which the characters are less people than
abstractions representing the stages of man's life, occurs after Patrick's vision,
but sheds greater light on the subtlety and complexity of Vitrac's thematic
development if examined first; for it makes almost explicit the symbolism
that is at the heart of the vision:

> From the left, enter a Young Man in evening dress. From the
> right, an Old Man with his beard trailing on the ground. The
> Young Man divests himself of his cane, his hat and his gloves,
> which he places on the floor of the stage. The Old Man raises
> his arms heavenward, and smiles.
> THE YOUNG MAN (pulling a bird out of his pocket): Dad,
> you have before you one who is about to die.
> THE OLD MAN: Then you will spread out my beard on the
> sheet. It needs to dry out.
> THE YOUNG MAN: Don't you ever wash it? Look how dirty
> it is!
> THE OLD MAN: Ah! When I was a child, Justin, it was as
> white as milk.
> The Young Man opens his hand. The bird flies off. Both go off
> stage to the left, weeping.
> The curtain falls abruptly. A shot is heard. (238-39)

The symbolism becomes both clearer and richer in Patrick's vision, in which
the bird is certainly dead. The Young Man will never grow now to be an Old
Man:

> Listen. A stroll in the mountains. The spruce trees are frozen.
> Ah, youth! Chandeliers under ice. And then the swamps! The
> swamps? So many beds with childless women. And suddenly
> there's the sparrowhawk. It's he. He is dead, I tell you. He falls

like a flashing of lightning. There are no wings on either side of
his naked body on the ground. There are two eyes. (234)

Here the bird is at the center of the action; deprived of his wings, this
symbol of freedom gains vision instead. But neither wings nor eyes are useful
to one dead before his time. "Chandeliers under ice" conveys the paradox of
youth: fire under ice can not yet burn strongly, but it is preserved for future
use. Here, however, it is quenched by swamps and the responsibilities of
adulthood. The fire disappears, but re-emerges as the sparrowhawk falls "like
a flashing of lightning."

The imagery of fire, of the thwarted promethean hero, recurs, ambiguous-
ly, still early in the play, in terms of explosive materials—Patrick promises
Leah, "Don't worry, my bed will smell neither of fulminate nor of powder,
the way it does here" (234). Leah's response, "What! It already smells like
brains," joins the explosive possibilities of the intellect with those of chemi-
cals and gunpowder. But she is not happy with such possibilities, as she
wishes, longingly, that "I wouldn't have to sleep with phosphorus tonight"
(235). Leah clearly appreciates neither Patrick's brain nor its creative capacities—the smell of phosphorus, the flash of lightning are too strong for her—as
she makes increasingly clear during the marriage:

> And that brain that you're so proud of. There's certainly a
> good-time Charlie: before a meal, all he dreams about is knife
> wounds, animals dying in the forest—and such language!
> And after that there's the prairie, the country with its delicate
> herbs where Mr. Patrick lies down like the cloud called cirrus
> which in shape looks like a pike and in color like fire. (247)

Certainly Leah is referring to the vision of the sparrowhawk, but she alludes
as well to Patrick's earlier brief vision:

> for a moment I took the lamb's part. It was bleating. Baa . . .
> Baa . . . Baa . . . The grass was getting off the train. It was
> putting on airs. The lamb pissed all over it. That's what it's
> like to be young. (232)

A little later he tells his wife, "You remind me of a slashing knife. A wound"
(235). She responds, "Ah! That animal that pissed, how dear it is to your
heart." Clearly the two visions are linked, with Patrick, both visionary and

protagonist of his own visions (as Leah is of her dreams), appearing as the sacrificial sheep (and pissed-on grass), as the bird which loses its wings and the sensitive victim, the *poète maudit* trampled on by life—and specifically by marriage.

It is easy to recognize Leah as his antagonist in each of these dramas. Insensitive to Patrick's needs, hostile to his creative potential, she is equated with a weapon of violence, in imagery—"*slash*ing" and "wound"—evocative of the vagina, primordial castrator. A related image in scene three intensifies this connotation while linking Patrick's earlier and later visions. Patrick says of Leah, "it's the mouth that lights your way. It's like a quarry of blood" (248). The mouth that is a "quarry of blood"—her own or her victim's— epitomizes woman through her sexual organs. A "white quarry," one devoid of blood, is the locale of Patrick's final vision. This time it is not youth that is cut down but, appropriate to his position in life, the mature workingman. Again, Patrick is victimized, both within and outside his vision. He again is the visionary, but Leah too sees the images in his eye. "The daylight," he says, "is in my left eye."

> LEAH: . . . And in your right eye, Patrick?
> PATRICK: There is a mountain.
> LEAH: Can I see?
> PATRICK: If you want.
>> Leah bends over Patrick's eye, and looks.
> LEAH: What is it?
> PATRICK: It's a wheel.
> LEAH: And behind it?
> PATRICK: Behind it, there's a white quarry.
> LEAH: Yes, the workers are taking it easy.
> PATRICK: Aren't they, though!
> LEAH: What's that shining among the stones?
> PATRICK: Their tools. They're pretty, aren't they? They're made of nickel. The smallest one looks like a pink finger-nail, and the biggest one like an ax. One of the men is holding the ax. Do you see him, Leah?
> LEAH: Very well. He seems tired.
> PATRICK: Still, he's got food and drink there.
> LEAH: He's taking a bath. That's curious.
> PATRICK: What's so curious about that?
> LEAH: He's melting. He's white. Now the animals are eating him.

PATRICK: Poor creatures.

LEAH: Poor creatures? Those vipers? Those flaming, scaly things?

PATRICK: They haven't done anything to you.

LEAH: In that case, kiss my hands.

> Patrick kisses her hands but suddenly leaps back.

PATRICK: Ouch!

LEAH: What have I done?

PATRICK: You've burned me.

> Smoke is rising from Leah's hands. (244-45)

Patrick is burned by Leah, just as the worker-protagonist of his vision is melted by bathwater and eaten by animals. The sexuality of the scene is obvious—the pretty nickel "tools," the smallest one "like a pink fingernail," the largest one "like an ax," which the workers bring to the quarry, the sperm-like liquid into which the worker dissolves—but it is Leah who brings in negative connotations. "Vipers," she calls them, "flaming, scaly things," adding sexuality to the promethean imagery she rejected earlier.

Leah's ability to see the vision in Patrick's eye is rather uncanny, of course, but the point that Vitrac more strongly stresses is that such perception may be an intrusion—"PATRICK: So in the future take care of your eyes, and leave mine alone" (245)—and possibly a distortion as well—if the outside viewer is unsympathetic. We need not accept Leah's view of the animals, which Patrick refers to as "poor creatures"; indeed, he seems undisturbed that they should eat the protagonist, who is, after all, merely a worker, and not a visionary like himself. Perhaps, too, the sexuality of the vision seems quite natural to him. For in the last scene he tells Leah, at her request, a story (another vision?) in which he quietly equates man's sexual and militaristic tendencies and shows woman both satisfying and overcoming these desires:

> The factory chimneys are harvested at the end of November. First they are polished by being rolled in sand. They come out smooth and bright after that operation. Some are set aside for reproduction, on the right; the others are placed on the left. The latter are divided into two parts. One part is for armaments. Cannons are made from them. The rest are sold at auction. These are therefore scattered. But as they change hands

they wear out and soon nothing is left of these former factory
chimneys. All that remains are the factories and the cannons.
Then the cannons are aimed at the factories. A cannon is given
away to every lady who asks for one, so that finally not a
single cannon remains.

LEAH: And, dear Patrick, what do the ladies do with all those
   cannons?

PATRICK: My dear, you don't have to believe me—but they
   eat them. (263)

In his visions Patrick has progressed from the youthful victim, fearfully antic-
ipating his own death, to the mature man who recognizes the Elizabethan
significance of dying, the giving up of self, sexually, in the hope of achieving
spiritual growth. Vitrac conveys this development through clusters of images,
apparently meaningless as they are isolated within individual speeches and
seemingly chaotic as they occur in separate scenes, but ultimately revealing
the coherent and meaningful pattern of Patrick's maturity.

IV

   Patrick has returned, he tells Leah, "to conclude . . . LEAH: To conclude
what? PATRICK: To love each other" (263). It is unclear whether he wishes
to destroy or to consolidate their love. The Author is similarly ambiguous
when he presents Patrick with a revolver, insisting that "a shot at the end of
the play is absolutely necessary for the development of the plot" (264). He
does not explain, however, why this is so, or who is to be shot. Moreover, The
Author in this Surrealist play may not have ultimate control over the plot or
his characters. "I didn't think you'd turn out so well" (265), he says to
Patrick, and indeed, Patrick has grown even more creative and sensitive than
his visions reveal. Now he can give life to inanimate vision; now for the first
time he can share his greater vision with his wife. In this final conversation
with The Author he alludes to his vision of the quarry, identifying himself
with the worker by stressing the whiteness of his skin, and speaking also of
the mountain, site and source of his vision, the raw material of his creation:

PATRICK: See how white my skin is.

THE AUTHOR: That wouldn't prove very much.

PATRICK: It wouldn't prove anything, actually, if it were not
   for the perpetual snows. The perpetual snows, sir, if you

care to know, have taught me to see clearly into this. The mountains, it is true, did somewhat disturb me. But do you know what I did with the mountains?

THE AUTHOR: What did you do with the mountains?

PATRICK: I turned them into men.

THE AUTHOR: Your words make everything impossible, my friend.

PATRICK: Well, then, write plays without words.[32]

THE AUTHOR: Did I ever intend to do otherwise?

PATRICK: Yes, you put words of love into my mouth.

THE AUTHOR: You should have spat them out.

PATRICK: I tried to, but they turned into gunshots or dizzy spells.

THE AUTHOR: That's hardly my fault. Life is like that.

PATRICK: Leave life alone, then, and increase the size of your brain. (265)

In turning mountains into men, Patrick is converting his visions into flesh and blood, resurrecting, in a sense, the bodies that were so denigrated earlier in the play and in his life. It is the "perpetual snows," he tells us, which have taught him, which have given him understanding, and, in his last speech in the play we see why, for there "snow on the mountain" is equated with death, and it is the knowledge of death which enables us to appreciate life—to join vision with reality in order to revitalize our lives—to live, in short, a Surrealist life.

The Author's preference for "plays without words" is also Artaud's, and we are reminded of his comment that in *Mysteries* "every feeling is instantly turned into action."[33] In the last moments of the play, feelings and words literally turn into actions, "into gunshots" specifically, as Patrick's final speech builds to its climax:

death like forgiveness. Like snow on the mountain. Forgiveness, like fire you slice with a knife. Forgiveness, like the water houses are made of. Forgiveness, like the murderer other crimes are made of. Forgiveness, like the living other dead are made of. . . . Forgiveness, like me, whom I am making a criminal of. Forgiveness, like you whom I am making a deadly acid of. The heart is red already. Flow. Leah. Hands on the copper of shadows. The heart is red already as far as the end of

> the theatre where someone is about to die.
> LEAH: Enough, Patrick! (She fires a shot.)
> PATRICK: What have you done, Leah? What have you done?
>   You've just killed a spectator. (267)

It is Leah, not Patrick as The Author presumably intended, who fires the shot which abruptly ends the play. Vitrac thus conveys the Surrealist notion that a play is not completed by its author alone, but by his characters as well, and even by the audience. For in a truly Surrealist play the audience partici-pates fully, is so drawn in that its members too become actors in the drama, a drama in which reality and illusion are merged completely. The death which ends the play does not occur on stage. As it began, *The Mysteries of Love* ends in an arena beyond the limits of the proscenium arch; the drama of the stage invades life itself, predicting in the process much of modern theatre, from Genet to the Environmental drama.

It is Leah who has become the criminal, the role which Patrick, following The Author's advice, anticipated for himself. She has also become "a deadly acid," not the substance which Patrick's bullet would have reduced her to, and not only as the result of her own bullet. This "deadly acid," like the other explosive materials equated with creative potential, has until now been associated with Patrick, and Leah has rejected it in him. Here, linked with "the copper of shadows," it implies a specific creative activity, that of etching, and for the first time it is applied to Leah. She has changed—for the "heart is red already"—presumably "pumped up" by Leah, as Patrick had earlier requested. She too has undergone much and has grown in sensitivity. Indeed, Leah herself has acknowledged the value of imagination by asking The Author for "two little brains. One for the child and the other for me" (266). It is Leah as well who suggests to Patrick the ultimate components of love: pain ("the great genesis," as Patrick describes it), forgiveness ("like returning"), and death ("like forgiveness"). In shooting a member of the audience she acts out both Breton's definition of "the simplest Surrealist act" and her own definition of love: death equals love or, as Patrick pre-sents it, "Forgiveness, the living other dead are made of."

To the Surrealists love epitomizes alchemically the meeting of two distant realities, the destruction of the barriers between them, and the sudden revelation of their mysteries. Vitrac has told us in his preface that these mysteries cannot simply be revealed, that they must "burst forth to closed eyes." *"Le tout,"* he continues, *"est de s'entendre. Ici, c'est un dialogue d'échos."*[34] (The essential thing is to understand one another. Here, there is a dialogue of echoes.) Patrick and Leah are finally able to communicate, but we are never able to hear them clearly. Love itself, Vitrac is saying, is not an obvious situation; in representing it one must suit the form to the content, with all of its ambiguities and complexities.

Throughout *The Mysteries of Love* Vitrac's method is the juxtaposition of unlike elements: reality against dream, chaos against order, the mundane against the fantastic, the modes of Surrealism against those of traditional drama. His themes themselves, the renewal of the love relationship and the freeing of the imagination, pursue parallel and contradictory courses at various times, and each theme in itself represents a contradiction of traditional views. Love is not just courtship, marriage, and children, but also the sometimes violent disruption of these patterns and the revelation of deeper, often painful fears and desires which may lead to fuller understanding. Creativity too lies in the release from accustomed patterns and in the acceptance of the creations of our unconscious, our dreams and visions, as viable materials for art. Vitrac develops these themes with incredible richness, offering a linear structure of schematic clarity within which he weaves the phantasmagoria of the unconscious. He interrupts the relentless progression of daily life with the shocking intrusions of the oneiric; he confounds the chaos of Surrealist imagery by the meaningful patterns through which he develops it. His characters come alive as they reveal the selves which they themselves do not truly know. Vitrac gives us, in short, a play which is truly Surrealist and which functions in a truly dramatic way.

Obviously, not all surrealist plays are as rich as *Mysteries*—not even all of Vitrac's. (Some of his later plays are all too commercial to be Surrealistic, and at least one early play, *Poison,* is perhaps too surreal to be stageable.) Some Surrealist plays are certainly limited by "an aesthetic predilection for the static or, at the very most, for a dynamics based on the interaction of static objects . . . ," as Eric Sellin laments,[35] and some fall into Nahma Sandrow's "two extreme categories of plays which emerged from Dada and surrealism . . . one sort which was not really surrealistic, and another which was not really drama."[36] But more of the drama of Surrealism than critics have acknowledged is both surreal and dramatic—and capable of literary analysis as well.

Today, fifty years after the birth of Surrealism, it is time for us to begin to recognize these progenitors of so much of what we still call the *avant garde.* As Eugene Ionesco wrote a decade ago in *Notes and Counternotes,* "I can well understand why a Surrealist theatre has been produced only recently; the theatre is always twenty or thirty years behind poetry."[37]

Criticism, in this case, is still further behind. We must not be intimidated by the drama of Surrealism, by its seeming chaos in form, by the display of primordial instincts in its content. We should be accustomed by now to such modes and revelations in the plays of Ionesco himself, in those of Genet and Arrabal, and of Handke and Weiss; we have known them as well in the world we inhabit. Our time is not so very different from that which created Dada and Surrealism, and we see in recent literature the emergence of what has been called "Neo-Surrealism." In the role of literary critic one may not perhaps change the world which has prompted, for the second time in fifty years, renewed attacks on the fruitlessness of reason. We will certainly need time to gain perspective on this newest movement—if movement it is. But it is high time that we tried to understand the old.

END NOTES

[1] André Breton, "Manifesto of Surrealism (1924)," in *Manifestoes of Surrealism*, tr. Richard Seaver and Helen R. Lane (Ann Arbor: Univ. of Michigan Press, 1972), p. 14. (Italics his.)

[2] *The Breasts of Tiresias*, tr. Louis Simpson, in *Modern French Theatre: The Avant-Garde, Dada, and Surrealism*, ed. Michael Benedikt and George E. Wellwarth (New York: Dutton, 1966), p. 66.

[3] Publication of Breton's first "Manifesto of Surrealism" in 1924 is generally acknowledged as the official birthdate of the movement.

[4] Subtitled *Explorations in Modernism* (LaSalle, Ill.: Library Press, 1973), p. 135.

[5] *Theatre in Dada and Surrealism* (Syracuse: Syracuse Univ. Press, 1974), p. 9.

[6] *Collected Works*, II, tr. Victor Corti (London: Calder and Boyars, 1971), p. 137. (Hereafter referred to as *Works*, to distinguish it from the French edition.)

[7] *The Theatre of the Absurd* (New York: Garden City, 1961), pp. 275-76.

[8] Esslin, p. 276.

[9] Benedikt and Wellwarth, p. xxix. (See footnote No. 2.)

[10] Breton, p. 12.

[11] Breton, p. 11.

[12] Breton, p. 13.

[13] The attribution is debatable, and there is the possibility that Vitrac himself made the statement. Although the line appears in Artaud's *Oeuvres complètes*, II (Paris: Gallimard, 1961), p. 38, and is cited by Eric Sellin, "Surrealist Aesthetics and the Theatrical Event," *Books Abroad*, 43, No. 2 (Spring, 1969), pp. 169, 172, Matthews regards it as "almost certain" that Vitrac wrote it (pp. 119-20), and cites for evidence Henri Béhar, *Roger Vitrac: Un réprouvé de Surréalism* (Paris: A. G. Nizet, 1966), pp. 281-301. See also p. 176.

[14] *Surrealism: The Road to the Absolute*, rev. ed. (New York: Dutton, 1970), p. 166.

[15] Matthews, p. 10.

[16] Béhar (*op. cit.*, p. 176) insists that these dreams are Patrick's, but offers no evidence for this view. Matthews recognizes the first as Leah's dream and points out that she "has the last word in scene two, and we see her lying in bed as the next tableau opens the second act" (p. 123).

[17] *The Mysteries of Love*, tr. Ralph J. Gladstone, in Benedikt and Wellwarth, p. 228. All quotations in English are from this text; future page references will be given parenthetically.

[18] Published as *Entrée Libre* in Roger Vitrac, *Théâtre*, III (Paris: Gallimard, 1964), and published first in English as an Appendix in Nahma Sandrow, *Surrealism: Theatre, Arts, Ideas* (New York: Harper and Row, 1972).

[19] Sandrow, p. 43.

[20] Victor Corti, Introduction to Antonin Artaud, *Works*, II, p. 7.

[21] Béhar elaborates on this issue, pp. 170-73.

[22] Artaud, *Works*, II, p. 136.

[23] Balakian, p. 169.

[24] Breton, p. 34.

[25] Pierre Reverdy, in *Nord-Sud*, March 1918. Cited in Breton, p. 20.

[26] Roger Vitrac, *Les Mystères de l'Amour* in *Théâtre*, II (Paris: Gallimard, 1948), p. 11.

[27] *Ibid.*

[28] Balakian, p. 143.

[29] Balakian, p. 147.

[30] Benjamin Péret, from "Dormir Dormir dans les Pierres" (1927), cited in Balakian, p. 150.

[31] In *Nadja*, tr. Richard Howard (New York: Grove Press, 1960), André Breton disclaims the value of work, concluding, "There is no use being alive if one must work" p. 60.

[32] Roger Vitrac published a "play without words," entitled *Poison,* in *Littérature,* 8, January 1923.

[33] Artaud, *Works,* II, p. 136.

[34] Vitrac, *Théatre,* II, p. 11.

[35] Sellin, p. 171.

[36] Sandrow, p. 55.

[37] As quoted in Ruby Cohn, "Surrealism and Today's French Theatre," *Yale French Studies,* 31 (May, 1964), p. 164.

Love, Death, and Resurrection in The Great Gatsby

Robert J. Emmitt

In a letter to Maxwell Perkins on May 1, 1925, Fitzgerald lamented that no one, neither readers nor critics, understood his novel.[1] Since *Gatsby* was less than a month old at the time, the statement might well seem a classic example of literary hypochondria. But when one considers the extent to which Fitzgerald's subtle and powerful use of complex symbols remains unappreciated after fifty years of commentary, criticism, and adulation, the statement begins to seem prophetic.

This essay suggests that despite a half-century of insights and intimations, the central metaphor of *The Great Gatsby* has been overlooked.[2] Its recognition can bring a new depth of understanding to interpretation of the novel and a new appreciation of Fitzgerald's scope and artistry. This presentation of the novel differs from previous accounts in systematically comparing its structure and imagery with the common ancestors of waste land, Grail legend, and Gospel story—the ancient Semitic and Egyptian resurrection myths of Tammuz, Adonis, Attis, and Osiris, and their divine consorts. These seminal myths about the annual rebirth and death of life and vegetation, reconstructed by Sir James Frazer in *The Golden Bough* and Jessie L. Weston in *From Ritual to Romance*,[3] seem to me to have provided Fitzgerald with a central armature around which he modeled the novel, as well as a resource for much of the elaborative symbolism which adorns it.

The myth themes give coherence to the novel's images of color, season, vegetation, heat and coolness, dust and water, light and stars, and they clarify their connotations of materialism, transience, and death. The images identify Gatsby with Adonis—as lover, son of god, ritual victim, priest, and votary. Simultaneously, they identify Daisy with Astarte, Isis, Cybele, and Aphrodite—dualistic goddesses of love and fate, generation and destruction. By means of parallels of color, action, and situation, Nick is identified with Gatsby, Jordan with Daisy, and thus both with the divine figures their models personify.

Even the climaxes of the plot are meaningfully correlated with the turning points of the seasonal and vegetational cycles, from summer solstice to autumnal equinox. By such analogical devices, plot and subplot, primary and secondary characters are bound together in a common denouement and re-enactment of the myth themes. In the end, through the working out of the metaphor, Gatsby's romance and sacrifice are given epic significance and Nick's potential becomes a pledge for the continuation of the cycle of quest and conquest, death and resurrection, beyond the confines of the novel.

Proof of direct influence is beyond the scope of this paper and the nature of the internal evidence it is based on, but it seems probable that Fitzgerald was led to Frazer and Weston by Eliot's introductory footnote in *The Waste Land,* where the works of both are highly praised as sources of inspiration.[4] The comprehensive explanatory power of the myth themes and their ability to unify diverse strains of *Gatsby* criticism may ultimately prove to be the only argument for their influence. Readers will decide for themselves whether the detailed parallels are more likely to be the result of a common source, coincidence, or unpremeditated art. The view presented here is that from the choice of symbolic color words and character names to the largest overall constructions of scene and sequence, the composition of *The Great Gatsby* reveals the concentrated intention of its author.[5]

The earliest written accounts of the Semitic divinities who became the major figures in the vegetation, fertility, and resurrection myths reconstruct-ed by Frazer and Weston are found among the Accadians, who invaded Sumer and adopted the Sumerian pantheon about 3500 B. C. Most prominent among these adopted divinities was the earth goddess, Astarte, whose mythol-ogy goes back to the Sumerian Ininni-Ashdar-Ishtar, goddess of the morning star Venus and mother, wife, and lover of the Sumerian dying god Tammuz. Through processes of syncretism, conquest, and cultural assimilation, this primal pair became identified with Attis and Cybele, Osiris and Isis, Adonis and Aphrodite.[6] Despite variations and overlapping details of doctrine and ritual, the main elements of the story are invariable and are best represented in the Adonis ritual, which may be taken as the classic form of the cult: a beautiful youth, beloved by a great but also capricious goddess, is wounded in his generative organs and dies, and the earth falls sterile at his death to be restored only by his resurrection.[7]

Certain accidental and variable attributes of the myth are also relevant to interpreting *Gatsby.* Among the Babylonians, Ishtar-Astarte, owing perhaps to the appearance of Venus as both the morning and evening star, was the god-dess of fate, war, and discord as well as of love, beauty, fertility, and harlotry. In Egypt, between 3000 and 4000 B. C., Sirius, the dog-star, associated with the related goddess, Isis, appeared at dawn in the east during the summer solstice to herald the annual rising of the Nile. As Cybele in Phrygia, the goddess was the object of human sacrifice and of self-castration by her male votaries.[8]

Tammuz, addressed as *adonai,* or lord, by his worshippers, is the immediate precursor of the Adonis of Phoenicia and Cyprus and the prototype of the Semitic dying gods and human scapegoats, including Christ and Dionysus. Originally a god of vegetation or a resurrected human victim who became a god, "Tammuz" originally meant faithful "son of god." His worship and sacrifice were inseparably linked with the annual rains or rise of the waters and from this he became associated with the progress of the seasons and was generalized into a lord of life.[9]

From its center at Byblus in Phoenicia, the Adonis cult spread to Cyprus and from there throughout the Aegean Isles. Frazer relates how several cultic symbols were associated with the myth. Each year at Byblus, the ritual casting of the god's effigy into the waters was accompanied by the blooming of the scarlet anemone, while rivers and sea were incarnadined as the annual rains washed the blood-red earth down from the mountains of cedared Lebanon.[10]

While Frazer stresses local variations in the seasonal observance of the ritual, Weston emphasizes the chronology at the great center of Adonis worship in Cyprus, a chronology significant for the interpretation of *Gatsby:* "In Cyprus, at the autumnal equinox, i.e., the beginning of the year in the Syro-Macedonian calendar, the death of Adonis [fell] on the 23rd of September, his resurrection on the 1st of October, the beginning of a New Year."[11] Weston also notes that elsewhere "the Tammuz celebrations were held from June 20th to July 20th, when the Dog-star Sirius was in the ascendant, and vegetation failed beneath the heat of the summer sun."[12] Since the days of the Babylonian captivity, this month has been designated "Tammuz" in the Jewish calendar, a time of universal lamentation preceding rebirth.

On a first reading, the dominant images in *The Great Gatsby* are material —the Long Island setting of the rich, the mansions of Gatsby and Tom Buchanan, their clothing, and those consumptively wild parties that are somehow reminiscent of the potlatch ceremonies of the Kwakiutl Indians. Clothing, jewelry, and silver abound in gross profusion, whole orange groves are stripped of their produce or herds of ponies transported cross-country and housed in garages converted into polo stables. Conspicuous consumption seems the battle cry of the age and the Protestant Ethic is manifested in all its glory and vulgarity.

Yet beneath these symbols of an age run amuck with the brute substance of wealth are innuendoes of romantic and spiritual significance concealed by the gaudy parade of ostentation. Color and material are admirably
compact symbols of identification and characterization. The use of white,
gold, and silver throughout the book is the most notable example. Fitzgerald
uses white in conjunction with the adjective cool to suggest physical and
emotional poise, privilege, and sanctity. The images of beauty and of desirability are all white—beginning with the fashionable mansions of East Egg and
including the fashionable women who inhabit them: "Across the courtesy
bay the white palaces of fashionable East Egg glittered along the water."

Daisy and Jordan, like idols, "were both in white, and their dresses were
rippling and fluttering." Even their conversation is white, with illusory connotations of chastity and coldness: "a bantering inconsequence that was
never quite chatter, that was as cool as their white dresses and their impersonal eyes in the absence of all desire."

Their vacuity and shallowness are ironically underscored by Tom
Buchanan's concern about "The Rise of the Colored Empires" and his fear
that "if we don't look out the white race will be—will be utterly submerged."
The terror the thought inspires is suggested by the catch in his speech, but the
objects of all this solicitude are characteristically unmoved. Obviously, Daisy
and Jordan are too vacantly secure in their privileges to seriously consider the
prospect of their submergence. Thus, by means of white clothes and autumn
gold hair, parallels of situation, and similar origins, the figurative identity of
the two women and their affiliation with an indefinably soiled whiteness is
established in the opening chapter.

The white façades of the lower classes are even more clearly blemished.
The whiteness of ash land, which dominates the second chapter, is as depleted
and disreputable as the appearance of its people—it is, in fact, no longer
white, but gray. The one creature of vitality in this "waste land" is Myrtle
Wilson, and escaping the depleted soil and faded gaze of T. J. Eckleburg, she
pursues her own path to the renovated whiteness that is the preserve of Tom
Buchanan and his class. But an irretrievable vulgarity attends the white ambitions of the poor. Myrtle and her friends are blurred, milky, powdered, and
blotched, and not at all godlike.

But these distinctions between rich and poor, divine and profane are not
limited to white. From the beginning of the novel, the appearance of white
is allied with gold and silver. The obvious identification of gold and money is
established in the first chapter, when Nick remarks that he bought "a dozen
volumes on banking and credit" that stood on his shelf "in red and gold like

new money from the mint." At Gatsby's parties, where the radiance of wealth is at its most opulent, gold oranges and yellow lemons are mechanically disemboweled. Turkeys are "bewitched to a dark gold." The moon rises during the course of the party and casts a "triangle of silver scales" on the water of the Sound.

The same device that earlier identifies Daisy and Jordan is used to associate Gatsby and Nick. To the first party Nick wears white flannels, and on the afternoon when he is to meet Daisy once again, Gatsby, who is given to striking messianic poses on his porch or lawn, wears "a white flannel suit, silver shirt, and gold-colored tie." Thus white, and to a lesser degree, gold and silver function to identify Daisy and Jordan, Gatsby and Nick, as members of a select class and variations on a common theme. All share an aura of brittle insouciance, youth, and privilege, all are in effect gods or demigods, as significant for their resemblances as for the details which distinguish them.

But these mythic implications of white, gold, and silver are most explicit in relation to Daisy. When he left her in Louisville during the war, Gatsby was "overwhelmingly aware of the youth and mystery that wealth imprisons and preserves, of the freshness of many clothes, and of Daisy, gleaming like silver, safe and proud above the hot struggles of the poor." She is an idol, a grail, and her voice is "full of money—that was the inexhaustible charm that rose and fell in it, the jingle of it, the cymbals' song of it . . . High in a white palace the king's daughter, the golden girl. . . . "

Besides being the colors of the daisy, white and gold are the colors traditionally used to depict Venus, from the multi-stage tower of Barsippa near Babylon to the vision of Botticelli.[13] White enchased with gold has been immemorially used to distinguish gods, goddesses, and sacrificial victims. From the chryselephantine statues of the Acropolis to the rams and bulls of the Old Testament, god and oblate must always be immaculate, unstained.

All the major color values in the novel are consistent with their meanings in the Semitic myths and scriptures, specifically, those of the Old Testament.[14] Most of these values are by now a common heritage and have been successfully interpreted.[15] But the green light which beckons Gatsby eastward across the waters of the Sound toward Daisy's dock is no mixture of blue dream and yellow reality. Green is the color of reviving vegetation, and thus of hope and resurrection. Above all, it is the color of Isis, "Green goddess whose green color is like unto the greenness of the earth,"[16] and whose star, rising annually in the east, promises the renewal of life. Rose, as color and flower, is emblematic of the death of Adonis, the effect of red blood on white petals,[17] and this is why Gatsby wears a pink suit near the end and stands in the center of Daisy's crimson carpet just before his emasculating confrontation with Tom. This and the identification of Nick with Gatsby is probably why Nick is abruptly compared to an "absolute rose" when Daisy wishes to thrust him upon the gentle solaces of Jordan Baker.

One of the more impressive accomplishments of *The Great Gatsby* is the sense of transience that pervades it from its first chapter to its final image of a romantic past. The flow of time runs like a tidal current throughout the novel, but is made explicit only at the end. "So we beat on, boats against the current, borne back ceaselessly into the past." This sense of the impermanence of earthly joys and pains is somehow impressive in so young a man as Fitzgerald. It is the very substance of realistic fiction—or of an art that is more real and poignant than reality—and it gives a depth to the novel that no static conception of character or of existence can convey.

On a broad scale, Fitzgerald's effect is achieved by having the drama of Gatsby's defeat and death take place against the changing natural scenery of a Long Island summer, whose progress is accentuated by images of drift, decay, and death. The fate of the characters is so integrated with the movement of the season from first promise to final reflection that men and nature seem to share a common fate. Like Adonis, Gatsby partakes of natural vitality and mortality—a fact signified by his name.[18]

At the beginning of the novel, the season is full of promise, expressed by the sunlight and vegetation: "And so with the sunshine and the great bursts of leaves growing on the trees, just as things grow fast movies, I had that familiar conviction that life was beginning over again with the summer." Nick is impressed by the profusion of grass and vines at the Buchanan mansion, by grass that seems almost to reach up inside the house. Gatsby's mansion seems "spanking new under a thin beard of raw ivy . . . and more than forty acres of lawn and garden."[19]

At first the sunlight is beneficient and seems to gild whatever it touches. Daisy glows golden in the rays of the setting sun: "For a moment the last sunshine fell with romantic affection upon her glowing face." Even Tom's sordid affair is touched by its vitality: "until after eight o'clock the apartment was full of cheerful sun." When Gatsby realizes the cherished dream of re-encountering Daisy that he has hoarded for five years, "He literally glowed. . . . he smiled like a weather man, like an ecstatic patron of recurrent light, and repeated the news to Daisy. 'What do you think of that? It's stopped raining'."

But as the summer wears on and the emotional climate becomes more intense, the sunlight suddenly becomes oppressive: "The next day was broiling, almost the last, certainly the warmest, of the summer." These are the dog-days, and madness and passion are in the air. "The straw seats of the car hovered on the edge of combustion; the woman next to me perspired delicately for awhile into her white shirtwaist, and then, as her newspaper dampened under her fingers, lapsed despairingly into deep heat with a desolate cry." It is the rutting season, and Gatsby and Tom approach their battle of male supremacy. That it is passion without fruition is signalled by Daisy's echo of *The Waste Land:* " 'What'll we do with ourselves this afternoon?' cried Daisy, 'and the day after that, and the next thirty years?' " Jordan's response, " 'Don't be morbid,' 'Life starts all over again when it gets crisp in the fall,' " is perhaps more heavily freighted with meaning than it appears.

The scene in the hotel brings the crisis into the open, and mixed with the connotations of desire and combat are implications of impending death. As Tom and Gatsby confront each other, a wedding march breaks out below, reminding us that Daisy in her heat could not wait for Gatsby's return. " 'Imagine marrying anybody in this heat!' cried Jordan dismally. 'Still—I was married in the middle of June,' Daisy remembered, 'Louisville in June!' " "As Tom took up the receiver the compressed heat exploded into sound and we were listening to the portentous chords of Mendelssohn's Wedding March from the ballroom below."

Superimposed on these associated images of heat and lust is the image of that final term in the temporal succession, death. There is the seemingly strange digression about Blocks Biloxi who fainted in the heat and was carried to Jordan's house to remain for three weeks until ordered to leave by her father, who died the next day. Thus heat and death are somehow obliquely associated. And amid all this heat, seasonal and emotional, Gatsby, who "always looks so cool," is at his nadir.

In his confrontation with Tom and Daisy, Gatsby's insistence that she say she always loved only him betrays his obsession with an idealization of the affair that defies reality, for the very form of his demand prompts the defeat that unmans him. As Nick observes, Gatsby's view of the affair as something beyond the "just personal" love of Daisy and Tom conveys "an intensity in his conception . . . that couldn't be measured." And it is precisely by means of this conception that Gatsby emasculates himself. He demands a concession from Daisy that she will not make. So complete is his degradation that Tom dismisses him like an eunuch to drive home with Daisy: " 'Go on. He won't annoy you. I think he realizes that his presumptuous little flirtation is over'.' "

After they leave, the motif of impending death is reinforced by Nick's "coincidental" revelation that he has just turned thirty and the prophetic, "So we drove on toward death through the cooling twilight."

Following the death of Myrtle Wilson, Gatsby's sacrificial assumption of guilt, and Daisy's betrayal, the weather suddenly breaks and the season moves toward its close. After the vigil during which Nick learns the true history of Jay Gatsby and his earlier affair with Daisy, Nick notes that "The night had made a sharp difference in the weather and there was an autumn flavor in the air." And with the death and burial of Gatsby, the myth cycle is almost completed: "So when the blue smoke of brittle leaves was in the air and the wind blew the wet laundry stiff on the line I decided to come back home."

So casually are these symbols of seasonal change handled and so much do they resemble the commonplaces of familiar conversation that they are easily overlooked. After all, everybody talks about the weather and nobody does anything about it. But a close analysis of the chronology indicates that there is every evidence in the novel that Fitzgerald orchestrated the events of the romance and the images of death, color, vegetation, heat and coolness, and drifting water and dust to conform to the chronology of the Adonis myths. So emphatic and deeply ingrained is the dating that this alone would justify considering the vegetation myths a primary source for the novel.

The earliest major event in the novel is Gatsby's "incarnation" in the fall of 1917 when he meets and falls in love with Daisy in Louisville. In relating the history of the romance to Nick, Jordan Baker is quite definite about the month and year. "One October day in nineteen-seventeen—" When Nick hears the account from Gatsby, it was "one autumn night," "a cool night with that mysterious excitement in it which comes at the two changes of the year." Nick mentions the romance a third time, just before he relates the events of Gatsby's death, "eventually he took Daisy one still October night, took her because he had no right to touch her hand."

Weston, as we have seen, reports the resurrection of Adonis as taking place in Cyprus on October 1, one week after the autumnal equinox on September 23, which marks his death. Daisy's first apostasy takes place during the winter of 1917-18 and by the next autumn she is "gay again, gay as ever." By Armistice Day, November 11, 1918, her letters to Gatsby are restless. When he fails to return, Daisy begins "to move again with the season." "She wanted her life shaped now, immediately, by some force." "That force took shape in the middle of spring," 1919, and in mid-June, in the heat of the month of Tammuz, she married Tom Buchanan of Chicago. Thus the date of

Gatsby's decisive loss closely corresponds to the summer solstice on June 21, when the dog-star rages, Isis-Astarte is in the ascendant, and "vegetation fails beneath the heat of the summer sun." Gatsby revisits Louisville in the heat of early July, while Tom and Daisy honeymoon in the South Seas and the baby, born the following April, is conceived.[20]

The same pattern marks the events of the climactic summer. The novel opens "in the spring of twenty-two" and "the history of the summer really begins" on the evening Nick dines with the Buchanans. It is "two weeks before the longest day in the year," the eve of the summer solstice, and Nick returns home to find Gatsby, arms extended, facing eastward towards the green light. The day of Gatsby's degradation and Myrtle's death comes little more than three months later on "almost the last, certainly the warmest" day of the summer. The ensuing night marks the sharp change in the weather and the day of Gatsby's death is the first of which it is remarked that there is "an autumn flavor in the air."[21]

Short of an outright statement, it would appear that Fitzgerald has done everything possible to intimate that Gatsby's defeat and death take place on or about the autumnal equinox on September 23, the traditional date for the death of Adonis.

A second series of images parallels the course of seasonal change and reinforces the sense of evanescent time and impending death. Water and dust drift through the pages of the novel, and both are related to attrition and death. The images and their connotations are established early in the book, and they run their course through it to the very end. Drifting waters are clearly related to the Adonis myth and ritual, while drifting dust is their logical counterpart in the absence of resurrection and the freeing of the waters. Dust is associated with the celebrated valley of ashes and carries the additional overtones of that controlling symbol of desiccation and death. This repository of dust, at once a graveyard and a dumping ground, is the end to which the human and inanimate materials of the novel are destined, the counterpart of the white, golden, vegetating paradise that Nick has been exposed to in the first chapter.

But the sinister implications of drifting dust are clear even before the valley of ashes is introduced. In the opening pages of the book Nick writes that "Gatsby turned out all right at the end; it is what preyed on Gatsby, what foul dust floated in the wake of his dreams that temporarily closed out my interest in the abortive sorrows and short-winded elations of men."

"Wake," with its connotations of water and funeral procession, is repeated at Myrtle Wilson's death as "Some one, kind or curious, took her in his car and drove her in the wake of her sister's body." The association with water is amplified in the next sentence: "Until long after midnight a changing crowd lapped up against the front of the garage." Like "daisy," her name carries a mythic association with the cycle of plant life—the myrtle was sacred to Adonis and Aphrodite, whose Nereids crowned her with myrtle when she rose from the sea.

Gatsby's parties seem to take place at the bottom of the sea. Guests drift from nothingness to nothingness, just as, at the end of the novel, Gatsby drifts from the fresh flow of water at one end of the pool to the drain at the other. The image is a symbol for the whole of life in a transient world. Significantly, the green light that represents Daisy beckons Gatsby across the water. Though Gatsby cherishes the illusion that he can recapture the past, the wash of time and the river goes on despite him, and by trying to resist he only sacrifices himself to it.

The proximate meaning of the myth themes is a fated death. Death is the major pivot of the cycle, the turn of the year, the nadir of the abundance curves of water and vegetation which the cultic rituals have sought, since the dawn of cultivation, to master by sympathetic magic and ritual sacrifice. And both Myrtle and Gatsby are insistently marked for death throughout the novel.

In her apartment, Myrtle recalls that at her first meeting with Tom, "All I kept thinking about, over and over was 'You can't live forever; you can't live forever'. " Among the things she must buy is "a wreath with a black silk bow for her mother's grave that'll last all summer." Shortly thereafter, in a scene that foreshadows her death, Tom Buchanan breaks her nose with "a short deft movement" and the floor of the bathroom is littered with bloody towels. Gatsby, too, is marked. It is repeatedly suggested that he "killed a man once." Death is associated with automobile accidents and a general irresponsibility in a premonitory scene following Gatsby's party. When Gatsby and Nick visit Wolfsheim they travel in what is subsequently to be called the "death car," through the valley of ashes, where Nick catches a "glimpse of Mrs. Wilson," and on the way they are stopped by a funeral.

Even during the rendezvous of Gatsby and Daisy, the romantic climax of the novel, images of death litter the path. Gatsby appears at the front door, "pale as death." Nick seeks shelter from the rain under a huge black tree in the yard and recollects that the brewer who built Gatsby's house went into a decline when his neighbors refused to have their roofs thatched. "His children sold his house with the black wreath still on the door."

The culminating death-image of the book, which epitomizes the entire action, the death of Gatsby, and Nick's final rejection of the East in five brief sentences, is clearly a compressed rendition of modern seasonal rituals related to the death and resurrection of Adonis:

I see it as a night scene by El Greco: a hundred houses, at once conventional and grotesque, crouching under a sullen, overhanging sky and a lustreless moon. In the foreground four solemn men in dress suits are walking along the sidewalk with a stretcher on which lies a drunken woman in a white evening dress. Her hand, which dangles over the side, sparkles cold with jewels. Gravely the men turn in at a house—the wrong house. But no one knows the woman's name, and no one cares.[22]

In *The Golden Bough,* Frazer describes customs, called Burying the Carnival and Carrying out Death, that are observed in a score of European Lenten festivals and Orthodox Easter ceremonies, all resembling the ancient rites of Adonis. The common feature of these observances is that a representative or effigy of the ritual victim or Death-figure is carried about the town on a litter, then buried, thrown in the water, burned, or returned to the church. In some cases drunkenness is part of the ritual, in others the figure or bearers are dressed in white or black. Sometimes the procession is welcomed to homes in the community with gifts or incense; sometimes it is rejected and driven forth, depending on the character attached to the principal figure. Summarizing these practices, Frazer theorizes that in many cases they represent the banishment of death in anticipation of the resurrection of the dying god.[23]

To understand the full implications of this scene and its crucial place in the novel, it is first necessary to appreciate the mythic dimensions of Gatsby's quest and death and the moral implications of Nick's rejection of that death and of the East.

In terms of spiritual and moral significance, Gatsby's romantic quest, with its search for a grail and its parodic connotations of the Christian sacrifice, is a parable of the fate of idolatry, and a commentary on its particular American manifestations. But an evaluation of the novel's moral significance must include consideration of Nick's role and changing perception as well. In Nick's view, "Gatsby turned out all right in the end." He turned out all right because of his momentary recognition of the illusion and because his "crimes" were committed in a kind of invincible ignorance, like the sins of Rudolph Miller in Fitzgerald's "Absolution."

Gatsby's romantic illusion about himself began early: "Jay Gatsby of West

Egg, Long Island, sprang from his Platonic conception of himself. He was a
son of God—a phrase which, if it means anything, means just that—and he
must be about His Father's business, the service of a vast, vulgar, and meretricious beauty." Here the parody of the Christian account is the clearest source
of the characterization, if not the only one, but Gatsby's devotion to the
American success myth is first elaborated in a description of his ambitions before he had met either Daisy or Dan Cody:

But his heart was in a constant, turbulent riot. The most grotesque and
fantastic conceits haunted him in his bed at night. A universe of ineffable
gaudiness spun itself out in his brain while the clock ticked upon the floor.
Each night he added to the pattern of his fancies until drowsiness closed
down upon some vivid scene with an oblivious embrace. For awhile these
reveries provided an outlet for his imagination; they were a satisfactory hint
of the unreality of reality, a promise that the rock of the world was founded
securely on a fairy's wing.[24]

With amazing compression, almost the whole of Gatsby's life is prefigured
in the imagery: the universe of ineffable gaudiness which he constructs for
himself, the clock ticking in the background, his tangled clothes soaked with
"wet" moonlight, the vivid scene closed with an oblivious embrace, and
finally, the rock of the world with its connotations of the hardness against
which Gatsby is to break and the religious connotations of the Church,
with its fatal distinction between material and spiritual.

The passage suggests that Gatsby's fate is in some measure determined by
the irreality of his vision even before he meets Daisy. She determines only the
form of his disillusion. The Platonic and mythic dimensions of Gatsby's
romance with life doom him to a collision with experience. His reluctance to
reify and thereby limit the object of his quest is made clear in the luminously
lyrical passage which describes Gatsby's first encounter with Daisy:

Gatsby saw that the blocks of the sidewalks really formed a ladder and
mounted to a secret place above the trees—he could climb to it, if he climbed alone, and once there he could suck on the pap of life, gulp down the
incomparable milk of wonder.

His heart beat faster and faster as Daisy's white face came up to his own.
He knew that when he kissed this girl, and forever wed his unutterable visions
to her perishable breath, his mind would never romp again like the mind of
God. So he waited, listening for a moment longer to the tuning-fork that had

been struck upon a star. Then he kissed her. At his lips touch she blossomed for him like a flower and the incarnation was complete.[25]

The passage is replete with hidden ironies, for as suggested, the act of worship is an act of idolatry, and the incarnation is as much the fall of Adam as it is the descent of a son of God. Gatsby seems somehow aware of the contradiction, and the imagery suggests his confusion, for while the images of the breast of life and the blossoming flower are both associated with kissing Daisy, they are opposed to each other. Christian and pagan strains are clearly mixed. Daisy is at once mother, bride, goddess, and grail. On one level the images suggest blasphemous parody; on another, they invoke all the romantic richness of the myth theme.

After he loses Daisy, Gatsby's obsession is that he can recapture the past, and Nick understands: "I gathered that he wanted to recover something, some idea of himself perhaps, that had gone into loving Daisy." Gatsby wants to recapture his lost innocence, the illusion of freedom and invincibility that he had before he submitted his divine capacity for wonder to Daisy's mundane image. The theme is one of the most venerable in American literature, but *Gatsby* gives it new relevance by applying it to the American affair with love and money, and timeless implication by conveying it through the most storied romantic myths of antiquity.

In death, Gatsby subsumes the major religious figures and implications of the book. He is Christ, who carries the emblem of death upon his back, and even more clearly, he is Attis, Osiris, Adonis, who die at the end of the summer and whose image is cast in the water. The transformation of the ideal world into a material one with the death of illusion is equally explicit, for in a sense he is also the unnamed Platonic god of the romantic ideal: "He must have looked up at an unfamiliar sky through frightening leaves and shivered as he found what a grotesque thing a rose is." And as the illusion that lent reality to the ideal perishes, Gatsby's blood, tracing a line in the water, recalls the sacramental mingling of wine and water and the sanguinary death of Adonis, which annually dyes the rising waters of life.

The themes of romantic illusion, diabolic waste, and tragic death are concluded in the chapter in which Gatsby is killed. The moral significance of the book and the application of the parable to the American situation are made in the final chapter, in which Nick arranges the burial and prepares to leave West Egg for home. It is the death of illusion for Nick, too, and the experience leads him to a moral re-evaluation of life.

If there is a moral to be drawn from Gatsby's fate, Nick Carraway must be the one to draw it. He alone is sensitive to the ideal tendency in things and consistently realistic in his perceptions. Of the characters in the novel, only Nick has Fitzgerald's valued "ability to hold two opposed ideas in mind at the same time." As his last name implies, only he has the potential for rebirth and growth.[26]

Of the critics who have noted the similarities between *The Waste Land* and *Gatsby,* none has remarked that only Nick becomes capable of the *datta*-give, *dayadhvam*-sympathize, and the *damyatta*-control, to which Eliot points as the way out of the waste land. Some critics have been almost totally critical of Nick's character, and particularly of his final break with Jordan. But this view overlooks the essential fact of Nick's development from passive onlooker and diffident panderer into the novel's only active agent of what is ethically right.

There is some justice in the condemnation. At the beginning of the novel, Nick is that typical young American, an example of what Kierkegaard called the esthete. He drifts casually from America to Europe, casually from the Mid-West to the East Coast, and casually from one affair to another. He shows much of the "vast carelessness" in human relationships that he later condemns in Tom, Jordan, and Daisy, but he alone has the ill grace to rationalize his indifference as "honesty."

But by the end of the novel, Nick is ready to commit himself—and is, we suspect, at last really capable of love. Instead of the ironic and smug claim, "I am one of the few honest people that I have ever known," we have the genuinely contrite admission that he is "tremendously sorry." Breaking off with Jordan is Nick's first act after burying Gatsby in the rain and rejecting death in the image of the mummers' parade. In his insistence on performing his penance in person, we see that Nick has gained the courage to give, sympathize, and control by what he has learned from Gatsby's downfall. Though "angry, and half in love" with her, Nick must relinquish her with the past which went into loving her, if he has gained any insight into the radical defects which identify her with Daisy and in fact learned anything from Gatsby's fall.

Thus, if there is hope—realistic hope as opposed to Gatsby's "romantic readiness"—anywhere in the novel, it is in Nick's ability to say no to the romantic illusions of the East and return to the unexciting moral affirmations of his youth. In mythic terms, the cycle does not end with the death of Gatsby. It ends instead with an ambiguous resurrection—and this is the meaning of Nick's rejection of the burial, of the image of Carrying out Death, and of the whole Eastern seaboard in favor of the Midwestern Christmases of his youth. In a sense, Nick's return to the Mid-West and to the birth of Christ is a rejection of strange eastern gods, and at the same time it is his rededication to the ideal of all the resurrection myths in their most traditional American form.

Like the conclusion of *The Waste Land,* the final message of *The Great Gatsby* is equivocal and the symbols are self-correcting. Gatsby's death and Nick's rebirth are partly ironic, partly a parody on the religious myths, and also partly a reaffirmation of them. It is not Gatsby's dream but what preyed upon it that is rejected. There remains something gorgeous about Gatsby and his incorruptible dream—the magnanimity of a life thrown away in a gesture —but at a time when lives grow meaningless, there is something worthy in a beautiful gesture.

Thus, finally, Gatsby's fate becomes an exemplum of the unguarded pursuit of the American dream, that recreation of pagan myths of youth, rebirth, and abundance to which the eternal romantic sacrifices his life, but from which the realist may learn to seek the ideal with wisdom and compassion.

END NOTES

[1]Andrew Turnbull, ed., *The Letters of F. Scott Fitzgerald* (New York: Scribner's, 1963), p. 181.

[2]Jackson R. Bryer, *Sixteen Modern American Authors* (Durham, North Carolina: Duke Univ. Press, 1974), pp. 300-02, lists a dozen essays published since 1953 that deal with the waste land, American and Near-Eastern myth themes. None notes the extensive parallels discussed here, nor, to my knowledge, does any previous criticism.

[3]For convenience, references to Frazer are to *The Golden Bough* (New York: Macmillan, 1948), one-volume abridged edition, except where volume references indicate the original thirteen-volume edition (New York: Macmillan, 1963). References to Weston are to the Peter Smith edition, New York, 1941.

[4]T. S. Eliot, *The Complete Poems and Plays, 1909-1950* (New York: Harcourt, 1962), p. 50.

[5]Unpremeditated art of this complexity may be a conception without a corresponding reality. Elementary probability theory suggests that the odds against a chance articulation of ten such meaningful symbols are greater than one followed by fifty zeros. Thus, until a more plausible explanation of the evidence is advanced, one may reasonably entertain the theory that Fitzgerald consciously worked in the symbolic and mythopoeic tradition of Eliot and Joyce, following their example in combining myths, cycles, and symbols for his own artistic ends.

[6]Stephen H. Langdon, *Semitic Mythology*, volume V of *The Mythology of All Races* (New York: Cooper Square, 1964), ed., Canon John A. MacCulloch, pp. 1-99 and 336-51. A brief history of the origins and descent of the Tammuz-Ishtar mythology.

[7]Weston, pp. 32-48; 136-37.

[8]Frazer, pp. 370; 347.

[9]Langdon, pp. 342, 343; 346.

[10]Frazer, pp. 329; 336.

[11]Weston, p. 43.

[12]Weston, p. 44.

[13]Langdon, p. 159.

[14]James Hastings, ed., *Encyclopedia of Religion and Ethics* (New York: Scribner's, 1921), XII, p. 150.

[15]Daniel J. Schneider, "Color Symbolism in *The Great Gatsby*," *University Review*, 31 (October, 1964), 13-17.

[16]Frazer, p. 382.

[17]Frazer, p. 336.

[18]"Gatsby" is probably a Joycean multiple pun containing *gat*-gun and *gad*-god associations, but derived primarily from the Middle Irish *gat*, a willow rod or pole. (See the etymology of *gad*, *Webster's New International Dictionary* . . . , Second Edition Unabridged; Springfield, Massachusetts: G. & C. Merriam, 1961; p. 1024.) The name thus carries connotations of mourning, lost or forsaken love, the generic tree-spirits behind the resurrection gods, and of the vital, regenerative, and reproductive powers attributed to the phallic Maypole. Cf. Gertrude Jobes, *Dictionary of Mythology, Folklore, and Symbols* (New York: Scarecrow, 1962) II, pp. 1079, 1681; *Brewer's Dictionary of Phrase and Gable,* rev. (New York: Harper & Row, 1970), p. 1157; Hastings, II, 832; Frazer, II, 75-76 and XI, 294.

[19]The ivy was sacred to Attis and Osiris, and was also associated with Dionysus. Frazer, pp. 352; 381; 387.

[20]*Three Novels of F. Scott Fitzgerald: The Great Gatsby* (New York: Scribner's, 1953). The passages cited in this section appear on pages 57-59; 84; 97-98; 113-17.

[21]*Gatsby*, pp. 4; 6; 11; 18; 87; 110; 116.

[22]*Gatsby*, p. 134.

[23]Frazer, IV, *The Dying God*, pp. 220-54; V, *Adonis Attis Osiris*, pp. 254-55.

[24]*Gatsby*, p. 75.

[25]*Gatsby*, p. 84.

[26]Though not mentioned by Frazer, the pungent caraway, both seed and plant, is an appropriate symbol of recurrence or resurrection. Introduced into the Mediterranean area from Asia in ancient times by spice traders and later naturalized in Europe, it now grows wild in Europe, Asia, and America. When sown in the fall, the herb develops flowers and seeds the following summer, and if left alone, self-sows from year to year thereafter.

Notes on Contributors

John Balaban is Assistant Professor of English at The Pennsylvania State University. His first book of poetry, *After Our War,* was the Lamont Selection of the Academy of American Poets and was nominated for the National Book Award in Poetry in 1974. John studied with Maurice Cramer at Penn State.

Harry Fisher studied with Maurice Cramer at the University of Chicago. He is a widely published poet whose latest volume is entitled *Advice to Divers.* He is an advertising executive in Saint Louis.

Lana Balaban is part-time Instructor of English at The Pennsylvania State University where she studied with Maurice Cramer. In 1971-72, she was Instructor of English at the University of Saigon.

Elizabeth Coleman is the Associate Dean of the New School for Social Research, a member of its faculty in Humanities and Literature, and Director of the Freshman Year Program. She studied with Maurice Cramer at the University of Chicago.

Marilyn M. Carens is Assistant Professor of English at Bucknell University. She has published essays and read papers on a variety of Old and Middle English topics. She was a student of Maurice Cramer's at Penn State.

Gerald B. Kinneavy is Associate Professor of English and Chairman of Graduate Studies at the University of Colorado. He has published essays on Medieval and Victorian literature. He studied with Maurice Cramer at Penn State.

Donald R. Wineke is Assistant Professor and Chairman of English at Wichita State University. Donald was a student of Maurice Cramer's at Penn State.

Jo Ann Davis has taught at Syracuse University and Chapman College. She has delivered papers to and chaired the Shakespeare and Satire Sections of NEMLA and published essays on Shakespeare and Restoration drama. Jo Ann studied with Maurice Cramer at Penn State.

Arthur J. Weitzman is Professor of English at Northeastern University. He is an editor of *The Scriblerian* and has published on Milton, Swift, Pope, Dr. Johnson, and others. He is currently working on a study of the relationship of literature to urban life and in 1976 is a visiting fellow at William Andrews Clark Memorial Library. Professor Weitzman studied with Maurice Cramer at the University of Chicago.

Keith A. Gould, formerly a student under Maurice Cramer at The Pennsylvania State University, presently teaches English at Norwich University, Northfield, Vermont.

John G. Rudy is Assistant Professor of English at Indiana University at Kokomo. He studied with Maurice Cramer at Penn State. His professional interests include Nineteenth-Century British and American literature, Science Fiction, Children's literature, and the novel.

Robert J. Cornet is the Public Information Specialist for Hamilton County, Tennessee government with County Judge Don Moore, chief executive officer. He is a former Assistant Professor of English at the University of Tennessee, Chattanooga and studied with Maurice Cramer at Penn State. His essays have appeared in *The Markham Review, Four Quarters,* and *The Segouyah Review.*

Donna G. Fricke is Assistant Professor of English at Bowling Green State University. She has published on Herbert, Swift and Hogarth, Tennyson and others. She was a student of Maurice Cramer's at Penn State.

Apostolos Marmaras is formerly a student of Maurice Cramer's at The Pennsylvania State University and is presently completing his Ph.D. at the University of Colorado.

Lilika Marmaras, who worked with Maurice Cramer at Penn State and did graduate work at the University of Colorado, is currently Assistant Director of Studies at the Hellenic-American Union in Athens, Greece.

Douglas C. Fricke, Assistant Professor of English at Bowling Green State University, studied with Maurice Cramer at Penn State. His publications include articles on Wordsworth and Coleridge, George Eliot, Tennyson, and Swinburne.

Sallie J. Hall is Associate Professor of English at the University of South Florida. Recent scholarship includes a paper on Melville delivered at the 1975 convention of SAMLA. She studied with Maurice Cramer at The Pennsylvania State University.

Marshall Ledger specializes in Nineteenth-Century literature and composition. He has taught English at the University of Pennsylvania, the University of New Hampshire, and LaSalle College. He has also established a freelance writing career, having done a book on American farming seen through the eyes of *Farm Journal* as well as articles on education and community action. Currently, he is staff writer for *The Pennsylvania Gazette,* alumni magazine of the University of Pennsylvania. Marshall studied with Maurice Cramer at The Pennsylvania State University.

Annette Shandler Levitt, Assistant Professor of English at Temple University, has published articles and reviews on William Blake, Surrealist drama, and Federico Garcia Lorca. She has delivered papers on Blake, James Joyce and Surrealism, and Modern American Poetry in Paris, Edinburgh, Zagreb, and Philadelphia. Since 1973, she has chaired the MLA Seminar on Blake and Moderns. She studied with Maurice Cramer at Penn State.

Robert J. Emmitt is Senior Education Specialist, Job Corps, Office of Manpower Development Programs, U. S. Department of Labor. Formerly an English editor, Managing Editor of Curriculum Advisory Service, and Assistant Academic Director of The Great Books Foundation, he is currently completing a Ph.D. in National Higher Education Policy. He studied with Maurice Cramer at the University of Chicago.